In These Last Days

WORD STUDIES IN
THE GREEK NEW TESTAMENT
For the English Reader

by Kenneth S. Wuest

THE NEW TESTAMENT
IN EXPANDED TRANSLATION

In These Last Days

II Peter, I, II, III John, and Jude

in the

Greek New Testament

FOR THE ENGLISH READER

by
Kenneth S. Wuest

WM. B. EERDMANS PUBLISHING CO.

Grand Rapids   Michigan

IN THESE LAST DAYS
by KENNETH S. WUEST

Copyright, 1954, by
Wm. B. Eerdmans Publishing Company

———————

Set up and printed, January 1954
Tenth printing, November 1975

Library of Congress Number 53-9735
ISBN 0-8028-1238-4

PHOTOLITHOPRINTED BY GRAND RAPIDS BOOK MANUFACTURERS, INC.
GRAND RAPIDS, MICHIGAN, UNITED STATES OF AMERICA

PREFACE

The title of this book, *In These Last Days,* was suggested by Paul's words to Timothy (II Tim. 3:1), "This know also, that in the last days perilous times shall come." In II Timothy, Paul predicts the end-time apostasy in the professing Church, and speaks of the fact that the laity will be infected with what we today call Modernism or Liberalism. Peter in his second epistle, traces the source of this apostasy to false teachers. In II Peter, false teachers deny redemption truth. In I John they deny the truth concerning the Person of our Lord. In II John, the denial of the Incarnation is treated, and the correct attitude of the saints towards teachers who are Unitarians is enjoined. In III John, Diotrephes, a petty tyrant in a local church, and of Modernistic tendencies, is presented. In Jude, various characteristics of the apostasy are brought out. Thus, we have in these five books, a picture of the Church in the days in which we are living, a guide for the saints, acquainting them with the nature of the false teachers and their heretical doctrines, and a warning against both. In view of all the foregoing, a study of these books should prove most timely and salutary, since we are living in the very last days of the Church Age, and in the midst of the apostasy which these Books predict.   K.S.W.

INTRODUCTION

This book is written for the student of the New Testament who does not have access to the Greek text, but who would like to work beneath the surface of the English translation in the untranslatable richness and added accuracy which the original text affords.

This is done by the use of Greek word studies, interpretive material, and an expanded translation. The word studies bring out a far richer, more developed, and clearer meaning of the Greek word than any single English word could do. In the interpretive material, the author gives the English student access to the work of the great Greek masters in addition to his own work in the Greek text. In the expanded translation, a translation using more English words than the standard versions do, the author gives the student what the Greek reader of the first century read. In the process of translating, the standard versions leave much rich material behind in the Greek text, since these are held down to a minimum of words. This added material, the Bible student should know if he expects to do work of a high calibre.

This book is not armchair reading. Its place is next to the student's open Bible on his study desk. With its aid, he can work through the Greek texts of the Bible Books treated, and obtain a far clearer and richer understanding of their contents than he could from a study of any number of different translations. After he has worked through these epistles, he can use this book as a reference work in future Bible study.

The authorities used in the writing of this book are as follows: In *Expositor's Greek Testament*, R. H. Strachan, M.A., writing on II Peter; David Smith, M.A., D.D., writing on the Epistles of John; and J. B. Mayor, Litt.D., writing on Jude;

Marvin R. Vincent, D.D., in his *Word Studies in the New Testament;* Henry Alford, D.D., in *Alford's Greek Testament;* A. T. Robertson, A.M., D.D., LL.D., Litt.D., in his *Word Pictures in the New Testament;* Richard C. Trench, D.D., in his *Synonyms of the New Testament;* Joseph H. Thayer, D. D., in his *Greek-English Lexicon of the New Testament;* James H. Moulton, D.D., Th.D., and George Milligan, D.D., in their *Vocabulary of the Greek Testament;* Hermann Cremer, D.D., in his *Biblico-Theological Lexicon of New Testament Greek;* H. E. Dana, Th.D., and Julius R. Mantey, Th.D., D.D., in their *Manual Grammar of the Greek New Testament.*

The Greek text used is that of Nestle. The translation quoted is the Authorized Version. The expanded translation offered must not be used as a substitute for but as a companion translation to the standard version the student is using.

K. S. W.

CONTENTS

THE
EXEGESIS
OF
SECOND PETER

In order to reap the most benefit from his
study, the student is urged to work through
Peter's letter verse by verse, with his Bible
and this exegesis before him, seeking to understand the meaning of the Word in the
light of the word studies, interpretations, and
expanded translation.

CHAPTER ONE

(1:1) For the significance of the name "Simon Peter," see notes on I Peter 1:1.[1] The apostle calls himself a servant of Jesus Christ. The word is *doulos,* the most abject and servile term for a slave of the five words the Greeks used when speaking of one who serves. The verb form is *deō,* "to bind." Thus, a *doulos* is one bound to another as a slave. The word designated one who was born as a slave. This classical usage fits in very well with the doctrinal significance of the word as it is used in the Christian system. Sinners are born into slavery to sin at physical birth, and into a loving, willing, glad servitude to Jesus Christ by regeneration. The word referred to one whose will is swallowed up in the will of another. Before salvation, the sinner's will is swallowed up in the will of Satan. After salvation has wrought its beneficent work in his being, his will is swallowed up in the sweet will of God. The word spoke of one who is bound to another in bands which only death can break. The sinner is bound to Satan in bands which only death can break. In the case of the believing sinner, his identification with the Lord Jesus in His death on the Cross broke the bands which bound him to Satan. Now, the believer is bound to Christ in bands which only death can break. But the Lord Jesus will never die again, and since He is the life of the saint, that saint will never be severed from his Lord, but will be His loving bondslave for time and eternity. Again, *doulos* refers to one who serves another to the disregard of his own interests. Before salvation, the sinner served Satan to his own detriment. Since he has been saved, a Spirit-filled believer serves his Lord with an abandon that says, "Nothing matters about me, so long as the Lord Jesus is glorified."

1. *First Peter in the Greek New Testament for the English Reader.*

As to the significance of the Greek word for "apostle," please see notes on I Peter 1:1.[2] The names, "Jesus" and "Christ" have important meanings. "Jesus" is the English spelling of the Greek word *Iēsous*. This, in turn, is the Greek spelling of the Hebrew word which in English is "Jehoshua," and which means, "Jehovah saves." Thus, there are three cardinal doctrines of the Christian faith in the name "Jesus," the deity of our Lord, His humanity, and His sacrificial atonement. Jehovah could not save sinners except on the basis of justice satisfied, this, in order that He might maintain His righteous government. Justice, to be satisfied, demanded that sin be paid for, and only God can satisfy His own demands. So, He in the person of His Son, stepped down from His judgment throne in heaven, and took upon Himself the guilt and penalty of human sin. But He could not do this except by the incarnation and the Cross. The word "Christ" is the English spelling of the Greek *Christos* which means "the anointed," and this Greek word is the translation of the Hebrew word which comes into our language in the name "Messiah." In the case of the Gospel according to Matthew, the name is a designation of the Lord Jesus as the Messiah of Israel. In the Church epistles, it speaks of Him as the Anointed of God.

"Obtain" is *lagchanō*, "to obtain by lot, to receive by divine allotment." The faith here is appropriating faith exercised by the believing sinner when he places his trust in the Lord Jesus. This faith is given in sovereign grace by God to the sinner elected (chosen out) to salvation, and is part of the salvation which is given him. It is given him, Peter says here, by divine allotment. See notes on I Peter 1:2[3] concerning the setting-apart work of the Spirit in which He brings the sinner foreordained to salvation to the act of appropriating faith. Paul speaks of the same thing in Ephesians 2:8, the word "that" referring to the general idea of salvation spoken of in the context. Should an unsaved person perchance read these lines and wonder whether he has been thus

---

2. *First Peter in the Greek New Testament.*
3. *First Peter in the Greek New Testament.*

chosen to salvation, he is exhorted to place his heart-faith in the Lord Jesus as his Saviour from sin, and he will find that he has been chosen out to be a recipient of salvation.

This faith is described as "like precious faith with us." The word "precious" is *isotimon,* made up of *isos,* "equal in quantity or quality," and *timios,* "held as of a great price." The compound word means either "like in honor," or "like in value." Vincent suggests that both meanings are applicable here. His comment is as follows: "not in the same measure to all, but having equal value and honor to those who receive it, as admitting them to the same Christian privileges." How priceless is this gift of faith which admits us to the salvation which God has provided through the death and resurrection of His Son! And what an honor is conferred upon those who are the recipients of this gift of faith! Peter, a Jew, writing to the Gentiles here, says that the latter have been given this faith by divine allotment together with the Jews. Paul speaks of the same thing in Ephesians 3:6.

This faith which was given to both Jew and Gentile alike was given through the righteousness of God. The word is *dikaiosunē,* and its distinctive meaning here is that of "justice, the virtue which gives each one his due." It precludes the showing of partiality. The thought is not here that the gift of salvation was due a sinner in the sense that God was obligated to give it to him, or that the sinner deserved it, but that if the Jew was given it, it should also be given to the Gentile, lest God show partiality in giving it to one class of individuals and not to another.

The expression, "God and our Saviour" is in a construction in the Greek text which demands that we translate, "our God and Saviour, Jesus Christ," the expression thus showing that Jesus Christ is the Christian's God; this, in opposition to the cult of the Caesar in which the Roman emperor was the god of the pagan Roman citizen. Because Peter continued to insist upon this teaching, he was martyred.

Translation. *Simon Peter, a bondslave and an ambassador of Jesus Christ, to those who have been divinely allotted like precious faith with us by the equitable treatment of our God and Saviour, Jesus Christ.*

(1:2) This is sanctifying grace, the work of the Holy Spirit producing in the yielded believer His own fruit. This peace is sanctifying peace, the tranquility of heart that is the result of the ministry of the Holy Spirit in the believer. "Knowledge" here is *epignōsis,* full, perfect, precise knowledge as opposed to *gnōsis,* imperfect, partial knowledge. Strachan says: *"epignōsis,* 'involving the complete appropriation of all truth and the unreserved acquiescence in God's will, is the goal and crown of the believer's course' (Lightfoot) . . . *epignōsis* implies a more intimate and personal relationship than *gnōsis.* It would be a useful word, seeing that *gnōsis* had become associated with Gnosticism, then incipient in the Church. . . . Grace and peace are multiplied in and through this more intimate heart knowledge of Jesus Christ, in contrast to a mere barren *gnōsis.*" "Knowledge" is locative of sphere and instrumental of means. This grace and peace are in the sphere of this knowledge and are produced by it. The particular word for "knowledge" here, *epignōsis,* speaks of experiential knowledge, that is, knowledge gained by experience. This knowledge of the Lord Jesus possessed by the believer therefore, is not a mere intellectual knowledge of the facts concerning Him acquired by a study of the Gospels, for instance, but a heart experience of what and who He is gained by such a study plus a personal association with Him by means of the Word and the ministry of the Holy Spirit. It is a person with Person knowledge through intimate fellowship.

The construction in the Greek text translated by the words "God and our Saviour Jesus Christ" is the same as in verse one, and requires the rendering, "our God, even Jesus the Lord."[4]

Translation. *Grace to you, and peace, be multiplied in the sphere of and by the full knowledge of our God, even Jesus, the Lord.*

(1:3) This grace and peace multiplied to the saints is further described in this verse. "According as" is *hōs,* "assuming that,

---

4. The words "Saviour" and "Christ" are not in Greek text.

seeing that." Alford, commenting on its use here says: "It is characteristic of this Epistle, to dilate further when the sense seems to have come to a close." The word "divine" is *theias,* which Peter borrowed from the classical Greek usage. It was used of Zeus, the greatest of the Greek gods. Paul uses it in Acts 17:29 and Romans 1:20, and in both places he uses it to speak of the attributes of God, or of God seen from the standpoint of His attributes. Here Peter uses it to describe the power of God, *dunamis,* "that which overcomes resistance, inherent power, power residing in a thing by virtue of its nature, power which a person exerts or puts forth." "Hath given" is *dōreō,* a stronger and more expressive word than *didōmi,* "to give." It means "to grant or bestow." Strachan says that "this word and its cognates always carry a certain regal sense describing an act of large-handed generosity." It is a perfect participle, speaking of the past completed act of presenting the gift with the present result that it is in the possession of the believer with no strings tied to it. It is his permanent possession, having been given by pure grace.

"Pertain" is in italics in the A.V. However, it is the translation of the preposition *pros* which appears in the Greek text, which preposition here could be translated, "with reference to." "Godliness" is *eusebeia.* Vincent's note on this word is most helpful: "It is from *eu,* 'well,' and *sebomai,* 'to worship,' so that the radical idea is 'worship rightly directed.' Worship, however, is to be understood in its etymological sense, 'worth-ship,' or reverence paid to worth, whether to God or man. Wycliffe's rendering of Matthew 6:2, 'that they be *worshipped* of men'; and '*worship* thy father and thy mother' (Matt. 19:19). In classical Greek, the word is not confined to religion, but means also *piety* in the fulfilment of human relations, like the Latin *pietas.* Even in classical Greek, however, it is a standing word for *piety* in the religious sense, showing itself in right reverence; and is opposed to *dussebeia,* 'ungodliness,' and *anosiotēs,* 'profaneness.' 'The recognition of dependence upon the gods, the confession of human dependence, the tribute of homage which

man renders in the certainty that he needs their favor — all this
is *eusebeia,* manifest in conduct and conversation, in sacrifice
and prayer.' (Nägelsbach, cited by Cremer). This definition
may be almost literally transferred to the Christian word. It
embraces the confession of the one living and true God, and life
corresponding to this knowledge."

As to the inclusion of the idea "life" with that of godliness,
Strachan comments; "The conjunction of the two ideas 'life'
and 'godliness' is significant. Religion does not narrow, but
expands the province of life. The life in Christ is not 'a little
province of peculiar emotion. . . . If we fear that it may lose
itself in the vast and often lawless universe of life beneath, the
danger is to be averted not by wilfully contracting it within a
narrower field, but by seeking greater intensity of life in deeper
and more submissive communion with the Head Himself in the
heavens' (Hort, *The Way, the Truth, and the Life*)." The
word "life" here is not *bios,* "the necessaries of life," such as food,
clothing, and shelter, but *zōē.* This word speaks of life in the
sense of one who is possessed of vitality and animation. It is
used of the absolute fulness of life, both essential and ethical,
which belongs to God. It is used to designate the life which
God gives to the believing sinner, a vital, animating, spiritual,
ethical dynamic which transforms his inner being and as a result,
his behavior.

The Lord Jesus is now described as the One who called us by
means of His own uniquely possessed glory and virtue. The
words are in the instrumental case in the Greek text, and the
word *idios* is included, of which the A.V. takes no notice, and
which means "one's own private, unique, peculiar possession."
It was the attracting power of our Lord's beautiful life that
worked effectively in the act of God calling us into salvation.
Strachan says; "The phrase contains one of the finest ideas in
the New Testament. What could be a more effective answer to
the intellectualism of the Gnostic teacher or its modern equivalent,
than the impression produced on the lives of men, and especially
the early disciples, by the personality of Jesus? They beheld His

glory in the evidences of miraculous knowledge and power which Jesus showed at the time of their call (John 1:42, 47-51; Luke 5:4). Their sense of His moral greatness overcame all resistance on their part (Luke 5:8; John 1:49). If II Peter is lacking in devotional expression, his apologetic for the person of Christ is cast on most effective lines. Reason can only compass the facts of Revelation, in terms of antimonies (oppositions), and it is vain to meet inadequate theories of the person of Christ by dogmatic subtlety. The Life and Death of our Lord, if its significance is to be fully understood, must be looked upon largely as an acted parable, and Christian experience — the *impression* of 'glory' and 'virtue' — is an indispensable constituent of dogmatic *expression*." All of which goes to say that the convincing power of a Christlike life is of greater effect than all of the learned disquisitions of scholars concerning the Person and Work of our Lord. These latter are basic and absolutely necessary to the maintenance of true doctrine, but in themselves are helpless to answer the gainsayings of the destructive critic. But the latter has no answer for the supernatural transformation of a sinner's life into that of a Christlike life.

Translation. *Seeing that the all things to us His divine power has generously given, the things which pertain to life and godliness, through the full knowledge of the One who called us by means of His own glory and virtue.*

(1:4) "Whereby" goes back to "glory and virtue." It is through these that are given to us the promises. Strachan's explanation is helpful; "No doubt what II Peter has chiefly in view is the particular, comprehensive promise of His Second Coming (compare 3:4, promise, and 3:13). The Parousia (personal presence) will be the vindication of all moral and spiritual effort. Christ promised forgiveness to the sinful, rest to the weary, comfort to the sad, hope to the dying, and life to the dead. If the reference adopted above of 'whereby' is correct, the sense would be that in the character and deeds of the Incarnate One, we have a revelation that is itself a promise. The promises are given, not only in word but also in deed. The very life of

Christ among men, with its glory and virtue, is itself the Promise and Life, and the Parousia expectation is also a faith that He lives and reigns in grace."

Through these promises, the saints have become partakers of, sharers in the divine nature. Peter is here referring to regeneration as in I Peter 1:23. This divine nature implanted in the inner being of the believing sinner, becomes the source of his new life and actions. By its energy in giving him both the desire and the power to do God's will, he has escaped the corruption that is in the world. "Escaped" is *apopheugō*, "to escape by flight." That is, the believer has run away from the corruption which is in the world (*kosmos* world system of evil), this corruption being within the sphere of lust (*epithumia*, "craving, passionate desire") here in the widest sense of inordinate affection.

Translation. *By means of which (glory and virtue) there have been generously given to us the precious and exceedingly great promises in order that through these you might become partakers of the divine nature, having escaped by flight the corruption which is in the world in the sphere of passionate cravings.*

(1:5-7) Concerning the words, "and besides this," Vincent says; "Wrong. Render, *for this very cause.*" Robertson concurs in this translation, and adds that this is a classic idiom. "Giving" is *pareispherō*, made up of *pherō*. "to bring," *eis*, "into," and *para*, "alongside," thus, "to bring in alongside, to contribute besides" to something. The R.V. translates, "adding on your own part." Strachan says that the words "and besides this" emphasize the fact of the gifts spoken of in verse four as having their logical outcome in character, and quotes Bunyan as saying, "The soul of religion is the practical part."

"Diligence" is *spoudē*. The verb is *spoudazō* which means "to make haste, be eager, give diligence, to do one's best, to take care, to exert one's self." In verses two and three we have the divine provision and enablement given the believer in salvation, an inner dynamic, the divine nature which impels to a holy life, giving both the desire and power to do God's will (Phil. 2:13). In verses five to seven, we have human responsibility, that of seeing to it that the various Christian virtues are included in one's life. The divine nature is not an automatic self-propelling machine that will turn out a Christian life for the believer irrespective of what that believer does or the attitude he takes to the salvation which God has provided. The divine nature will always produce a change in the life of the sinner who receives the Lord Jesus as Saviour. But it works at its best efficiency when the believer cooperates with it in not only determining to live a life pleasing to God, but definitely stepping out in faith and living that life in dependence upon the new life which God has implanted in him. And this must not be a mere lackadaisical attempt at doing God's will, but an intense effort, as shown by the word *spoudē,* translated "diligence."

As to the translation, "add to your faith," Vincent says; "The A.V. is entirely wrong. The verb rendered 'add' (*epichorēgeō*) is derived from *chorus,* a chorus, such as was employed in the representation of Greek tragedies. The verb originally meant 'to bear the expense of a chorus,' which was done by a person selected by the state, who was obliged to defray all the expense of training and maintenance." Strachan adds, "It was a duty that prompted to lavishness in execution. Hence *chorēgeō* came to mean 'supplying costs for any purpose,' a public duty or religious service, with a tending, as here, towards the meaning, 'providing more than is barely demanded.'" Thus, the word means "to supply in copious measure, to provide beyond the need, to supply more than generously."

Saints are to supply or provide in their faith, virtue. Vincent says; "The A.V. exhorts *to add* one virtue to another; but the Greek, *to develop one virtue in the exercise of another;* each new grace springing out of, attempting and perfecting the other. Render, therefore, as Rev. *In your faith supply virtue,* and in your *virtue, knowledge, etc.*" The exhortation is that in the faith which the saints exercise in the Lord Jesus, they should provide for virtue. The believer exercises faith in the Lord

Jesus to supply his needs, to guide him along life's way. He
should also exercise faith for the generating of virtue in his inner
being by the Holy Spirit. This virtue, Vincent says, is in the
form, "not of moral excellence, but of the *energy* which Christians
are to exhibit, as God exerts His energy upon them. As God
calls us by His own *virtue* (v. 3), so Christians are to exhibit
virtue or energy in the exercise of their faith, translating it into
vigorous action." They are to provide in this virtue, knowledge
(*gnōsis*), and in this knowledge, temperance (*egkrateia,* self-
control), holding the passions and desires in hand. The word
was used of the virtue of one who masters his desires and passions,
especially his sensual appetites. The Greeks used it of the one
who had his sex passions under control. The papyri (Moulton
and Milligan) quote the phrase, "a trusty dispenser of continence."
One can see what a blessing the fruit of the Spirit is when it
provides the saint with a mastery of his sex passions (Gal. 5:23,
temperance, *egkrateia,* self-control).

The saints are to provide generously in this self-control,
patience. The word is *hupomonē,* literally, "to remain under,"
thus, "to remain under trials and testings in a way that honors
God." Vincent translates, "remaining behind or staying." He
says further, "not merely endurance of the inevitable, for Christ
could have relieved Himself of His sufferings (Heb. 12:2, 3,
compare Matt. 26:53) ; but the heroic, brave patience with which
a Christian not only *bears* but *contends.* Speaking of Christ's
patience, Barrow remarks, 'Neither was it out of a stupid
insensibility or stubborn resolution that He did thus behave
Himself; for He had a most vigorous sense of all those grievances,
and a strong (natural) aversation (act of turning away from)
from undergoing them . . . but from a perfect submission to the
divine will, and entire command over His passions, an excessive
charity toward mankind, this patient, and meek behaviour did
spring.' The same writer defines patience as follows: 'That
virtue which qualifies us to bear all conditions and all events, by
God's disposal incident to us, with such apprehensions and
persuasions of mind, such dispositions and affections of heart,

such external deportment and practices of life as God requires and good reason directs.' "

Godliness is to be provided generously in patience. This is *eusebeia*, a thorough treatment of which word was presented in the material of verse three, which please see. In this virtue of godliness is to be provided brotherly kindness. The word is *philadelphia*, made up of *phileō*, "to have an affection for," and *adelphos*, "a brother." This affection or fondness for one's Christian brethren is to be saturated with charity. The word is *agapē*, "that divine love which God is as to His nature, which is produced in the heart of the yielded believer by the Holy Spirit, and which impels him to deny himself for the benefit of the one loved."

Translation. *And for this very cause, having added on your part every intense effort, provide lavishly in your faith, virtue, and in your virtue, knowledge, and in your knowledge, self-control, and in your self-control, patience, and in your patience, godliness, and in your godliness, an affection for the brethren, and in your affection for the brethren, divine love.*

(1:8) "Be" is *huparchō*. The word refers to an antecedent condition protracted into the present. It speaks of possession. Vincent says: "In the sense of *being* the verb is stronger than the simple *einai*, 'to be'; denoting being which is *from the beginning*, and therefore attaching to a person as a proper characteristic, something belonging to him, and so running into the idea of rightful possession as above." Thus, the possession of the Christian virtues by the believer is a natural, expected thing by reason of the fact that he has become a partaker of the divine nature. And they are not a spasmodic possession either, present one day and absent the next. Indeed, if they were not present in the life, one could well discount the person's claim of being a child of God.

"Abound" is *pleonazō*, used of one possessing in the sense of "super-abounding." The Spirit-filled life is the overflowing life. It is like an artesian well whose source is higher than its outflow, the outflow being spontaneous by reason of that fact. The source of the Christian life is God; the outflow, through the believer. But the Christian life that does not run over, or overflow with spiritual blessings to others, is never a source of spiritual refreshment to others. A farmer once said to his helper who always filled the buckets of grain only three fourths full when they should have been full, "the buckets are never full until they are running over." So a Christian is never filled with the Spirit and spiritual blessings until his life is running over with the good things of God, refreshing the lives of others. "Make" is *kathistēmi*, "to constitute, to render, make, cause." "Barren" is *argos*, from *ergon* "work" and *a*, "not," thus, "no work," hence, "idle." "In" is *eis*. Vincent says: "Rev., more correctly, *unto*. The idea is not idleness *in* the knowledge, but idleness in pressing on and developing *toward* and finally reaching the knowledge."

Translation. *For if these things are your natural and rightful possession, and are in superabundance, they so constitute you that you are not idle nor unfruitful in the full knowledge of our Lord Jesus Christ.*

(1:9) "But" of A.V. is *gar* in Greek text, and should be "for." As to the words, "He that lacketh these things," the literal translation of the Greek text here is, "to whom these things are not present." Vincent comments: "Note that a different word is used here from that in verse eight, *are yours*, to convey the idea of possession. Instead of speaking of the gifts as belonging to the Christian by habitual, settled possession, he denotes them now as merely *present* with him."

"Cannot see afar off" is *muōpazō*, used by Aristotle of a near-sighted man. It is used in Ecclesiasticus of a soul on which the light shines (blinking and turning away). Here the word "limits the word *tuphlos*, blind as a short-sighted man screwing up his eyes because of the light" (Robertson). The two words together speak of a person who is short-sighted spiritually, seeing only things present and not heavenly things (Vincent). Strachan quotes Mayor, "He cannot see the things of heaven, though he may be quick enough in regard to worldly matters."

"Hath forgotten" is in the Greek text literally, "having taken forgetfulness." "Purged" is *katharismos*, "cleansing." This is the case of a saint who has wandered far from the sanctifying work of the Holy Spirit. He is carrying around with him his justification, but not availing himself of his sanctification. He is not stone blind. He has some spiritual sight. But the light of the Word dazzles his sin-sick soul as he turns his dimmed, spiritual eyes away, a sad situation in which to be.

Translation. *For he to whom these things are not present is blind, being short-sighted, having taken forgetfulness of the cleansing of his old sins.*

(1:10) "Wherefore" is, "because of the exhortation and argument in verses five to nine" (Robertson). "Rather" is *mallon*, a comparative adverb meaning "more," and is to be construed with "give diligence." The verb is ingressive aorist, "become more diligent." It is the word *spoudazō*, "to do your best, bend every effort." "To make" is a middle infinitive, "make for yourselves," that is, "satisfy yourselves that you are saved." "Sure" is *bebaios*, "stable, fast, firm." Strachan says of the word: "The word has a legal sense. It is the legal guarantee, obtained by the buyer from the seller, to be gone back upon should a third party claim the thing. Here the readers are exhorted to produce a guarantee of their calling and election. This may be done by the cultivation of the Christian graces." "Calling" is *klēsin*, from *kaleō*, "to call," and refers to the divine call of God to a participation in salvation. "Election" is *eklogē*, "the act of picking out from a number," and refers to the act of God choosing certain out of mankind for salvation. Alford says of the Christian's act of making his calling and election sure, secure, firm, "for both (the calling and election), in as far as we look on them from the lower side, not able to penetrate into the counsels of God, are insecure unless established by holiness of life. In His foreknowledge and purpose, there is no insecurity, no uncertainty; but in our vision and apprehension of them as they exist in and for us, much, until they are pointed out." The exhortation is that the believer should make sure of the fact that he is saved by seeing to it that the Christian graces superabound in his life. There is no idea here of making sure that we *retain* our salvation but that we *possess* salvation. "Fall" is *ptaiō*, "to stumble, fall into misery, become wretched."

Translation. *Wherefore, brethren, exert yourselves the more, and bend every effort to make for yourselves your calling and choosing out sure, for doing these things, you will never stumble.*

(1:11) "Entrance" is *eisodos*, made up of *eis*, "into," and *hodos*, "road," thus, "the road into," the definite article appearing before the word in the Greek text, pointing to a particular road. Our Lord said that He was the way (*hodos*, John 14:6). The writer to the Hebrews (10:19, 20) says, "Having therefore, brethren, boldness to enter the holiest by the blood of Jesus, by a freshly-slain and living way (*hodos* road)." Our Lord is the road to heaven by virtue of His precious blood. The words "shall be ministered" are *epichorēgeō*, "to richly supply." Vincent comments: "We are to furnish in our faith: the reward shall be furnished to us. *Richly,* indicating the fulness of future blessedness. Professor Salmond observes that it is the reverse of 'saved, yet so as by fire' (I Cor. 3:15)."

Translation. *For in this way the entrance shall be richly supplied to you into the eternal kingdom of our Lord Jesus Christ.*

(1:12) Vincent says of the words, "I will not be negligent"; "The A.V. follows the reading *ouk amelēsō*, which it renders correctly. The better reading, however, is *mellēsō*, I *intend*, or, as often in classical Greek, with a sense of *certainty*, I shall *be sure*, which the Rev. adopts, rendering *I shall be ready*." The verb here is in the future tense. Strachan comments: "What is the exact significance of the future? It can hardly be a simple periphrastic future. 'The idea is rather that the writer will be prepared in the future, as well as in the past and in the present, to remind them of the truths they know, whenever the necessity arises' (Zahn)." "Be established" is *stērizō*, a perfect tense participle. The word means "to make stable, place firmly, set fast." These saints had become stabilized in the truth and were in a state of being set fast, placed firmly on it. Their knowledge

of the Word and the cardinal doctrines of the Christian faith were
set in their thinking. As to the words, "in the present truth,"
Vincent says: "namely, the truth which is present with you
through the instruction of your teachers; not the truth at present
under consideration."

Translation. *Wherefore, I intend always to remind you concerning these things even though you know them and have become
firmly established in the truth which is present with you.*

(1:13, 14) "Think" is *hēgeomai*, "to consider, deem, account."
"Right" is *dikaios*, "to render each his due." Thus, Peter's idea
in using the word was that it was his solemn duty to stir up his
readers. Strachan translates, "I consider it a duty," and remarks,
"The language in verses 13 and 14 is studiously solemn and
impressive." "Tabernacle" is *skēnōma*, "a tent." He refers
here to his physical body. Paul, in II Corinthians 5:1, 4 uses
the same figure when referring to the body, but uses the shorter
word, *skēnos*. Peter uses his word again in Matthew 17:4,
where he speaks of making three tents. Vincent says, "The word,
as well as the entire phrase, carries the idea of *brief duration* —
a frail *tent,* erected for the night."

"Stir up" is *diegeirō*, "to wake up, awaken, arouse," metaphorically, "to arouse the mind, stir up, render active." The
prefixed preposition adds the idea of doing a thorough piece of
work in arousing their minds. Robertson translates, "keep on
rousing you up." Peter purposed to do this by reminding them
of the things which they had been taught. The phrase is instrumental of means. He would arouse their minds to action by
reminding them of the truth they had learned from the Word of
God. The preacher and teacher should be an intense student of
the Word, bringing to his hearers fresh, new truth with the dew
of heaven upon it. But there is a place for the repetition of the
old truths which the saints know well. Much of it has not yet
been put into practice, and the fact that it is repeated gives the
Holy Spirit an opportunity to make it experiential in the life of
the believer.

As to the words, "shortly I must put off this my tabernacle," Vincent says, "Literally, *quick is the putting off of my tabernacle*. Rev. *the putting off of my tabernacle cometh swiftly*. Possibly an allusion to his advanced age. *Putting off* is a metaphor, from "putting off a garment." So Paul (II Cor. 5:3, 4), *being clothed, unclothed, clothed upon . . . Cometh swiftly*, implying the speedy approach of death though others understand it of the *quick, violent* death which Christ prophesied he should die. 'Even as our Lord Jesus Christ hath showed me.' See John 21:18, 19. Compare also John 13:36, and note the word *follow* in both passages. 'Peter had now learnt the full force of Christ's sayings, and to what end the following of Jesus was to bring him' (Lumby)."

Translation. *Indeed, I consider it due you as long as I am in this tent, to keep on arousing you by means of a reminder, knowing that very soon there is the putting off of my tent, even as also our Lord Jesus Christ gave me to understand.*

(1:15) "Endeavor" is *spoudazō*, "to bend every effort, to do one's best." "Always" is *hekastote*, "on each occasion when you have need." "That ye may be able" is *echein humas*, literally, "that you may have it." "These things" refers back to verse 12 and to the Christian virtues of verses 5-7. Strachan says: "It must have reference as in verse 12 to the practice of the Christian graces, and the larger reference must be to some systematic body of instruction. This might easily take the form of reminiscenses of the example of Jesus Himself, and the allusion may be to the Petrine reminiscences contained in the Gospel of St. Mark . . . Surely, nothing could be more appropriate, more helpful to a godly life, than that Peter should leave behind the picture of the glory and virtue drawn from his own recollection."

"Decease" is *exodos*, "the road out." The word comes into our language in the title "Exodus." The word is used only three times in the Greek N. T.: Luke 9:31, where the heavenly visitors speak of our Lord's decease, His road out of this earth to heaven; Hebrews 11:22, where the reference is to the departing of the children of Israel; and in this passage. Alford says:

"It is at least remarkable that, with the recollection of the scene on the Mount of Transfiguration floating in his mind, the apostle should use so close together the words which were there also associated, *tabernacle* and *decease*. The coincidence should not be forgotten in treating of the question of the genuineness of the epistle."

Translation.   *Indeed, I will do my best also that, on each occasion when you have need, after my departure, you will be able to call these things to remembrance.*

(1:16) "Followed" is *exakoloutheō*, "to follow out to a conclusion, to pursue a line of thought to its termination." "Cunningly devised" is *sophizō*, in a good sense, "to make wise, teach"; in a bad sense, "to invent, play the sophist, to devise cleverly or cunningly." Vincent translates, *"artfully framed by human cleverness."* "Fables" is *muthos* (myths). Vincent says: "The reference here may be to the Jewish myths, rabbinical embellishment of O.T. history; or to the heathen myths about the descent of the gods to earth, which might be suggested by his remembrance of the Transfiguration; or to Gnostic speculations about aeons or emanations which rose from the eternal abyss, the source of all spiritual existence, and were named *Mind, Wisdom, Power, Truth,* etc."

"Coming" is *parousia,* made up of *para,* "alongside," and *ousia,* "to be," thus, "to be alongside"; thus, "personal presence." Strachan quotes Dr. Milligan as authority for the statement that the word "occurs frequently in the papyri as a kind of *terminus technicus* with reference to the visit of a king, or some other official." Dr. Milligan then says: "The word must, therefore, have come into use, in this application to the Second Advent, in apostolic times, as faithfully representing the meaning of Jesus Himself (compare Matt. 24:3, 27, 37, 39). The usual classical sense of the word as 'presence,' must not be regarded. Taken together with the other meaning illustrated by the Koine, *parousia* would thus seem to combine in itself the meaning of 'actual presence' and a near 'coming.' This combination of meaning in the consciousness of the early Church, with its perplexity as to the interpretation of our Lord's promise, would seem to be reflected in John 16:16-18." "Power" is *dunamis*, "inherent power, power residing in a person or thing by virtue of its nature, power which a person exerts."

"Eyewitnesses" is *epoptēs*, "a spectator." Thayer says: "Inasmuch as those were called *epoptai* by the Greeks, who had attained to the third degree of the Eleusinian mysteries, the word seems to be used here to designate those privileged to be present at the heavenly spectacle of the transfiguration of Christ." Robertson says that "Peter clearly felt that he and James and John were lifted to the highest stage of initiation at the transfiguration of Christ." Strachan says: "used here to enhance the splendor of the vision, and the honor done the disciples at the transfiguration, 'admitted to the spectacle of His grandeur.'" "His" is a demonstrative pronoun in the Greek text, literally, "that One." It is emphatic, pointing out the greatness of the Person to whom reference was made. "Majesty" is *megaleiotētos*. The positive adjective *megas* means "great." Here we have the superlative form, "greatest." The word means "magnificence." It is used here, Thayer says, "of the visible splendor of the divine majesty as it appeared at the transfiguration."

Translation. *For we did not follow out to their termination cleverly devised myths when we made known to you the power and personal coming of our Lord Jesus Christ, but became spectators of that One's magnificence.*

(1:17) There is a participial construction in the Greek text which should be translated as follows; "For, having received from the presence of God the Father," the phrase referring back to our Lord in the previous verse. "Came" is the translation of *pherō*, "to bear, carry," literally, "there was borne along," the participle here being in the passive voice. "From" is the translation of *hupo*, "by means of." The voice was borne or carried along by "the excellent glory." "Such" is *toiasde*, "such," generally with an implied suggestion of something excellent or admirable. The word "excellent" describing "glory" is *megaloprepēs*, made up of *megas*, "great," and *prepei*, "it is becoming," thus, "that which is becoming to greatness." Thayer defines the word as follows: "befitting a great man, magnificent, splendid, full of majesty." Vincent defines, "sublime." The word is used in the LXX (Septuagint, Greek translation of the O.T.) in Deuteronomy 33:26 as an epithet of God. The A.V. translates by the word "excellency." Vincent says that "the phrase excellent *glory* refers to the bright cloud which overshadowed the company on the transfiguration mount, like the shekinah above the mercy-seat." It has always been the opinion of the present writer that that cloud was the Shekinah.

Translation. *For having received from the presence of God the Father honor and glory, there was borne along by the sublime glory such a voice, My Son, the beloved One, this One is, in whom I am well pleased.*

(1:18) The word "holy" means "set apart for God's use, or rendered sacred by the divine presence." Hence, the latter meaning is applicable. Robertson says that the scene of the transfiguration was probably one of the lower slopes of Hermon. Vincent quotes Lumby as follows: "Of all places to which special sanctity would be ascribed by Christ's followers, surely that would be the first to be so marked where the most solemn testimony was given to the divinity of Jesus. To the Jewish Christian this would rank with Sinai, and no name would be more fitly applied to it than that which had so constantly been given to a place on which God first revealed Himself in His glory. 'The holy mount of God' (Ezek. 28:14) would now receive another application, and he would see little of the true continuity of God's revelation who did not connect readily the old and new covenants, and give to the place where the glory of Christ was most eminently shown forth the same name which was applied so oft to Sinai."

Translation. *And this voice we heard borne along, out from heaven, when we were with Him in the holy mountain.*

(1:19) The statement, "We have also a more sure word of prophecy," could be understood in either one of two ways: (1) "We are better certified than before as to the prophetic word by reason of this voice," or, (2) "We have the word of prophecy as a surer confirmation of God's truth than what we saw ourselves, i.e., Old Testament testimony is more convincing than even the voice heard at the transfiguration" (Vincent). The context (vv. 20, 21) decides for the latter, for Peter goes on to speak of that which makes the O.T. scriptures unmistakably reliable, their divine inspiration.

Vincent quotes two authorities on this matter: "To appreciate this we must put ourselves somewhat in the place of those for whom St. Peter wrote. The New Testament, as we have it, was to them non-existent. Therefore we can readily understand how the long line of prophetic scriptures, fulfilled in so many ways in the life of Jesus, would be a mightier form of evidence than the narrative of one single event in Peter's life" (Lumby). "Peter knew a sounder basis for faith than that of signs and wonders. He had seen our Lord Jesus Christ receive honor and glory from God the Father in the holy mount; he had been dazzled and carried out of himself by visions and voices from heaven; but nevertheless, even when his memory and heart are throbbing with recollections of that sublime scene, he says, 'we have something surer still in the prophetic word.' . . . It was not the miracles of Christ by which he came to know Jesus, but the word of Christ as interpreted by the Spirit of Christ" (Samuel Cox).

"More sure" is the comparative of *bebaios,* "stable, fast, firm," metaphorically, "sure, trusty." The idea here is of something that is firm, stable, something that can be relied upon or trusted in. The idea in the Greek text is, "We have the prophetic word as a surer foundation" than even the signs and wonders which we have seen. "Light" is *luchnos,* "a lamp." "Dark" is *auchmēros;* Vincent defines it, "Literally, *a dry place.* Rev. gives *squalid* in margin. Aristotle opposes it to *bright* or *glistering.* It is a subtle association of the idea of darkness with squalor, dryness, and general neglect." Strachan defines: "dry, parched, squalid, rough," and comments: "Here it means 'murky.'" Thayer comments: "To a lamp is likened the prophecies of the O.T. inasmuch as they afforded at least some knowledge relative to

the glorious return of Jesus from heaven down even to the time
when by the Holy Spirit that same light, like the day and the
day-star, shone upon the hearts of men, the light by which the
prophets themselves had been enlightened and which was necessary to the full perception of the true meaning of their prophecies."

Translation. *And we have the prophetic word as a surer
foundation, to which you are doing well to pay attention, as to a
lamp which is shining in a squalid place, until day dawns and a
morning star arises in your hearts.*

(1:20, 21) The phrase, "knowing this first," refers back to
the words "whereunto ye do well that ye take heed." That is,
as Peter's readers give their attention to the Old Testament
prophecies, they are to keep in mind what follows in the rest of
the verse and the succeeding one. The word "private" is *idios,*
"unique, one's own." "Interpretation" is *epilusis,* "a loosening,
unloosing," metaphorically, "interpretation." The verb is *epiluō,*
"to unloose, untie, to explain what is obscure and hard to understand." The interpretation is here not that of the student of
scripture, but of the inspired prophet or writer of the scriptures
himself, since verse 20 speaks of the method by which these
prophecies came with relation to these writers. "It is the prophet's grasp of the prophecy, not that of the readers, that is here
presented, as the next verse shows" (Robertson). No prophecy
is of any private interpretation, so far as the writer of the
prophecy is concerned. Strachan says: "It seems most satis-
factory to understand this expression as the meaning of the
prophet himself, or what was in the prophet's mind when he
wrote; the fulfilment in any particular generation or epoch. 'The
special work of the prophet is to interpret the working of God
to his own generation. But in doing this, he is laying down the
principles of God's action generally. Hence there may be many
fulfilments of one prophecy, or to speak more exactly, many
historical illustrations of some one principle of providential government' (Mayor)." Strachan translates, "No prophecy is of
such a nature as to be capable of a particular interpretation."

In verse 20, the apostle explains what he means by the
expression, "private interpretation." The meaning or interpretation of the prophet does not come from the writer himself but
from the Holy Spirit. Robertson says: "Peter is not here warning against personal interpretation of prophecy as the Roman
Catholics say, but against the folly of upstart prophets with no
impulse from God."

Strachan continues the explanation of this verse in the words:
"Here we have the only reference to the Holy Spirit in the
epistle, and only in this connection, namely, as the source of
prophetic inspiration. The Spirit is an agency rather than an
agent. The men speak. The Spirit impels. It is of much
significance for the interpretation of the whole passage that 'men'
occupies a position of emphasis at the end of the sentence, thus
bringing into prominence the human agent. The prophets were
not ignorant of the meaning of their prophecies, but they saw
clearly only the contemporary political or moral situation, and
the principles involved and illustrated therein." All of which
means that the inspired prophets themselves, while understanding
only the contemporary application of their prophecies, did not
know their full implications and could not therefore limit that
meaning to their own time, which would be private or particular
interpretation.

Translation. *Knowing this first, that every prophecy of
scripture is not of a particular or limited meaning. For not by
the desire of man did prophecy come aforetime, but being carried
along by the Holy Spirit, men spoke from God.*

This process of men being carried along by the Holy Spirit and
thus speaking from God is explained by the apostle Paul in his
classic passage on that subject in I Corinthians 2:9-16. It was
written to a racial group that stands out in history as the most
intellectual of all peoples, the Greeks. They were a race of
creative thinkers. The sole instrument which they used in their
attempt to pierce through the mysteries of existence was human
reason. This they sharpened to a keen edge. But it was inadequate to solve the great mysteries of origins, of the wherefore

of human existence, of God, and of evil. Plato, one of their great
philosophers, said, "We must lay hold of the best human opinion
in order that borne by it as on a raft, we may sail over the dangerous sea of life, unless we can find a stronger boat, *or some
sure word of God,* which will more surely and safely carry us."
This great philosopher acknowledged that mere human reason
was not sufficient to answer the riddles with which man is confronted, and that the only sure foundation for a system of religious
truth was, not even the best of human opinion, but a revelation
from God.

The man who wrote this passage, declaring to these intellec-
tuals that the Bible has come not from human reason but by
divine revelation, was himself trained in their schools. He was a
native of Tarsus, a city where Greek culture predominated. The
University of Tarsus was known all over the world. Strabo
placed it ahead of the universities of Athens and Alexandria in
its zeal for learning. Paul's people were Roman citizens, and
also citizens of Tarsus, which latter fact tells us that his family
was one of wealth and standing, for during the time of Paul, only
people of wealth and standing in the community were allowed to
possess Tarsian citizenship. This explains Paul's statement, "I
have suffered the loss of all things" (Phil. 3:8). The city was
noted for its intense activity, its atmosphere of what we today call
"drive." Paul was not reared in the lassitude and ease of an
oriental city, but in an atmosphere of physical and mental
achievement. That he had a thorough training in the University
of Tarsus is evident from his words to the Corinthians: "And I
having come to you, brethren, came, not having my message
dominated by a transcendent rhetorical display or by philosophical subtlety . . . and my message and my preaching were not
couched in specious words of philosophy" (I Cor. 2:1, 4). He
could have used these had he wanted to. He was schooled in
Greek rhetoric, philosophy, and sophistry, also in Greek literature.
Thus in giving the Greeks his teaching of verbal inspiration, Paul
was not looking at the subject from only one angle, that of a
mystic who knew what fellowship with God was and who had

received communications from God, but he had had the other side of the problem in the Greek university, where he was brought into contact with human reason at its best.

He begins the treatment of his subject by telling the Greeks that neither scientific investigation nor human reason has ever been able to discover a sure foundation upon which a religious system could be built. He says, "Eye hath not seen, nor ear heard, . . . the things which God hath prepared for them that love him." The context makes it clear that these "things" consist of the revelation of truth, the holy Scriptures. But not only has scientific investigation never discovered this truth, but this truth has not been produced by the activity of man's reason, for he said, "neither have entered the heart of man." The Greek word translated "entered" does not refer to something entering the mind from the outside, but was used of things that come up in one's mind. We use the expression today, "It never entered my mind," meaning by that that the thing never occurred to us. Thus we have the statement of Paul that the truth of Scripture never arose in the consciousness of man, never found its source in the reason of man. Observe the bearing this has upon teaching that finds its basis in the theory of evolution, teaching to the effect that all that the human race knows is the result of divinity resident in man, and that therefore, all knowledge has come from within the race, none from without. After asserting the fact of the final inadequacy of reason in solving the riddle of existence, Paul proceeds to describe the three successive steps in the transmission of truth from the heart of God to the heart of man. These are, *revelation,* the act of God the Holy Spirit imparting to the Bible writers, truth incapable of being discovered by man's unaided reason (2:10-12) ; *inspiration,* the act of God the Holy Spirit enabling the Bible writers to write down in God-chosen words, infallibly, the truth revealed (2:13) ; and *illumination,* the act of God the Holy Spirit enabling believers to understand the truth given by *revelation* and written down by *inspiration* (2:14-16).

We will deal first with *revelation*. The first word in our English translation in verse nine, Authorized Version, is "but," and is the translation of the strong adversative particle in the Greek. But the first word in verse ten should not be "but," but "for," since the Greek word here is not adversative but explanatory. Paul explains that the Bible did not come by the way of scientific investigation and human reason, but that it came in another way, by revelation. Then he shows that the very fact that God gave this truth by revelation proves that in the nature of things it could not have been given in any other way, and proceeds in verse eleven to show that this is true. The word "revealed" is the translation of a Greek word which means "to uncover, to lay open what has been veiled or covered up." The word "us" refers to the Bible writers, for Paul is explaining to the Greeks his knowledge of the truth. The Holy Spirit who searches the deep things of God uncovered this truth to the vision of these men.

Then Paul by the use of pure logic proves to these Greeks the impossibility of discovering God's Word through scientific investigation or human reason. The word "man" in the Greek is not the word which refers to an individual male member of the human race, but is the generic term for man, which includes individuals of both sexes. The second use of the word "man" is accompanied by the definite article which in Greek points out individuality. Thus, our translation is, "For who is there of men who knows the things of the (individual) man." That is, no individual knows the inner thoughts and heart-life of another person. Man is inscrutable to his fellow-man.

The word "spirit" in the Greek refers here to the rational spirit, the power by which a human being feels, thinks, wills, and decides. Again, the word "man" in the phrase, "save the spirit of man," is preceded by the article. The Greek article originally came from the demonstrative pronoun, and it retains much of the demonstrative's force of pointing out. Therefore, we translate, "For who is there of men who knows the things of the (individual) man except the spirit of (that) man which is in him." Only the individual knows what is in his heart of hearts. To his fellow-man he is inscrutable.

Just so, Paul says, logic will lead us to the conclusion that if a man is inscrutable to his fellow-man, so God must be inscrutable to man. And just as only the individual person knows what is in his own heart, so only God knows what is in *His* own heart. Therefore, if man finds it impossible through scientific investigation and human reason to discover the inner secrets of his fellow-man, it is clear that he cannot find out the mind of God by the same methods. The only way in which a person can come to know the inner heart-life of another person is to have that person uncover the secrets of his inner life to him. It likewise follows that the only way in which a person can know the mind of God is to have God uncover His thoughts to man. Thus Paul has demonstrated to these Greeks the absolute need of a revelation from God if we are to know what is in His heart. The first step therefore, in the transmission of truth from the heart of God to the heart of the believer is *revelation,* the act of God the Holy Spirit uncovering the things in the heart of God to the Bible writers, thus imparting the truth of Scripture to them.

This brings us to the doctrine of verbal inspiration which Paul states in verse thirteen. After the Bible writers had been given the truth by means of the act of the Holy Spirit in uncovering it to them, the apostle says that they were not left to themselves to make a record of it. It is one thing to know a certain fact. It is quite another to find the exact words which will give someone else an adequate understanding of that fact. And right here is where the need of verbal inspiration comes in. Paul first makes the negative statement, "Which things we speak (put into words, *laleō*), not in words taught by human wisdom." That is, the words which the Bible writers used were not dictated by their human reason or wisdom.

Then the apostle makes the positive statement, "but in words taught by the Spirit." He says that the words which the Bible writers used were taught them by the Holy Spirit. That is, as they wrote the Scriptures, the Holy Spirit who had revealed the truth to them, now chooses the correct word out of the writer's vocabulary, whose content of meaning will give to the believer the exact truth God desires him to have. This however does not imply mechanical dictation nor the effacement of the writer's own personality. The Holy Spirit took the writers as He found them and used them infallibly. Luke's Greek is the purest and most beautiful. He was a native Greek. Paul's Greek is far more involved and difficult than John's, for Paul had a university training, while John's knowledge of Greek was that of the average man of the first century who knew Greek as his second language but never had any formal training in it. Professor John A. Scott in his excellent book, *We Would Know Jesus,* speaks of "the superb control of the Greek language" which Luke everywhere showed, and of the "hard and crabbed Greek of Paul as shown in Romans," also of the flowing language of Paul's speeches recorded in the Acts, which quality is not due to Paul's delivery but Luke's literary excellence.

However, whether it is the pure Greek of Luke, the difficult Greek of Paul, or the simple Greek of John, it is all correct as to grammar and syntax. The Holy Spirit observed the rules of Greek grammar as they existed in the *koine* Greek of that time. And the wonder of it all is seen in the fact that John brings to his readers just as precious, just as deep truth, in his simple Greek, as Paul does in his intricate constructions and involved sentences. God the Holy Spirit is above language. Thus we have in the original Hebrew and Greek texts of the Bible manuscripts the very words that God taught the writers to use as they recorded the truth which they had received by revelation. This is what is meant by verbal inspiration.

Then Paul in the words "comparing spiritual things with spiritual" explains this process of choosing the right word in each case. We will look carefully at the Greek word translated "comparing," for it throws a flood of light on Paul's teaching of verbal inspiration. The word is a compound of the verb meaning "to judge" and a preposition meaning "with," thus "to judge with." It speaks of the action of judging something with something else. For instance, a milliner wishes to trim a red hat with ribbon of the same color. She takes the hat over to the spools of ribbon and "judges" the various shades of red ribbon "with" the hat. She compares the hat with ribbon after ribbon in an attempt to find one which will exactly match the color of the hat. She rejects one after another until she finally finds one ribbon that exactly matches the hat. And that is exactly what the word means, "to join fitly together, to combine, to compound." That is just the procedure which the Bible writers went through in writing their books. As led by the Holy Spirit, they searched their vocabularies for the exact word which would adequately express the truth they wished to record. By the process of comparing the word with the truth they wished to write down, they rejected all those words which the Holy Spirit showed them would not correctly express the thought, and finally chose the word to which the Holy Spirit led them, and upon which the Holy Spirit put His stamp of approval. Thus the Holy Spirit allowed the writers the free play of their personalities, vocabulary, and training, while at the same time guiding them to make an infallible record of truth infallibly revealed.

The words, "spiritual things with spiritual," are from two adjectives in the Greek. The first word translated "spiritual" is in the accusative case, the direct object of the verb "comparing," and in the neuter gender. It refers to the spiritual truths already given the writers by revelation. The second use of the word "spiritual" is in the instrumental case, the instrumental of association. As to gender this word could be either masculine or neuter, for these two genders have the same form in the genitive through the dative cases. The English reader will please excuse these technicalities. We must look at the context to decide which gender is meant. The two things in the context which are compared and then combined are the truth revealed and the words which would correctly convey this truth. The words "spiritual things" refer to this truth. Therefore the word "spiritual" in its second use in verse thirteen refers to "words." The gender is therefore masculine since the word "words" in this verse is masculine. Vincent translates this phrase, "combining spiritual things with spiritual words." G. C. Findlay translates, "wedding kindred speech to thought." Alford renders it, "putting together spiritual words to spiritual things."

We come now to the doctrine of *illumination*, namely, the act of God the Holy Spirit enabling the believer to understand the truth given by *revelation*, and by *inspiration* written down. Paul says, "the natural man receiveth not the things of the Spirit of God." The word "natural" is the translation of a Greek word which Paul uses to describe to the Corinthian Greeks the unregenerate man at his best, the man whom Greek philosophy commended, the man actuated by the higher thoughts and aims of the natural life. The word used here is not the Greek word which speaks of the sensual man. It is the word coined by Aristotle to distinguish the pleasures of the soul, such as ambition and the desire for knowledge, from those of the body. The natural man here spoken of is the educated man at the height of his intellectual powers, but devoid of the Spirit of God. This man, whose powers of apprehension are limited to the exercise of his reason, does not admit these spiritual things into his heart. The reason for this rejection is that they are foolishness to him.

Then Paul states the impossibility of his knowing them, and its reason, because they are spiritually discerned. The Greek word translated "discern" means "to investigate, inquire into, scrutinize, sift, question." Thus the investigation of, inquiry into, scrutinizing, and sifting of scripture truth is done in the energy of the Holy Spirit who illuminates the sacred page of Scripture to the believer. It is "he that is spiritual" that judgeth all things. The word "judgeth" is the translation of the same Greek word rendered "discerneth." The Spirit-controlled Christian investigates, inquires into, and scrutinizes the Bible and comes to an appreciation and understanding of its contents.

The expanded translation of this important passage is as follows: *But just as it stands written: The things which eye did not see and ear did not hear, and which did not arise within the heart of man, as many things as God prepared for those that love Him. For, to us God uncovered them through the agency of His Spirit. For the Spirit explores all things, yes, the deep things of God. For who is there of men who knows the things of the (individual) man, unless it be the spirit of (that) man which is in him. Even so also the things of God no one knows, but the Spirit of God (knows the things of God). But as for us, not the spirit which animates the world did we receive, but the Spirit who proceeds from God, in order that we might know the things which by God have been freely given to us; which things we speak, not in words taught by human wisdom, but in words taught by the Spirit, matching spiritual things with Spirit-taught words. But the man whose powers of apprehension are limited to the exercise of his reason rejects the things of God since they are foolishness to him. And he is powerless to know them, because they are investigated through the instrumentality of the Spirit. But the man equipped by the Spirit comes to an apprehension of all things, yet he himself is comprehended by no one. For who knows the Lord's mind, that he should instruct Him? But as for us, we have the mind of Christ.*

In 1:1-11, Peter has dealt with the subject of the divine provision for a holy life in days of apostasy. A holy life is the most powerful antidote to the false doctrine to which the saint is subject, and a preventive of becoming entangled in the heresies of Modernism. As the believer lives close to the Lord Jesus, controlled by the Holy Spirit, he is constantly being warned against the false doctrines with which he is confronted.

In 1:12-21, the inspired apostle speaks of another safeguard against Modernism, namely, a rigid adherence to the doctrine of the full, verbal inspiration of the holy Scriptures, which he has just presented. After all, this is the crux of the whole controversy between the conservative position, sometimes called

Fundamentalism, and Modernism. Did God really speak? Is every Hebrew and Greek word in the original autographs which left the hands of the inspired writers a God-chosen word? If so, all the other doctrines of the Christian system are shown to be from God, since they are clearly reiterated in the pages of holy writ, such doctrines as the deity, virgin birth, vicarious atonement, and bodily resurrection of the Lord Jesus.

CHAPTER TWO

(2:1) After treating the subject of the Divine Provision for a Holy Life (1:1-11), and the Divine Inspiration of the Scriptures (1:12-21), the inspired apostle deals with the matter of false teachers in the Church (2:1-22). He had been speaking of the true prophets of God who wrote the O.T. scriptures (1:21). Now, he warns against false ones. The chief ministry of the O.T. prophet was a hortatory one to his own generation. That is, he was a preacher who rebuked Israel because of its sins, and pointed to the way of righteousness. His predicting of the future was but one of his ministries. In the case of the N.T. prophet in the Church, the preaching of the gospel of grace to the unsaved and the exposition of the Word to the saints constitute his responsibilities. The designation "teachers" which Peter uses, refers to any man who is engaged in Christian activity, whether a pastor, evangelist, teacher. In short, he is speaking in this section of anyone who teaches the Bible.

"There were" is *ginomai*, "there arose." These were self-appointed prophets. "Who" is *hoitines*, speaking not only of identity but including the idea of class or kind, namely, "who were of such a kind or class that" etc. "Privily shall bring in" is *pareisagō*, made up of *agō*, "to bring," *eis*, "into," and *para*, "alongside," thus, "to bring in alongside." That is, these false teachers, teaching much true doctrine, would cleverly include false teaching with it. Vincent says that the metaphor in the word is that of a spy or traitor. Strachan says: "The idea of 'stealth' or 'secrecy' — 'stealthily to introduce' — is hardly in accord with their character described elsewhere . . . Rather the idea seems to be of the introduction of false teaching alongside the true, whereby the way of truth is brought into disrepute."

"Damnable heresies" is better rendered (Vincent) "heresies of destruction." The Revision gives, "destructive heresies."

46

"Destructive" is the translation of *apōleia*, "ruin, destruction, the destruction which consists in the loss of eternal life, eternal misery, perdition." The word speaks of the loss of everything that makes human existence worthwhile. The word "heresies" is interesting. It is the English spelling of the Greek word *hairesis*, the primary meaning of which is "choice." Vincent explains: "so that a heresy is, strictly, the choice of an opinion contrary to that usually received." Peter now mentions what was probably the most serious of the heretical teachings, the denial of the substitutionary death of our Lord. "Bought" is *agorazō*, one of the three words used in the N.T. which are translated "redeem." The word in classical use meant "to purchase in the market place," and was used of the purchase of slaves in the slave-market. Our Lord's precious, outpoured blood was the ransom paid to redeem slaves of sin from that slavery. His death satisfied the just demands of the High Court of Heaven, paying the penalty for the sinner, and making a way whereby a righteous God could be just and at the same time the justifier of the believing sinner. Strachan says: "The denial seems to have consisted in an inadequate view of the Person and Work of Christ, and their relation to the problem of human sin." Of course, such a person is unsaved. We make this point here in order that when we approach the subject matter dealing with the utter destruction of these false teachers, we may be guided by our context. These are not misguided Christians, but heretics. The word "destruction" is the same Greek word *apōleia* discussed above, and which refers to the loss of all that makes existence worthwhile. It is eternal misery apart from a holy God that is in view here.

Translation. *But there arose also false prophets among the people, even as also among you there shall be false teachers, who will be of such a character as to bring in alongside (of true doctrine) destructive heresies, even denying the Lord who purchased them, bringing upon themselves swift destruction.*

(2:2) "Follow" is *exakoloutheō*, "to follow out to the end, to pursue to its termination," a line of thought or activity.

"Pernicious" is *aselgeia,* "unbridled lust, excess, licentiousness, lasciviousness, wantonness, outrageousness, shamelessness, insolence." The term, therefore, does not refer to the heresies of the false teachers, but to their immoral lives. The latter are the result of the former. "Whom" refers back to the many who followed the false teachers. "The way of truth" is more accurately, "the road of the truth." The word "way" is to be understood here as a path or road, the road down which a person travels. It does not mean "method" or "manner," but refers to the outworking of the truth in the life of the Christian, his behavior or manner of life. Thus, Christianity is spoken against by the world by reason of the ungodly lives of professing, and alas, sometimes of possessing Christians. "Evil spoken of" is *blasphēmeō,* "to speak reproachfully of, rail at, revile, calumniate."

Translation. *And many will follow their licentious conduct to its consummation, on account of whom the way of the truth will be reviled at.*

(2:3) "Covetousness" is *pleonexia,* "greedy desire to have more, avarice." "Through" is *en* followed by the locative of sphere. It is in the sphere of a greedy desire to have more, that these false teachers operate. Robertson says: "These licentious Gnostics made money out of their dupes." "Feigned" is *plastos;* the verb form is *plassō,* "to mould" as in clay or wax. Vincent says: "The idea is, therefore, of words moulded at will to suit their vain imaginations." "Make merchandise" is *emporeuomai,* "to go a trading, to traffic, trade." The Greek word *emporion,* from which we get our word "emporium" means "a place where trade is carried on, a seaport, a mart." Strachan translates, "make gain of, exploit." Thayer translates, "whose punishment has long been impending and will shortly fall."

Vincent says (quoting Salmond and Lillie), "There is a graphic picture in the sentence. The judgment is not *idle.* It is represented as a living thing, awake and expectant. Long ago that judgment started on its destroying path, and the fate of sinning angels, and the deluge, and the overthrow of Sodom and Gomorrah were but incidental illustrations of its power; nor has it ever since lingered. . . . It advances still, strong and vigilant as when it sprang from the bosom of God, and will not fail to reach the mark to which it was pointed from of old." "Damnation" is *apōleia,* "utter ruin and destruction, the loss of all that makes existence worthwhile."

Translation. *And in the sphere of covetousness, with moulded words they will exploit you, for whom the judgment is not lingering, and their destruction is not sleeping.*

(2:4) "The angels that sinned" are the angels of Jude 6, 7 whose sin was that of fornication. There is no article before "angels" in the Greek text. They are looked upon as a class and with reference to their position in the scale of created beings, the argument being that if God did not spare a higher order of being to man, namely, angels, He will surely not spare human beings. "If" is *ei,* the particle of a fulfilled condition. It could be translated "since," or "in view of the fact." "Hell" here is *Tartarus.* This is the prison of the fallen angels until the Great White Throne Judgment, from where they will be sent to eternal misery in the Lake of Fire (Rev. 20:14), the final abode of the wicked dead, also called "hell." The Greek word is *geenna,* from which we get the name "Gehenna" (Matt. 5:22, 29, 30). The word *hāidēs,* translated "hell" (Matt. 16:18), means "the unseen" and refers to the unseen world of free moral intelligences, holy angels, fallen angels, departed saints, the unsaved who died, Satan, and the demons. The context speaks of the latter two in the unseen world who would destroy the Church if they could. For a full discussion of the three words, *geenna, tartarōsas,* and *hāidēs,* see the author's book, *Treasures in the Greek New Testament,* chapter 6, "Hell, Hades, and Tartarus." Here, Peter is speaking of that place in the unseen world where the fallen angels are imprisoned until the Great White Throne Judgment. The word *tartarōsas* is the Greek pagan name for the place of punishment of the evil. Strachan says: "In Homer, Hades is the place of confinement for dead men, and Tartarus is the name given to a murky abyss beneath Hades in which the sins of fallen immortals are punished. Hence II Peter uses this word in agreement with the Book of Enoch (where Tartarus is the place of punishment of fallen angels) and Greek mythology because he is speaking of fallen angels and not of men."

"Delivered" is *paradidōmi*, "to give over into the hands of another, to deliver to someone something to keep, to commit to another." God committed these fallen angels into "chains of darkness." "Chains" is *seiros*, "a pit, an underground granary." The word *seira*, meaning "a line, a rope," is found in some texts, but the best texts have *seiros*, "a pit." The English reader can see the similarity of the words and understand how the mistake could have occurred in the centuries when the Greek manuscripts were copied by hand. "Darkness" is *zophos*, "blackness, the blackness of (i.e., the densest) darkness," originally used of the gloom of the nether world. Homer uses the word in the lines, "These halls are full of shadows hastening down to Erebus amid the gloom" (Odyssey). When Ulysses meets his mother in the shades, she says to him, "How didst thou come, my child, a living man, into this place of darkness?" (Odyssey). Milton writes, "Here their prison ordained in utter darkness set, as far removed from God and light of heaven as from the centre thrice to the utmost pole" (Paradise Lost).

"To be reserved" is a present participle in the Greek text, showing action going on, thus, "being reserved" for judgment.

Translation. *For, in view of the fact that God did not spare angels who sinned, but having thrust them down into Tartarus, committed them to pits of nether-world gloom, being reserved for judgment.*

(2:5) "Saved" is *phulassō*, "to guard a person that he remain safe, that is, lest he suffer violence, be despoiled." Here it means "to preserve" Noah through the time of the flood. The word has no reference to spiritual salvation. Noah was already a saved man before he entered the ark. The words "the eighth *person*" are to be understood as referring to the fact that there were eight people preserved in the ark. "Preacher" is *kērux*, "a herald." A herald in ancient times was a highly honored person, frequently a spokesman for the emperor, or an ambassador of one country to another. The verbal form means "to proclaim or announce." Noah proclaimed the message of God for 120 years to the antediluvian world, warning the people of the coming judgment of the flood and showing the way of personal salvation. "Bringing in" is *epagō*, "to cause something to befall one, usually something evil." It is used of "setting on, letting loose" the dogs. "Flood" is *kataklusmos*. The verbal form is *katakluzō*, "to overwhelm with water, to submerge, deluge." The noun means, "an inundation, deluge." "Ungodly" is *asebēs*, "destitute of reverential awe towards God, impious."

Translation. *And did not spare the ancient world, but preserved Noah as the eighth person (to be preserved), a proclaimer of righteousness, having let loose the deluge upon the world of those who were destitute of reverential awe towards God.*

(2:6) "Turning into ashes" is *tephroō*, "to reduce to ashes, to consume, destroy." Strachan says: " 'to cover up with ashes,' not 'to reduce to ashes,' found in a description of the eruption of Vesuvius." "Overthrow" is *katastrophē*, "overthrow, destruction." The verb is *katastrephō*, "to turn over, turn under, throw down." Strachan translates: "constituting them an example to ungodly persons of things in store for them."

Translation. *And the cities of Sodom and Gomorrha having reduced to ashes, He condemned them to destruction, having constituted them as a permanent example to the ungodly of things about to come.*

(2:7) "Vexed" is *kataponeō*, "to tire down with toil, exhaust with labor, to afflict or oppress with evils." The vile lives of the people of these two cities wore Lot down as his soul rebelled against the filth he saw always about him. "Conversation" is *anastrophē*, "manner of life." "Wicked" is *athesmos*, "lawless," used of one who breaks through the restraints of law and gratifies his lusts. The word is stronger than *anomos*, "lawless," because "it is used especially of a divine ordinance, a fundamental law" (Strachan). "Filthy" is *aselgeia*, "unbridled lust, excess, wantonness, shamelessness." The word is in the locative of sphere following the preposition *en*. Peter is referring to the behavior of the lawless in the sphere of unbridled lust.

Translation. *And righteous Lot, completely worn down by the manner of life of the lawless in the sphere of unbridled lust, He delivered.*

(2:8) "Dwelling" is *egkatoikeō*, "to live in a home," *kata*, "down," and *eg (en)* "in," or "among." *Katoikeō* speaks of the act of settling down permanently. It was used of the permanent residents of a town as contrasted to the transients who lived there only for a time. Lot had settled down permanently among the inhabitants of Sodom. "Seeing" is *blemma* (from *blepō*), "a look, a glance." It is used of the look of a man from without. The person looking is an onlooker but not a participant of the thing viewed. "Vexed" is *basanizō*, "to torment, to torture." Strachan remarks: "It is somewhat peculiar that the active should be used. 'He vexed, distressed his righteous soul.' May it not be that in the use of the active a certain sense of personal culpability is implied? Lot was conscious that the situation was ultimately due to his own selfish choice." Strachan translates, "day in, day out."

Translation. *For, in seeing and hearing, the righteous one having settled down permanently among them, day in, day out, tormented his righteous soul with their lawless works.*

(2:9) Strachan says: "The idea here is primarily of those surroundings that try a man's fidelity and integrity, and not of the inward inducement to sin, arising from the desires. Both Noah and Lot were in the midst of mockers, and unbelievers. This *peirasmos* (testing, temptation) is the atmosphere in which faith is brought to full development. It was a condition even in the life of Jesus (Luke 22:28). It is the word used by St. Luke of the Temptation (Luke 4:13). On the one hand *peirasmos* is not to be lightly sought (Luke 11:4) nor entered into carelessly (Mk. 14:38); the situation of *peirasmos* may itself be the result of sin (I Tim. 6:9). On the other hand, it is a joyous opportunity for the development of spiritual and moral strength (James 1:2, 12). *Peirasmos* becomes sin only when it ceases to be in opposition to the will." The word originally meant "a test," and by use, came also to mean "a temptation," in the sense of a solicitation to do evil. "To be punished" is a present participle in the Greek text. It presents continuous action.

Translation. *The Lord knows how to deliver the godly out of testing and temptation, but to be reserving the unrighteous for the day of judgment under punishment.*

(2:10) Peter, having spoken of the sins of the Sodomites, now turns to those of the Libertines. "Walk" is *poreuomai*. This word means "to proceed along a road, go on a journey." It speaks of the act of leading or ordering one's life. The usual word translated "walk" is *peripateō*, "to order one's behavior." *Poreuomai* has the added idea of pursuing a course of action. "After" is *opisō*, which is used of the act of joining a certain person as an attendant and follower, of running after a thing that one lusts for. "Flesh" is *sarx*, and here has reference to the totally depraved nature. The picture in the Greek therefore is of these Libertines pursuing after the evil nature, eager to follow its behests. "Lust" is *epithumia*, "passionate desire, a craving." "Uncleanness" is *miasma*, "that which defiles." The same word is used in 2:20 in the phrase, "the pollutions of the world," which Thayer defines as "vices the foulness of which contaminates one in his intercourse with the ungodly mass of mankind."

"Despise" is *kataphroneō*, made up of *phroneō*, "to feel, think, have understanding," and *kata* "down," thus, "to think a thing down." We say, "look down our noses at a thing." The compound word means therefore, "to disdain, think little or nothing of, to condemn, despise." "Government" is *kuriotēs* "dominion, power, lordship," used in the N.T. of one who possesses dominion. Strachan says: "*Kuriotēs* cannot be taken in a purely abstract sense, 'despising authority.' *Kuriotēs* is used in the abstract sense of the Lordship of Christ in Didache 4:1. . . . As is suggested by this passage in the Didache, we may conclude that by 'despise government' is meant a despising of the Lordship of Christ, which was the central theme of the apostolic teaching and preaching."

"Presumptuous" is *tolmētēs*. The verb is *tolmaō*, "to dare, not to dread or shun through fear, to be bold, bear one's self boldly."

"Selfwilled" is *authadēs*, "self-pleasing, arrogant, selfwilled."
"Afraid" is *tremō*, "to tremble, to fear, be afraid." The trembling
spoken of in this word is predominantly physical. "Speak evil
of" is *blasphēmeō*, "to speak reproachfully of, rail at, revile,
calumniate." "Dignities" is *doxa*, used in the N.T. in the meaning of "splendor, brightness, a most glorious condition, most
exalted state, used of the majesty (glory) of angels, as apparent
in their exterior brightness (Luke 9:26); in a wider sense, in
which angels are called *doxa* as spiritual beings of preeminent
dignity (Jude 8, II Peter 2:10) (Thayer). Strachan says: "The
false teachers may have scoffed at the idea both of angelic help
and of diabolic temptation. Their tendency seems to have been
to make light of the Unseen, to foster a sense of the unreality
both of sin and of goodness, and to reduce the motives of conduct
to a vulgar hedonism, (the doctrine that pleasure is the sole or
chief good in life, and that moral duty is fulfilled in the gratifica-
tion of pleasure-seeking instincts and dispositions)."

Translation. *But especially those who proceed on their way,
hot in pursuit of the flesh in the sphere of the passionate desire
of that which defiles, and who disdain authority. Presumptuous,
arrogant, they do not tremble when defaming those in exalted
positions.*

(2:11) "Power" is *ischus*, "indwelling strength, especially
as embodied, which dwells in persons or things, and gives them
influence or value" (Vincent). "Might" is *dunamis*, "ability,
faculty, not necessarily manifest, as *ischus*" (Vincent). The
angels are greater in power and might than the false teachers
of verse 10. These latter presume to speak evil of the holy
angels. But, the holy angels do not presume to speak reproachfully of fallen angels. Strachan is helpful here: "We may note
the tendency in II Peter, exemplified here, to put in general terms
what Jude states in the particular, in the story of Michael and
Satan. . . . The sentence 'they bear not against them railing
accusation,' is only intelligible by reference to Jude 9, where
Michael does not himself condemn Satan, but says, 'The Lord
rebuke thee.'"

"Accusation" is *krisis*, "a judgment, an opinion or decision given concerning anything," especially concerning justice and injustice, right and wrong. "Railing" is *blasphēmos*, "reproachful."

Translation. *Whereas, angels being greater in power and might, are not bringing against them from the presence of the Lord reproachful judgment.*

(2:12) "These" refers to the false teachers of verse 10. They are described as "natural brute beasts." "Brute" is *aloga*, "unreasoning, irrational." Strachan says: "Their chief characteristic is that they are 'alive,' and have no sense of the moral issues of life. Like animals, they exist to be taken and destroyed." The word "natural" is *phusikos*, "produced by nature." "Made" is to be construed with this word. "Made" is *gennaō*, "to beget," passive, "to be born." Here the word is a perfect passive participle. Thayer translates, "born mere animals." The word he defines as "governed by (the instincts of) nature." Strachan translates, "born creatures of instinct," and says: "Instinct is here distinguished from the rational centres of thought and judgment." "To be taken and destroyed" is *eis halosin kai phthoran*, literally, "for capture and destruction." Vincent translates, "But these, as creatures without reason, born mere animals to be taken and destroyed." "Speak evil" is *blasphēmeō*, which Strachan here translates, "*speaking lightly* of things they are ignorant of." Vincent defines the word as "railing." In the words, "shall utterly perish in their own corruption," we have in the Greek text a cognate construction. The meaning of the verb is the same as the meaning of the noun in the predicate. Vincent reports the Revision translation as follows: "shall in their destroying surely be destroyed."

Translation. *But these, as irrational creatures, having been born as creatures of instinct, (destined) for capture and destruction, railing against things of which they are ignorant, shall in their destroying, surely be destroyed.*

(2:13) The word "receive" in the Greek text is *adikeō*, in passive as it is here, "receiving unrighteousness." Thus, the apostle is telling us here that these false teachers are receiving

unrighteousness as their hire for unrighteousness. "Riot" is
truphē, "softness, effeminacy, luxurious living." These count it
a pleasure to live a luxurious life in the day time, which means
that they do not work for a living but live off of the money they
get from those whom they lead astray into false doctrine. They
live luxuriously at a time when men are supposed to be sober and
at their daily occupations. See Acts 2:15 and I Thessalonians
5:7.

"Sporting" is the translation of the verb *entruphaō,* "to live in
luxury, to revel in." "Deceivings" is the translation of *apatais*
"deceitfulness." Vincent, Alford, and Robertson argue for the
meaning of *agapais,* as "a love-feast," a feast expressing and
fostering mutual love which was held by Christians before the
celebration of the Lord's Supper, and at which the poorer Christians mingled with the wealthier and partook in common with
the rest, of food provided at the expense of the wealthy. The
two words are very similar, *apatais* and *agapais.* A near sighted
or careless scribe could have easily made such an error. Jude
uses the word in verse 12 where he speaks of the Christian love
feast. This is most probably the case where these false teachers
ate with the Christians at the love-feast, enjoying the food provided by the rich. They were spots and blemishes at that occasion. "Spot" is *spilos,* used in secular manuscripts of a spot or
stain. Moulton and Milligan report its usage in the expression,
"the dregs of humanity from the city." The word is used metaphorically in Ephesians 5:27. It speaks of a fault or moral
blemish. Here it is used of these gluttonous false teachers.
"Blemish" is *mōmos,* "a blot, a disgrace," used here of men who
are a disgrace to society. "Feast" is *suneuōcheō,* "to feast sumptuously with." Vincent says: "The word originally conveys
the idea of *sumptuous* feasting, and is appropriate in view of the
fact to which Peter alludes, that these sensualists converted the
love-feast into a revel. Compare Paul's words (I Cor. 11:21),
'one is hungry and another drunken.' This seems to favor the
reading *agapais* (love-feast)."

Translation. *Receiving unrighteousness as the hire for
unrighteousness, deeming luxurious living in the day-time a*

pleasure; moral blemishes and disgraceful blots, living luxuri-
ously at your love-feasts, feasting sumptuously with you.

(2:14) Alford and Robertson translate, "having eyes full of
an adulteress." The latter says: "Vivid picture of a man who
cannot see a woman without lascivious thoughts toward her
(Mayor)." "Cannot cease" is *akatapauō*, "unable to stop."
"Beguiling" is *deleazō*, "to catch by bait." "Unstable" is
astērikos, "unsteadfast," from *stērizō*, "to make stable, place
firmly, set fast," and alpha privative which negates the word. It
speaks of a person who is not anchored securely, or who is not
solidly on a foundation, here, doctrinally and experientially.

The translation could better read, "having a heart exercised in
covetousness." The word "exercised" is *gumnazō*. It is the
word the Greeks used of an athlete exercising in the gymnasium.
Here it speaks of the exercise of the heart, the latter standing
for the reason, the will, and the emotions. The word is a perfect
participle, speaking of a past completed action having present
results. These false teachers had lived in a heart atmosphere
of covetousness for so long that their heart condition was one of
a permanent state. The Greek has it, "children of cursing," the
latter word, genitive of description. That was the character of
these false teachers. "Curse" is *katara*, "an execration, impre-
cation, curse." The word is used of one who is under the divine
curse.

Translation. *Having eyes full of an adulteress and which are
unable to cease from sin, catching unstable souls with bait, having a heart completely exercised in covetousness, children of a
curse.*

(2:15 16) "Have forsaken" is *kataleipō*, "to abandon." It
is in the present tense, "abandoning," emphasizing habitual action. "The right way" is "the straight road." "Way" here is
hodos, "a road," metaphorically, "a course of conduct, a way of
thinking, feeling, deciding." "Right" is *euthus*, "straight, level,
right." Abandoning the straight way, they went astray. "Following" is an aorist participle, "having followed out to the end."
The verb is *exakoloutheō*, the prefixed preposition being perfec-

tive in force, intensifying the already existing idea in the verb. These false teachers followed out most assiduously the way of Balaam. The verb means, "to tread in one's steps, to imitate one's way of acting." Balaam was the hireling prophet who commercialized his gift. These false teachers were in the profession for the money they could get out of it. The word "loved" is *agapaō*, "a love called out of one's heart by the preciousness of the object loved." The same word is used of Demas who loved this present age (II Tim. 4:10).

"Was rebuked" is literally "had a rebuke." "His iniquity" is *idias paranomias,* "his own transgression." The possessive speaks of what is one's own private, unique possession. The word translated "iniquity" (A.V.) is made up of *nomos,* "law," and *para,* "contrary to," thus, "one who acts contrary to law." "Ass" is *hupozugion,* literally, "that which is beneath the yoke," "namely, "a beast of burden." "Dumb" is *aphōnon,* "without the faculty of speech." The word "speaking" is *phtheggomai,* "to give out a sound, noise, cry"; used by the Greeks of any sound or voice, whether of man or animal or inanimate object, as of thunder, musical instruments. It denotes sound in its relation to the hearer rather than its cause. The inarticulate animal spoke in a human voice. "Forbad" is *kōluō,* "to hinder, check, restrain."

Translation. *Abandoning the straight way, they went astray, having followed assiduously the way of Balaam the son of Bosor, who set a high value upon and thus came to love the hire of unrighteousness, but had a rebuke for his own transgression, the inarticulate beast of burden having spoken in a man's voice, restrained the insanity of the prophet.*

(2:17) "Well" is *pēgē,* "a spring." The Greek word for a "well" is *phrear.* The word *pēgē* speaks of an ever-upleaping living fountain. The words "without water" are an oriental expression where the green verdure excites the traveller's hope of water, only to have it often disappointed. Such are these false teachers. Where one looks for a clear spring of water, the living Word of God, there is a spring gone dry. "Clouds" does not occur in the best manuscripts, rather *homichlē,* "a mist, a fog."

"Carried" is *elaunō*, "to drive"; used of the wind driving ships or clouds. "Tempest" is *lailaps*, "a whirlwind, a tempestuous wind, a squall, a violent wind." It is never a single gust, nor a steadily blowing wind, however violent, but a storm breaking forth from black thunder-clouds in furious gusts, with floods of rain, and throwing everything topsy-turvey (Thayer). "Mist of darkness" is "blackness of the darkness." "Is reserved" is perfect in tense, namely, "has been reserved with the present result that it is kept in store." False teachers are devoid of the Holy Spirit. Our Lord speaks of the one who drinks of the water that He shall give (John 4:14), and says that that water shall become in him a spring (*pēgē*) of water leaping up into eternal life. John in 7:39 says that our Lord's use of water here as a symbol points to the Holy Spirit.

Translation. *These are springs without water, and mists driven by a tempest, for whom the blackness of the darkness has been reserved.*

(2:18) "Speak" is *phtheggomai*, the same word used when Balaam's beast of burden was uttering sounds. It denotes sound in relation to the hearer rather than the cause. From this we judge that the inspired apostle used this distinctive word to indicate that "the great swelling words" were spoken with an oratorical flare that would impress the hearers. One could better translate "utter." "Great swelling" is *huperogka* from *huper* "over," and *ogkos*, "a swelling," thus "overswollen," used metaphorically with the meanings of "immoderate, extravagant"; Thayer says, "expressive of arrogance." Vincent comments: "The word means 'of excessive bulk.' It accords well with the peculiar word *uttering*, since it denotes a kind of speech full of high-sounding verbosity without substance." The word "words" is not in the Greek text, but is rightfully supplied.

"Vanity" is *mataios*, "empty, vain" in the sense of "futile, in vain." Strachan remarks that the reference no doubt is to Gnostic terms. *Mataios* (vanity) is used especially of moral insincerity. The verbose speech of these false teachers was futile in that it did not fulfil that for which speech was intended, to convey accurate and true information. All it did was to allure like bait the hearers so that they would become followers of the false teachers. "Allure" is *deleazō,* "to catch by bait, to beguile by blandishments, to entice." These false teachers allure through the lusts of the flesh, namely, the cravings of the totally depraved nature. That is, they appeal to these cravings and satisfy them. The evil nature is that which they catch hold of to lead their hearers astray. Our Lord said in this connection, "The prince of this world cometh, and hath nothing in Me" (John 14:30), that is, Satan found nothing, no fallen nature in our Lord to catch hold of. "Wantonness" is *aselgeia.* Thayer's note on this word as it is used in this passage is as follows: "plural, wanton acts or manners, as filthy words, indecent bodily movements, unchaste handling of males and females." The word is in apposition to "cravings." That is, the false teachers use bait to catch their hearers, satisfying the cravings of the fallen nature in the realm of *aselgeia,* these wanton acts or manners.

"Clean" is the translation of *ontōs,* "really, actually," the Greek word being found in the Received Text which the translators of A.V. used. The best texts today read *oligōs,* "in a little degree, just, scarcely." "Escaped" is a present participle, denoting a process going on. The translation reads, "those who are just about escaping," denoting, as Vincent says, "those who are in the early stage of their escape from error, and are not safe from it and confirmed in the truth." Strachan describes these as those "who have been impressed with Christian truth, and have had strength to separate themselves from their old surroundings and customs, but are led to return through the compromises suggested by the false teachers. The phenomenon is not uncommon in all missionary work, of men who have escaped from 'Gentile vices,' but are not yet established in Christian virtues."

Those "who live in error" are the false teachers. "Live" is *anastrephō,* "to conduct one's self." "Error" is *planē,* "a wandering, a straying about, error, wrong opinion relative to morals or religion."

Translation. *For when they are uttering extravagant things that are in their character futile, they are alluring by means of the cravings of the flesh (evil nature), by means of wanton acts, those who are just about escaping from those who are ordering their behavior in the sphere of error.*

(2:19) Strachan, commenting on the words, "while they promise them liberty," says: "Doubtless that Antinomianism (against law, thus lawlessness, not responsible to law) is indicated to which the doctrine of grace has ever been open. Compare Galatians 5:13. It arises from the ever-recurring confusion of liberty and license. The training of conscience is contemporaneous with the growth of Christian character. The Pauline teaching, which abrogated external legality, was open to abuse, and might easily be dangerous to recent converts from heathenism." The liberty spoken of in Galatians 5:1 is liberty from the Mosaic law, not liberty to do as one pleases. The one set at liberty from the law is under a stronger and more effective compulsion, namely, divine love as ministered to the yielded saint by the Holy Spirit (Gal. 5:13). These false teachers, not being saved and therefore not knowing grace, misrepresented the latter as license to sin. "Servants" is *doulos,* "slaves." The word is a designation of the most abject, servile form of slavery.

The Greek back of the translation, "of whom a man is overcome, of the same is he brought in bondage," is literally, "by whom a person has been overcome with the result that he is in a state of subjugation, to this one has he been enslaved with the result that he is in a state of slavery." The perfect tense is used by Peter.

Translation. *While they are promising them liberty, they themselves are slaves of corruption. For by whom a person has been overcome with the result that he is in a state of subjugation, to this one has he been enslaved with the result that he is in a state of slavery.*

(2:20, 21) The subject of false teachers is continued in this verse. These are the false teachers of 2:1 who deny the doctrine of atonement by the substitutionary death of the Lord Jesus.

Hence they are not saved, only professing Christians. They are said to have had a knowledge of the Lord Jesus. It is one thing to know Him personally, as a believer does, and another to know of Him, namely, the facts about Him, and to give a mental acquiescence to these, as an unbeliever does. Such a knowledge resulted in their escaping the pollutions of the world. The world here is *kosmos,* the world system of evil. That in this system which they escaped is given us in the word *miasma.* Thayer defines this word as "that which defiles," and explains it in its occurrence here as "vices the foulness of which contaminates one in his intercourse with the ungodly mass of mankind." Strachan says: "In the LXX (Septuagint, Greek translation of the Old Testament) the word seems to have a technical religious sense, the profanation of flesh by ordinary use which is set apart for sacrifice. This sense lingers here. The body is sacred to God, and to give licentious rein to the passions is *miasma* (pollution)." The moral and ethical influence of the Word of God had acted as a detergent and a deterrent upon these false teachers to the end that their outward lives had been relatively pure. But as they persisted in their false teaching that grace gave license to sin, they became entangled in their former licentious ways. "Entangle" is *emplekō,* "to inweave." The noun speaks of an interweaving, a braiding. Their going back to their former immoral lives was not the act of a moment, but a gradual process, as the word implies. Vincent quotes a classical author (Aeschylus) on the use of this word, "For not on a sudden or in ignorance will ye be entangled by your folly."

Translation. *For if, having escaped the pollutions of the world by a knowledge of the Lord and Saviour Jesus Christ, in these moreover again being entangled, they have been overcome with the result that they are in a state of subjugation, the last things have become to them worse than the first ones; for it were better for them not to have known the way of the righteousness, than, having known it, to turn back from the holy commandment which was delivered to them.*

(2:22)   Peter quotes Proverbs 26:11 in mentioning the dog. The second saying is not found in Scripture.   Pagan sources speak of the habit of hogs delighting to bathe in a filthy mudhole. Robertson refers to a story about a hog in ancient literature "that went to the bath with people of quality, but on coming out saw a stinking drain, and went and rolled himself in it."

These unsaved teachers, cleaned up on the outside, experiencing an outward moral reformation but not an inward regeneration, like the sow, went back to their wallowing in the gross forms of sin from which they had been outwardly delivered by the cleansing action of an intellectual knowledge of the Word of God.

Translation. *But it has happened to them according to the true saying: a dog returns to his own vomit, and a sow, having been bathed, to her rolling in mire.*

CHAPTER THREE

(3:1, 2) After dealing with the presence of false teachers in the first century church, Peter predicts that there will be such in the last times. "Pure" is *eilikrinēs*, "unmixed, unsullied, sincere," here, free from falsehoods. "Be mindful" is *mimnēskō*, "to remind."

Translation. *This already, divinely-loved ones, is a second letter I am writing to you, in which I am stirring up your unsullied mind by way of remembrance, that you should remember the words spoken previously by the holy prophets and the commandment of the Lord and Saviour spoken by your apostles.*

(3:3) "Scoffers" is *empaiktēs*, "a mocker, a scoffer." The cognate verb is *empaizō*, "to play with, to trifle with, to mock." "Lusts" is *epithumia*, "a desire," here, as the context shows, "evil desires."

Translation. *Knowing this first, that there shall come in the last of the days mockers with mockery, ordering their manner of life according to their own personal desires.*

(3:4) The question which faces the expositor now is as to the identity of this coming. Is it the coming of our Lord into the air to catch out the Church, or is it His Second Advent to this earth to reign? The following considerations indicate that it refers to the Advent. The word "coming" is *parousia*, literally, "a being alongside," hence a personal presence. The word is used of the Rapture and the Advent. So the word itself is not decisive. *First,* Peter had spoken of the Advent in 1:16 (see work on that verse), *second,* the false teachers are not to be judged at the Rapture but at the Advent, and *third,* the context (3:10) speaks of the day of the Lord, which occurs at the time of the second Advent.

There are four days in Scripture, the day of man (I Cor. 4:3, "man's judgment," Greek, "man's day"), that time starting with Adam's fall until the second Advent when unsaved man has liberty under the permissive will of God to do as he pleases; the day of Christ (Phil. 1:6), when Christ has His day in the catching out of His Bride at the Rapture; the day of the Lord (Isaiah 13:9, Rev. 6-20), the Great Tribulation and the Millennium, when the Lord has His day, visiting judgment upon the ungodly; the day of God (II Peter 3:12), when God has His day, the close of the Millennium, the Great White Throne judgment, and the restoration of the earth and its planetary heavens to their pristine glory.

The end-time mockers will mock at the promise of our Lord's second Advent. The basis of their rejection of the second Advent according to John in his second letter (v. 7) is that they deny that Jesus Christ comes in flesh. That is, they deny that the Jehoshua of the Old Testament (Jehovah who saves) who is designated as the Anointed One (Christ) in the New Testament, ever would become incarnate, assume a human body and put Himself under human limitations without its sin. The denial of an incarnation today is given a rationalistic basis in the theory of evolution which teaches that the universe and man are such today by reason of the operation of a resident force in matter and man that is developing both from a crude beginning toward a perfect conclusion without the aid of any outside force. In short, the theory will not permit the introduction of anything or anyone from the outside into the unbroken continuity of existence, hence, no incarnation.

The basis of the end-time mocker's rejection of the second Advent is that from the beginning of the creation, all things continue as they were. Here we have the unbroken continuity of existence given as a reason for rejecting the coming of the Lord Jesus, no introduction of anything from without into the affairs of the human race. The promise of the Lord's return must have been tied up in the minds of these mockers with the judgment of God upon the ungodly, for Peter in 3:5-12 speaks

of the past judgment of Genesis 1:2 and the future judgment of
the day of the Lord. The argument of the end-time false teachers is that since there was no judgment meted out upon the
ungodly in the past, there will be none in the future.

Alford explains the statement of the mockers as follows: "The
time of waiting for the promise necessarily dates from the death
of the fathers, and the duration of things continuing as they are
now extends back beyond the death of the fathers; so that the
meaning will be, ever since the death of those to whom the promise was made, things have continued as we now see them (and
as they have ever continued even before the fathers) from the
beginning of the creation." All of which echoes the intent of
the present day theory of naturalism which contends that nothing
happened in days gone by that does not happen today. The
fathers are evidently those to whom the promise of our Lord's
coming was made. Alford says that they are "largely and generally those to whom the promise was made; the same as are
indicated in Romans 9:5; yet not exclusively these, but simul-
taneously with them any others who may be in the same category,
namely, those who bear to the N.T. Church the same relation
as they to that of the O.T." The words, "fell asleep," are a
euphemism for death, that is, a pleasant way of speaking of
something that in itself is not pleasant.

Translation. *And saying, Where is the promise of His coming? for since the fathers fell asleep, all things are remaining
permanently in that state in which they were from the beginning
of the creation.*

(3:5, 6) The literal Greek is, "for this escapes them being
willing" (Robertson); Vincent translates, "this escapes them of
their own will," and quotes the Revision, "this they wilfully
forget." Alford suggests: "for (i.e., they speak thus because)
this (namely, this fact which follows) escapes them (passes un-
noticed by them) of their own will (i.e., they shut their eyes to
this fact)." All of which means that the denial of the second
Advent by these false teachers is due to a culpable ignorance on
their part.

The key to the understanding of the rest of verse five is in the word "world." It is *kosmos,* which speaks of a system where order prevails. This word refers here to the original perfect system of the material universe of Genesis 1:1 which was brought into being by the fiat of God. He spoke the universe into existence. What a commentary as to the condition of the first perfect earth, the surface of which was made up of land masses surrounded by water. This earth "being overflowed with water, perished." This refers to the cataclysm of Genesis 1:2 where we read, "and the earth became without form and void, and darkness was upon the face of the deep." It was the judgment upon the fall of the angel Lucifer and the consequent apostasy of the pre-Adamic race. This judgment the endtime mockers are wilfully ignorant of, like the fictitious ostrich who buries his head in the sand and thus thinks to escape danger. The ancient Greeks thought the primeval condition of the earth was one of chaos. The theory of evolution starts with a chaos. The New Testament writers, using *kosmos,* describe the original condition of the universe as one of perfection. The sons of God (the angels) did not shout for joy over a *chaos* (Greek for a rude, unformed mass), but a *kosmos* when they saw this universe come into existence by the creative fiat of God (Job 38:4-7). The word "overflowed" is *katakluzō,* "to overwhelm with water, to submerge, deluge," from which we get our word "cataclysm." "Perished" is *apollumi,* "to ruin so that the thing ruined can no longer subserve the use for which it was designed."

The Greek text back of the words, "the earth standing out of the water and in the water" is most difficult. The word "standing" is *sunistēmi,* "to place with" something else, thus, "to set or place together, to stand with or near" the former in a transitive sense, the latter in an intransitive. The word is a participle in the perfect tense. Thayer under this word states that the verb in this tense is used intransitively. It refers to the juxtaposition of the things, one next to another. Thus, the thought of Peter is that the land and water on the perfect earth of Genesis 1:1 were in juxtaposition, the earth rendered so out (*ek*) of water and by means of (*dia*) water. Alford offers the following explanation: "out of water, because the waters that were under the firmament were gathered together into one place and the dry land appeared; and thus water was the material *out of* which the earth was made; by means of water, because the waters below the firmament by furnishing moisture and rain, and keeping moist the earth, are the *means by which* the earth (*sunistēmi*) holds together."

Vincent says: "*out of water,* denoting not the *position* of the earth, but the *material* or mediating element in the creation; the waters being gathered together in one place, and the dry land appearing. . . . *By means of water,* (Bengel); The water served that the earth should consist, that is, cohere." Robertson says that it is not plain what is meant by "by means of water," and Strachan states that the meaning is obscure.

Translation. *For concerning this they wilfully forget that heavens existed long ago, and earth out of water as a source and by means of water cohering by the word of God, through which the ordered world of that time having been deluged by water, was ruined.*

(3:7) "Kept in store" is *thesaurizō*, "to gather and lay up, store up." We have what is called a periphrastic perfect participle speaking of a past storing up completed, with a present state of being stored with that which has been gathered and laid up. "Fire" is in the instrumental case, showing the thing which was instrumental in completing the action in the verb. The present heavens and earth have been stored with fire with the present result that the deposit of fire with which they were stored resides in them as a permanent deposit.

This present condition of the heavens and the earth, that of being stored up with fire, is being constantly maintained (reserved *tēreō*, guarded) with a view to the day of judgment of ungodly men, the Great White Throne judgment which will occur at the close of the Millennium, at which time the wicked dead, fallen angels, and demons will be judged, to be sent to an eternity of suffering, banished from the presence of a holy God (Rev. 20:11-15).

"Perdition" is *apōleia*. The verb is *apollumi*, "to be delivered up to eternal misery, to incur the loss of all things that make existence worth while." The noun (*apōleia*) means "eternal misery." "Ungodly" is *asebēs*, "destitute of reverential awe towards God."

Translation. *But the present heavens and the earth by the same word have been stored with fire, being kept so guarded with a view to the day of judgment and eternal misery of men destitute of reverential awe towards God.*

(3:8) "Be ignorant" is *lanthanō* which means literally "to be hidden," thus, "stop allowing (this) to be hidden from you." Robertson translates, "let not this one thing escape you." The present imperative with *mē* (not) is used in the Greek text, forbidding the continuance of an action or state already going on. The scoffing false teachers were deliberately allowing the fact Peter wishes to bring to their attention now to escape them. It was a culpable ignorance, as we saw in a previous verse.

How are we to understand the words, "With the Lord one day is as a thousand years, and a thousand years as one day"? Alford suggests: "We are not to judge God, in the case of delay, as we do men, seeing that His thoughts are not as our thoughts. . . . The saying is the completion of Psalm 90:4, setting forth also in a wonderful way, that one day may be in God's sight as productive of events as a millennium." Robertson says: "Peter applies the language of Psalm 90:4 about the eternity of God and shortness of human life to 'the impatience of human expectations' (Bigg) about the second coming of Christ. 'The day of judgment is at hand (I Pet. 4:7). It may come tomorrow, but what is tomorrow? What does God mean by a day? It may be a thousand years.' (Bigg)." Strachan comments: Infinite compassion overrides in the divine Mind all finite reckoning."

The false teachers argue that the second Advent has not occurred after so many years of delay, therefore, it will not occur.

Peter reminds them that God does not look at the passing of time as we do. He, in His eternal being does not experience time as such, and the passing of a thousand years is no different to Him than the passing of a day, so far as His predicted actions are concerned. Therefore, their argument is fallacious.

Translation. *But this one thing, stop allowing it to be hidden from you, divinely-loved ones, that one day in the sight of the Lord is as a thousand years, and a thousand years as one day.*

(3:9) "Is slack" is *brandunō*, "to delay or loiter." The Septuagint has it "to linger." Alford translates "to be tardy." "The word implies, besides *delay*, the idea of lateness with reference to an appointed time" (Vincent). Strachan comments: "The idea combated is that God has made a promise and has not kept it. He is, however, better than His promise. The additional element of His long suffering is brought into play. God is greater than men's conception of Him especially if their's is a mechanical view of the universe. . . . As nowhere else in the epistle, here the writer of II Peter enables us to view the summit of the Christian faith, and to rise to a magnificent conception of God. . . . Delay does not spring from an unwillingness or impotence to perform. His will is not even that 'some' should perish, though that is regarded by the writer as inevitable. . . . Some will perish, but it is not His will. His will is that all should come to repentance. The goodness of God should lead to repentance."

The word "willing" is *boulomai*. The synonyms *thelō* and *boulomai* mean "to wish, desire." Thayer says: "Many agree with Prof. Grimm that *thelō* gives prominence to the emotional element, *boulomai*, to the rational and volitional; that *thelō* signifies the *choice*, while *boulomai* marks the choice as *deliberate* and *intelligent;* yet they acknowledge that the words are sometimes used indiscriminately, and especially that *thelō* as the less sharply defined term is put where *boulomai* would be proper." Trench, in his *Synonyms of the New Testament* says regarding synonyms: "All that we certainly affirm is that, granting this, (namely, that there may be one hundred passages where it would be quite as possible to use the one as the other), there is a hundred and first, where one would be appropriate and the other not, or where, at all events, one would be *more* appropriate than the other."

It would seem that *boulomai* is used here advisedly by Peter. It is not God's considered will that any should perish. There is the sovereignty of God and the free will of man. God will not violate man's will. While it is His considered will that no one should be lost, yet in making man in His image He necessarily had to make him a free moral agent, with a will which is able to say "yes" and "no" to Him. While God is always willing to save man, man is not always willing to be saved.

"Longsuffering" is *makrothumia,* God's infinite patience with sinners who put Him to the test and provoke Him. Trench says: "Men may tempt (test) and provoke Him, and He may and does display an infinite *makrothumia* in regard of them (Ex. 34:6; Rom. 2:4; I Pet. 2:20); there may be a resistance to God in *men,* because He respects the wills which He has given them, even when those wills are fighting against Him."

Peter says that the seeming delay of God in fulfilling His promise of the second Advent is not any tardiness on His part to keep an appointment, but is due to His long patience with sinners, giving the human race an opportunity, generation after generation, to accept the salvation He has wrought out on the Cross.

Translation. *The Lord is not tardy with regard to the appointed time of His promise, as certain consider tardiness, but is long-suffering toward us, not having it as His considered will that certain should perish, but that all should come to repentance.*

(3:10) The Church is today in its last age, the Laodicean period (Rev. 3:14-19). The next prophetic event will be the Day of Christ or the Rapture of the Church. Following that will come the Great Tribulation, a period of seven years, the seventieth week of Daniel (9:24-27). That is to be followed by the one thousand year world empire of the Lord Jesus (Rev. 20:1-7). At its conclusion the Great White Throne judgment will occur, at which the wicked dead will be judged. This is what Peter has reference to in 3:7 when he speaks of "the day of judgment and perdition of ungodly men." At this time will occur

the renovation of the earth and its planetary heavens mentioned
in 3:7, 10, 12. The Day of the Lord comprises the Great Tribulation and the Millennium. This great conflagration occurs at
the latter's end. The Millennium merging into eternity is the
Day of God (3:12).

That aspect of the Day of the Lord which will come suddenly
and unawares as a thief will be the second half of the seven-year
period in which Anti-christ turns against the human race to become the ruthless dictator, and the judgments of God fall upon
a Christ-rejecting world. Not only will the beginning of the
Day of the Lord come suddenly, but its end at the close of the
Millennium will come unexpectedly. The Great White Throne
judgment and the great conflagration will come upon the earth
dwellers who are unsaved as suddenly as the judgment of the
Great Tribulation. The greatest harvest of souls this earth has
ever seen will come during the Millennium. Our Lord will rule
as earth dictator. There will be universal righteousness, peace,
and prosperity. Satan and his demons will be in the bottomless
pit, the nation of Israel will be saved, and only true doctrine will
be preached. But despite all this, there will be masses of humanity still unsaved at the end of the thousand years. To these the
final judgment of The Great White Throne and the earth-con-
flagration will come as a surprise.

"Noise" is *roizedon*. The sound of the word suggests the
meaning. The word was used of the whistling of an arrow, the
sound of a shepherd's pipe, the rush of wings, the splash of water,
the hissing of a snake, and the sound of filing. "Elements" is
stoicheia, referring here to the four elements of which the universe
is composed, fire, air, earth, and water. The words "pass away"
are the translation of *paraluō,* "to loosen, dissolve." "Melt" is
luō "to dissolve." "Fervent heat" is *kausoō,* "to burn up, to set
fire to." The word denotes a violent consuming heat. Literally,
"the elements being scorched up, shall be dissolved." As to the
original text back of the words "shall be burned up," authorities
differ. The Nestle text gives the future of *heuriskō,* "shall be

found." Robertson suggests *katakaēsetai*, "shall be burned up," which from contextual considerations seems to be the most likely.

Translation. *But there will come the Lord's day as a thief, in which the heavens with a rushing noise will be dissolved, and the elements being scorched up will be dissolved, and the earth also and the works in it will be burned up.*

(3:11, 12) The Greek has it, "all these things being in the process of dissolution." "Ought" is *dei*, "it is a necessity in the nature of the case." "To be" is *huparchō*, "to be" in the sense that an antecedent condition is protracted into the present. That is, saints are obligated to maintain the holy life of separation in which they started in the Christian life. "Holy conversation" is "holy manner of life." The Greek word "holy" (*hagios*), means basically, "set apart for the service of God." Thus, a holy life is a separated life, separated from the world and to God. "Godliness" is *eusebeia*, "piety toward God." Both "conversation" and "godliness" are plural. Robertson translates, "holy behaviours and pieties."

"Looking for" is *prosdokaō*, "to expect, look for, wait for." The prefixed preposition *pros* means "towards" and adds the idea of "mental direction" to the already existing meaning of the verb. "Hasting" is *speudō*, "to hasten, to desire earnestly." Vincent says: "I am inclined to adopt, with Alford, Huther, Salmond, and Trench the transitive meaning, *hastening on.* i.e., 'causing the day of the Lord to come more quickly by helping to fulfil those conditions without which it cannot come; that day being no day inexorably fixed, but one the arrival of which it is free to the church to hasten on by faith and by prayer' (Trench). See Matthew 24:14,[1] 'this gospel of the kingdom shall be preached in all the world for a witness unto all nations; and then shall the end come.' Compare the words of Peter, Acts 3:19,[2] 'Repent and be converted' etc., *that so* there may come seasons of refreshing,' and the prayer, 'thy kingdom come.' Salmond quotes a

---

1. Refers to Israel, not the Church.
2. Also refers to Israel, not the Church.

rabbinical saying, 'If thou keepest this precept thou hastenest the day of Messiah.'" All of which means that Peter teaches here that the saints can hasten the coming of the day of God by a holy life.

"Wherein," Vincent says is not correct. The Greek is *di' hēn,* the preposition *dia,* meaning "because of," and the relative pronoun.

Translation. *All these things in this manner being in process of dissolution, what sort of persons is it necessary in the nature of the case for you to be in the sphere of holy behaviors and pieties, looking for and hastening the day of God, on account of which (day) heavens being on fire shall be dissolved and elements burning up are being melted.*

(3:13) "New" is *kainos,* "the new as seen from the aspect of quality; the new, as set over against that which has seen service, the outworn, the effete or marred through age" (Trench). The present heavens and earth, beautiful as they are, are under the curse placed upon them because of Adam's sin. The new heavens and earth, new in quality, free from any curse, will surely be beautiful beyond the wildest expectation of man. "Dwelleth" is *katoikeō,* "to be permanently at home."

Translation. *But new heavens and a new earth according to His promise we are looking for, in which righteousness is permanently at home.*

(3:14) "Wherefore" is *dio,* "on which account, wherefore." "Beloved" is *agapētoi,* "divinely-loved ones." The word for "love" is *agapē,* used for the love that God is (I John 4:18), the love with which God loves the lost (John 3:16) and His own (John 13:34, 17:23). It is not Peter who is said to be loving the recipients, although he does, but God. Peter is reminding the saints that they are loved ones of God, loved with a divine and infinite love. "Be diligent" is *spoudazō,* "do your best, make haste, take care, hurry on." Paul uses this same word in II Timothy 2:15. The word speaks of intense effort. "Of Him" is *autōi,* the personal pronoun in the dative case. The idea is, "Do your best to be found with respect to Him, in relation to

Him," thus, with respect to His coming and at that time by Him. "In peace" refers to the saints living at peace with one another. "Without spot" is *aspilos*, "spotless," used metaphorically, "free from censure, irreproachable." "Blameless" is *amōmētoi*, "that which cannot be blamed or found fault with."

Translation. *On which account, divinely-loved ones, since you are looking for these things, do your best to be found with reference to Him irreproachable and unblameable, in peace.*

(3:15, 16) "Our Lord" refers to the Lord Jesus as the context (v. 18) indicates. Alford says in this connection, "Throughout this weighty passage, the Lord Jesus is invested with the full attributes of Deity. It is He who waits and is longsuffering; He in His union and co-equality with the Father, who rules all things after the counsel of His own will." The longsuffering of God gives opportunity for repentance and thus salvation for the lost who put their trust in the Lord Jesus.

Robertson, commenting upon the rest of verse 15 says: "Peter claimed wisdom for himself, but recognizes that Paul had the gift also. His language here may have caution in it as well as commendation. 'St. Peter speaks of him with affection and respect, yet maintains the right to criticise' (Bigg)." "Account" is *hēgeomai*, "to consider, deem."

"Wrest" is *strebloō*, "to twist, turn away." The noun form refers to an instrument of torture. The verb thus means also, "to torture, put to the rack, to twist or dislocate the limbs on the rack." Vincent says that "it is a singularly graphic word applied to the perversion of scripture." The words, "other scriptures" show that Paul's epistles were ranked as scripture at that time.

Translation. *And the longsuffering of our Lord, consider it as salvation, just as our beloved brother Paul according to the wisdom given to him, wrote to you, as also in all his epistles, speaking in them concerning these things, in which (epistles) are certain things hard to be understood, which those who are unlearned and lacking stability distort (from their proper meaning) as also the rest of the scriptures to their own destruction.*

(3:17, 18) Robertson suggests that, since the recipients of this letter had a knowledge of the things which Peter was telling them, "they are without excuse for misunderstanding Peter and Paul on this subject." "Beware" is *phulassō*, "to guard," a military term. That is, "be on your guard." "Being led away" is *sunapagō*, in passive as here, and in a metaphorical sense, "*to be carried away with*, so as to experience with others the force of that which carries away." "With the error" is instrumental case, "by the error." The word "error" is *planē*, "a wandering, a straying about," whereby one, led astray from the right way, roams hither and thither. Vincent says: "It is the word used by Paul of Barnabas, when he dissembled (played the hypocrite) with Peter at Antioch. 'Barnabas was *carried away* with their dissimulation.'" "Fall" is *ekpiptō*, "to fall out of." "Wicked" is *athesmos*, "lawless," of one who breaks through the restraints of law and gratifies his lusts.

Alford, commenting on the word "grow" says; "not only do not fall from your own steadfastness but be so firmly rooted as to throw out branches and yield increase." This growth should be in the sphere of "grace and the knowledge of our Lord and Saviour Jesus Christ." That is, this growth is in the spiritual sphere. This grace is "the grace of which Christ is the author and bestower" (Vincent), grace for daily Christian living, namely, the sanctifying work of the Holy Spirit in the yielded saint, and the Christian graces which are the product of His work. This knowledge is "the knowledge of which Christ is the object" (Vincent). This refers to the saint's knowledge of the Lord Jesus as his Saviour and Lord, as his friend and companion.

Translation. *As for you, therefore, divinely-loved ones, knowing (these things) beforehand, be constantly on your guard lest having been carried away by the rovings of the lawless ones, you fall from your own steadfastness. But be constantly growing in the sphere of the grace and knowledge of our Lord and Saviour Jesus Christ. To Him be glory both now and forever.*

THE
EXPANDED TRANSLATION
OF
SECOND PETER

Read this through at a single sitting. In that
way you will grasp the full sweep of Peter's
letter. Repeated readings will merge its various parts into one harmonious and connected
whole.

THE EXPANDED TRANSLATION
OF
SECOND PETER

Simon Peter, a bondslave and an ambassador of Jesus Christ, to those who have been divinely allotted like precious faith with us by the equitable treatment of our God and Saviour, Jesus Christ. Grace to you, and peace, be multiplied in the sphere of and by the full knowledge of our God, even Jesus, the Lord. Seeing that the all things to us His divine power has generously given, the things which pertain to life and godliness, through the full knowledge of the One who called us by means of His own glory and virtue, by means of which (glory and virtue) there have been generously given to us the precious and exceedingly great promises in order that through these you might become partakers of the divine nature, having escaped by flight the corruption which is in the world in the sphere of passionate cravings.

And for this very cause, having added on your part every intense effort, provide lavishly in your faith, virtue, and in your virtue, knowledge, and in your knowledge, self-control, and in your self-control, patience, and in your patience, godliness, and in your godliness, an affection for the brethren, and in your affection for the brethren, divine love, for if these things are your natural and rightful possession, and are in superabundance, they so constitute you that you are not idle nor unfruitful in the full knowledge of our Lord Jesus Christ, for he to whom these things are not present is blind, being short-sighted, having taken forgetfulness of the cleansing of his old sins.

Wherefore, brethren, exert yourselves the more, and bend every effort to make for yourselves your calling and choosing out sure, for doing these things, you will never stumble, for in this way the entrance shall be richly supplied to you into the eternal kingdom of our Lord Jesus Christ.

Wherefore, I intend always to remind you concerning these things even though you know them and have become firmly established in the truth which is present with you. Indeed, I consider it due you as long as I am in this tent, to keep on arousing you by means of a reminder, knowing that very soon there is the putting off of my tent, even as also our Lord Jesus Christ gave me to understand.

Indeed, I will do my best also that, on each occasion when you have need, after my departure, you will be able to call these things to remembrance, for we did not follow out to their termination cleverly devised myths when we made known to you the power and personal coming of our Lord Jesus Christ, but became spectators of that One's magnificence. For having received from the presence of God the Father honor and glory, there was borne along by the sublime glory such a voice, My Son, the beloved One, this One is, in whom I am well pleased. And this voice we heard borne along, out from heaven, when we were with Him in the holy mountain.

And we have the prophetic word as a surer foundation, to which you are doing well to pay attention, as to a lamp which is shining in a squalid place, until day dawns and a morning star arises in your hearts; knowing this first, that every prophecy of scripture is not of a particular or limited meaning, for not by the desire of man did prophecy come aforetime, but being carried along by the Holy Spirit, men spoke from God.

But there arose also false prophets among the people, even as also among you there shall be false teachers, who will be of such a character as to bring in alongside (of true doctrine) destructive heresies, even denying the Lord who purchased them, bringing upon themselves swift destruction. And many will follow their licentious conduct to its consummation, on account of whom the way of the truth will be reviled at. And in the sphere of covetousness, with moulded words they will exploit you, for whom the *judgment is not lingering, and their destruction is not sleeping.*

For, in view of the fact that God did not spare angels who sinned, but having thrust them down into Tartarus, committed them to pits of nether-world gloom, being reserved for judgment, and did not spare the ancient world, but preserved Noah as the eighth person (to be preserved), a proclaimer of righteousness, having let loose the deluge upon the world of those who were destitute of reverential awe towards God, and the cities of Sodom and Gomorrha having reduced to ashes, He condemned them to destruction, having constituted them as a permanent example to the ungodly of things about to come; and righteous Lot, completely worn down by the manner of life of the lawless in the sphere of unbridled lust, He delivered, for, in seeing and hearing, the righteous one having settled down permanently among them, day in, day out, tormented his righteous soul with their lawless works. The Lord knows how to deliver the godly out of testing and temptation, but to be reserving the unrighteous for the day of judgment under punishment.

But especially those who proceed on their way, hot in pursuit of the flesh in the sphere of the passionate desire of that which defiles, and who disdain authority. Presumptuous, arrogant, they do not tremble when defaming those in exalted positions. Whereas, angels being greater in power and might, are not bringing against them from the presence of the Lord reproachful judgment. But these, as irrational creatures, having been born as creatures of instinct, (destined) for capture and destruction, railing against things of which they are ignorant, shall in their destroying, surely be destroyed, receiving unrighteousness as the hire for unrighteousness, deeming luxurious living in the daytime a pleasure; moral blemishes and disgraceful blots, living luxuriously at your love-feasts, feasting sumptuously with you, having eyes full of an adulteress and which are unable to cease from sin, catching unstable souls with bait, having a heart completely exercised in covetousness, children of a curse. Abandoning the straight way, they went astray, having followed assiduously the way of Balaam the son of Bosor, who set a high value *upon and thus came to love the hire of unrighteousness, but had a rebuke for his own transgression, the inarticulate beast of burden having spoken in a man's voice, restrained the insanity of the prophet.*

These are springs without water, and mists driven by a tempest, for whom the blackness of the darkness has been reserved. For when they are uttering extravagant things that are in their character futile, they are alluring by means of the cravings of the flesh (evil nature), by means of wanton acts, those who are just about escaping from those who are ordering their behavior in the sphere of error. While they are promising them liberty, they themselves are slaves of corruption. For by whom a person has been overcome with the result that he is in a state of subjugation, to this one has he been enslaved with the result that he is in a state of slavery. For if, having escaped the pollutions of the world by a knowledge of the Lord and Saviour Jesus Christ, in these moreover again being entangled, they have been overcome with the result that they are in a state of subjugation, the last things have become to them worse than the first ones; for it were better for them not to have known the way of righteousness, than, having known it, to turn back from the holy commandment which was delivered to them. But it has happened to them according to the true saying: a dog returns to his own vomit, and a sow, having been bathed, to her rolling in mire.

This already, divinely-loved ones, is a second letter I am writing to you, in which I am stirring up your unsullied mind by way of remembrance, that you should remember the words spoken previously by the holy prophets and the commandment of the Lord and Saviour spoken by your apostles; knowing this first, that there shall come in the last of the days mockers with mockery, ordering their manner of life according to their own personal desires, and saying, Where is the promise of His coming? For since the fathers fell asleep, all things are remaining permanently in that state in which they were from the beginning of the creation.

For concerning this they wilfully forget that heavens existed long ago, and earth out of water as a source and by means of water cohering by the Word of God, through which the ordered world of that time having been deluged by water, was ruined. But the present heavens and the earth by the same word have been stored with fire, being kept so guarded with a view to the day of judgment and eternal misery of men destitute of reverential awe towards God.

But this one thing, stop allowing it to be hidden from you, divinely-loved ones, that one day in the sight of the Lord is as a thousand years, and a thousand years as one day. The Lord is not tardy with regard to the appointed time of His promise, as certain consider tardiness, but is longsuffering toward us, not having it as His considered will that certain should perish, but that all should come to repentance.

But there will come the Lord's day as a thief, in which the heavens with a rushing noise will be dissolved, and the elements being scorched up will be dissolved, and the earth also and the works in it will be burned up. All these things in this manner being in process of dissolution, what sort of persons is it necessary in the nature of the case for you to be in the sphere of holy behaviors and pieties, looking for and hastening the day of God, on account of which (day) heavens being on fire shall be dissolved and elements burning up are being melted.

But new heavens and a new earth according to His promise we are looking for, in which righteousness is permanently at home. On which account, divinely-loved ones, since you are looking for these things, do your best to be found with reference to Him irreproachable and unblameable, in peace. And the longsuffering of our Lord, consider it as salvation, just as our beloved brother Paul according to the wisdom given to him, wrote to you, as also in all his epistles, speaking in them concerning these things, in which (epistles) are certain things hard to be understood, which those who are unlearned and lacking stability distort (from their proper meaning) as also the rest of the scriptures to their own destruction.

As for you, therefore, divinely-loved ones, knowing (these things) beforehand, be constantly on your guard lest having been carried away by the rovings of the lawless ones, you fall from your own steadfastness. But be constantly growing in the sphere of the grace and knowledge of our Lord and Saviour Jesus Christ. To Him be glory both now and forever.

THE
EXEGESIS
OF
FIRST JOHN

In order to reap the most benefit from his study, the student is urged to work through John's letter verse by verse, with his Bible and this exegesis before him, seeking to understand the meaning of the Word in the light of the word studies, interpretations, and expanded translation.

CHAPTER ONE

(1:1) John begins his letter with a relative pronoun in the neuter gender, "that which." The reference is to things relating to the Lord Jesus. We are not to understand the expression as equivalent to "He who." The preposition "of" in the expression "of the Word of life" is *peri*, "concerning." This speaks of the things concerning our Lord, rather than of Him personally. John speaks of that which was true of our Lord from the beginning. "Was" is the verb of being in the Greek text (*eime*, "to be," not *ginomai*, "to become.") It is in the imperfect tense which speaks of an abiding state in past time. Thus, John has reference to those things that were true of our Lord since the beginning.

In his Gospel, he begins with the majestic words, "In the beginning was the Word." The context there identifies this beginning as the beginning of created things. That is, when all creation came into existence, our Lord was in existence. Since He antedated all creation, He must be uncreated. Since He is uncreated, He must be without beginning, and therefore Deity. In his Gospel, John reaches back into the eternity before the universe was brought into existence to speak of the Lord Jesus as in fellowship with the Father, and as the Light that shone through the darkness of sin through His creative acts (1:1-10). In his first epistle, he goes back only to the time when the created universe came into existence, and speaks of that which was true concerning Him since that time and until His incarnation ("that which was in the beginning," which would include the things true of Him mentioned in John 1:1-10), and then in the words "which we have heard, which we have looked upon, and our hands have handled," he speaks of His incarnation, as he does also in John 1:11-14 and on through the entire Gospel.

Vincent says: "By the words '*in* the beginning,' the writer places himself at the initial point of creation, and, looking back into eternity, describes that which was already in existence when creation began. 'The Word was in the beginning.' In the words, '*from* the beginning,' the writer looks back to the initial point of time, and describes what has been in existence from that point onward. Thus, 'in the beginning' characterizes the absolute divine Word as He was *before* the foundation of the world and *at* the foundation of the world. 'From the beginning' characterizes His development in time."

The inspired writer does not in his first letter deal with the preincarnate life of our Lord, which he merely mentions in the words "that which was from the beginning." But when he refers to His incarnation, he goes into careful detail as to His humanity. Robertson mentions the view of Westcott, that John wrote his Gospel to prove the deity of our Lord, assuming His humanity, whereas he wrote his first epistle to prove His humanity, assuming His deity. In the words, "which we have heard, which we have seen with our eyes, which we have looked upon, and our hands have handled," he is maintaining the real humanity of our Lord against its denial by a certain group in the Church at that time. These were the Gnostics. There were two groups among them, both agreeing in the essential evil of matter. Both groups had their own private opinions regarding the Person of our Lord. The Docetic Gnostics denied His actual humanity. The word "Docetic" comes from the Greek word *dokeō*, "to seem." These argued that our Lord had only a "seeming" body, not a real physical body. The Cerinthian Gnostics distinguished between the man Jesus and the *aeon* Christ that came on Him at His baptism and left Him on the Cross. As to Cerinthus, Smith says: "His distinctive heresy was a theory of the Person of Christ. . . . He supposed that Jesus had not been begotten by a virgin, but had been born of Joseph and Mary as a son in like manner to all the rest of men, and became more righteous and prudent and wise. And after the baptism the Christ descended into Him from the Sovereignty which is over the universe, in the form of a dove; and then He proclaimed the unknown Father and accomplished mighty works, but at the end the Christ withdrew from the Jesus, and the Jesus had suffered and had been raised, but the Christ had continued throughout impassible. The essence of this is the dissolution of the Person of our Lord, the distinction between the human Jesus and the divine Christ. St. John encountered Cerinthus at Ephesus, and strenuously controverted his error. Irenaeus and Eusebius quote a story of Polycarp's that the apostle once visited the public baths, and, seeing Cerinthus within, sprang out of the building. 'Let us flee,' he cried, 'lest the building fall, since Cerinthus, the foe of the Truth, is within it.' And all through our epistle, he has the heresy in view. See 2:18-23; 4:1-6, 13-15; 5:1-12." Some Gnostics practiced asceticism, while others went to the other extreme of licentiousness. John deals with both classes in his first letter. The word "Gnostic" comes from a Greek word gnōsis, which means "to know." They claimed a superior, private knowledge over and above that of the Bible. Nine times John presents tests for knowing the truth, and uses the verb ginōskō from which the Gnostics get their name. Therefore, in stressing the fact that he and his fellow-apostles had had personal experiential knowledge of the humanity of Jesus of Nazareth through the senses of hearing, seeing, and touching, he is combatting a doctrinal error in the early church known as Docetism, the teaching that our Lord had only a seeming body, not a real one.

The first proof the inspired apostle advances for the fact of the actual humanity of the Son of God is that he and his fellow disciples heard Him speak in a human voice. The verb is in the perfect tense, which tense in Greek refers to a process completed in past time having present results. Had John desired merely to refer to the fact of hearing the Lord, he would have used the aorist tense in Greek, which tense refers to the fact of an action without referring to its details such as completeness or incompleteness, whether it was an instantaneous act or a process. The fact that he goes out of his way to use another tense than the aorist indicates that he wishes to stress the details of the action. The first thing he tells us by the use of this tense is that his hearing the Lord speak was not confined to one single occasion, but that he heard Him speak at repeated intervals and at length. The impressions his auditory nerves received were correct, for he heard His voice over and over again. It is like repeating a scientific experiment over and over again so as to check results.

The second thing John wishes to tell his readers by the use of this tense is that this past process was a complete one. That is, he heard our Lord speak so often that the experiment, so to speak, was a finished one. It was complete, and a fair test of the question as to His actual or seeming humanity. The third thing he tells his readers is that the past completed process of hearing the Lord Jesus speak had present results, that is, present results with John at the time he was writing this letter. John wrote his first epistle about A.D. 90. He heard our Lord speak from A.D. 30-33. About sixty years had elapsed between the impression he had received and the time of the recording of the events in the Gospel which he wrote, the date of which is about the same as that of his first epistle. Sixty years is a long time to remember the discourses of an individual. John was an unlettered man. He was not trained in the Greek schools of the time, as was the apostle Paul.

However, there are several things which account for John's memory of the events in the life of our Lord. One is that in the first century books were few and men trained themselves to remember much, whereas today books are plentiful and men remember little. Another is that in the case of unlettered ancient peoples, a vast amount of their literature was remembered and repeated letter perfect through generation after generation. Still another is that our Lord's wonderful personality and discourses made an indelible impression upon those who were His constant companions for over three years. Finally, His words to His disciples, "He (the Holy Spirit) shall teach you all things, and bring to your remembrance, whatsoever I have said unto you" (John 14:26), account for any facts which it was necessary for

John to know in order to write the Gospel which bears his name, and which he may have forgotten. As John thought over those eventful years, often the Holy Spirit would, during those sixty years, bring back to his memory things that had slipped his mind. Thus John gives his readers the assurance that he is well equipped to write his Gospel, for he was a competent witness of the events recorded and remembered them accurately, this from the human standpoint. Of course, from the doctrine of verbal inspiration, and that division of it which we call the inspiration of superintendence, we are assured that the Holy Spirit superintended the recording of the historical facts so as to guarantee an infallible record of our Lord's life. John said in his Greek: "That which we have heard, and at this present moment is ringing in our ears."

For further proof of our Lord's actual humanity, John turns to the sense of vision. The distinctive word he uses for "seeing" here is *horaō,* which refers to the physical act of seeing, giving prominence to the discerning mind, to mental perception, and to mental activity. By the use of this particular Greek word for the act of seeing, John assures his readers that he not only had the sensory impressions on his retinae, but he understood what he was looking at. He was a correct interpreter of the events in our Lord's life for the reader. He says he saw the events in the Lord's life "with his eyes." How else can one see anything except by the aid of his eyes? While this is a self-evident thing, yet John felt it necessary to mention it in order to be absolutely sure that his readers understood him to be referring to sensory impressions from our Lord's actual human body. They were actual, discerning impressions, not an optical illusion or an hallucination.

Again, he uses the perfect tense. By doing that he tells his readers that the things he saw concerning our Lord were indelibly retained in his mind's eye. As he was writing this letter, he could close his physical eyes and see our Lord as He appeared to him during His humiliation on earth sixty years before. One could translate: "That which we have seen with discernment by means of our eyes, and which as a present result we have in our mind's eye."

But John did not only see our Lord with discerning eyes. He "looked upon" Him. Here he uses another word which means "to see." It is *theaomai*, which means, "to behold, view attentively, contemplate." In early classical usage it included the idea of wondering regard. Thayer says that this idea gradually faded out, to give place to "such a looking as seeks merely the satisfaction of the sense of sight." However, we can well conclude that after John and his fellow-disciples had seen our Lord with discerning eyes, they looked with a contemplation that was a mingling of wonder, awe, and admiration. The Greek word comes over into our language in the word "theatre." They looked at that unique life as upon a spectacle. Here John uses the aorist tense, referring merely to the fact of seeing without mentioning details. After having established the permanent accuracy of his observations in the use of the perfect tense in the previous verb which meant "to see," he did not feel the need of repeating that tense. The translation could read, "That which we gazed upon as a spectacle."

After establishing proof of our Lord's actual humanity through the scientific mediums of the senses of hearing and sight, John turns to that of touch. The words "have handled" are the translation of *psēlaphaō*, "to handle, touch, feel." In late Greek it meant "to examine closely." The verb means, "to handle with a view to investigation." The word is used in the Greek translation of the Old Testament when blind Isaac felt the hands of Jacob (Gen. 27:22). The old man, puzzled at the voice of Jacob, handled his hands with a view to investigating whether the speaker were really Esau. The same word is used in Luke 24:39, where our Lord said, "Handle Me with a view to investigation and see; because a spirit does not have flesh and bones as you see that I have." Our Lord's proof to the disciples that He was raised in the physical body in which He died was based on the scientific evidence of their sense of touch. They handled His body, investigating His claim to have a body of flesh and bones. John undoubtedly has reference to this occurrence here. It is the only reference to our Lord's resurrection in the epistle.

Thus far the expanded translation reads: "That which was from the beginning, that which we have heard and at this present moment is ringing in our ears, that which we have seen with discernment with our eyes and which is at this present moment in our mind's eye, that which we gazed upon as a spectacle and our hands handled with a view to investigation, concerning the Word of the life." Four times John uses the pronoun "that which." Each is qualified by the phrase, "concerning the Word of life." That is, the things John heard, saw, and felt concerned the Word of life.

The word *logos* (word), is John's particular designation of our Lord. *Logos* comes from *legō*, "to speak," and refers to the total concept of something. Our Lord is the *Logos* of God in the sense that He is the total concept of God seen through a human medium, His humanity consisting of His human body, His human limitations, and His human life lived on earth in the power of the Holy Spirit.

John calls Him here, "the Word of the life," the definite article appearing in the Greek text, not any general idea of life here, but the particular life that God is and which was revealed in concrete form in the humanity of our Lord.

Translation. *That which was from the beginning, that which we have heard with the present result that it is ringing in our ears, that which we have discerningly seen with our eyes, with the present result that it is in our mind's eye, that which we gazed upon as a spectacle, and our hands handled with a view to investigation, concerning the Word of the life.*

(1:2)   This life which God is, John says, "was manifested." The word "manifested" is *phaneroō*, "to make manifest or visible or known* what has been hidden or unknown" (Thayer). This life which is invisible was made visible to the human race through the humanity of our Lord. We put light which is invisible through a prism, break it up into its component parts, and it becomes visible. The beauty of the life that God is, broken up into its various parts such as love, grace, humility, kindness, etc., is seen through the prism of the human life of our Lord. Vincent's note is most helpful: "Was manifested; corresponding with *the Word was made flesh* (John 1:14). The two phrases, however, present different aspects of the same truth. *The Word became flesh,* contemplates simply the historic fact of incarnation. *The life was manifested,* sets forth the unfolding of that fact in the various operations of life. The one denotes the objective process of the incarnation as such, the other, the result of that process as related to human capacity of receiving and understanding it. 'The reality of the incarnation would be undeclared if it were said, *The Word was manifested;* the manifoldness of the operations of life would be circumscribed if it were said, *The life became flesh.* The manifestation of the Life was a consequence of the incarnation of the Word, but it is not coextensive with it' (Westcott)." Thus, the incarnation of the Son of God was the making visible to human understanding, the life which God is.

John repeats the fact that he has seen with discernment and still has in his mind's eye the visible disclosure of that life in the humanity of the Lord Jesus. He bears witness to what he has seen of that life in the Gospel which bears his name. The word is *martureō,* "to bear witness, testify, to affirm that one has seen or heard or experienced something." "Show" is *apaggellō,* "to bring tidings from" a person or thing, "bring word, report." He describes it as "that eternal life which was with the Father." "With" is an important word here. It is *pros,* which means "facing" and implies fellowship. All of which means that the life here referred to is a Person, for it requires a person to have fellowship. A mere abstraction can have no fellowship. The life here is none other than the Lord Jesus Himself who is said by John to have been in fellowship with the Father. "Which" is also important. It speaks of character or nature. The Life, the Lord Jesus, is of such a nature as to have been in fellowship with God the Father, very God of very God Himself, possessing co-eternally with God the Father and God the Spirit, the divine essence. This life, a Person, the Lord Jesus, is described by

John as *aiōnios,* "without beginning and without end, that which always has been and always will be, eternal." Since this life is without beginning, it must be uncreated, thus, deity in its essence. The particular word for "life" here is *zōē,* here used as Thayer indicates, as "the absolute fulness of life, both essential and ethical, which belongs to God." Thus, this life that God is, is not to be defined as merely animation, but as definitely ethical in its content. God is not the mere reason for the universe, as the Greeks thought, but a Person with the characteristics and qualities of a divine Person. The ethical and spiritual qualities of this life which God is, are communicated to the sinner when the latter places his faith in the Lord Jesus as Saviour, and this becomes the new, animating, energizing, motivating principle which transforms the experience of that individual, and the saint thus lives a Christian life. The message of John is that since the believer is a partaker of this life, it is an absolute necessity that he show the ethical and spiritual qualities that are part of the essential nature of God, in his own life. If these are entirely absent, John says, that person is devoid of the life of God, and is unsaved. The ethical and spiritual qualities of this life were exhibited to the human race in the earthly life of the Lord Jesus. His life thus becomes the pattern of what our lives should be in holiness, self-sacrifice, humility, and love.

Translation. *And this aforementioned life was made visible, and we have seen (it) with discernment and have (it) in our mind's eye, and are bearing witness to and bringing back to you a message concerning this life, the eternal, which is of such a nature as to have been in fellowship with the Father and was made visible to us.*

(1:3) John takes up the thought here of verse one, which was interrupted by the contents of verse two. The purpose for which he wrote the Gospel which bears his name and which contains the things which he had seen our Lord do and heard our Lord speak, was that his readers might have fellowship with him. This word "fellowship" is one of the important words in this letter. It becomes necessary for us right here to study the

Greek word which is translated "fellowship," and for the following reasons: first, the word is used in two different senses in this
epistle, and second, because the English word as it is normally
used today has a different meaning from that in which it was
used in A.D. 1611 when the A.V. was translated. The word is
koinōnia. Moulton and Milligan give instances of its use in the
papyri in their *Vocabulary of the Greek Testament*, as follows:
"belonging in common to, with whom I have no partnership."
The idea in the word is that of one person having a joint-participation with another in something possessed in common by both.
A very touching use of the verbal form of this word was found
in a fourth century inscription; a doctor of medicine had put up
an inscription to his wife who had also studied medicine, and
who had died. It read, "as with you alone I shared my life."
How beautiful it is when a sinner saved by grace comes to the
sunset of life and can say to the Lord Jesus, "as with you alone
I have shared by life."

Thus John writes, "That which we have seen with discernment
and at present have in our mind's eye, and have heard and at
present is ringing in our ears, we are reporting also to you in
order that, as for you also, a joint-participation you may be
having in common with us." Now to clear away some under-
brush that would impede our progress through the intricacies of
our interpretation. The word "fellowship" today means usually
"companionship, social intercourse." In this sense of the word,
it was impossible for John to have had fellowship with many of
his readers, for this is a general letter sent to the Church at
large, and John would never have had opportunity to see them
all personally and thus have fellowship with them. The word
"fellowship" cannot here be understood in its commonly accepted
usage. How are we to understand John here then? John wrote
his Gospel so that his readers who were not eyewitnesses of the
life of our Lord might enjoy joint-participation with him in his
first-hand knowledge of the Lord as gained through the senses
of sight, hearing, and touch. When his readers studied the
Gospel under the guidance of the Holy Spirit, they would be

looking at the Lord Jesus as He appeared on earth through John's eyes; they would be hearing Him speak through John's ears, and would be touching Him with John's hands. Thus, having a supernatural, Holy Spirit energized, first-hand knowledge of the Lord Jesus, they therefore would be able to have a real, practical, actual and more intimate companionship with Him. What if the Gospel records had not been written? We could find the way of salvation through the Pauline epistles and could be saved. We could have some mystical companionship with our Lord, but not such an intelligent, practical fellowship as we do have, since His portrait, painted by the Holy Spirit in the Gospels would be lacking. One cannot have very intelligent fellowship with a person whom we have never seen, even though reams of paper would be used in an effort to describe him. But as the child of God ponders the life of our Lord through Spirit-ground lenses, he sees Him in his spiritual mind's eye so that an intelligent fellowship can be enjoyed by the saint. To substantiate further the above use and interpretation of the Greek word "fellowship," we might add that the word "with" in "with us," is *meta,* and when used with the word "have" as it is here, means "partnership." Thus, a joint-participation on the part of the Christian in John's first-hand knowledge of the Lord Jesus, will issue in a real, practical, intelligent fellowship (companionship) with the Lord Jesus.

And that is exactly what John is saying in the words, "and the fellowship indeed which is ours, is with the Father and with His Son Jesus Christ." Here the word "fellowship" is the word we want. But even here it has a background of meaning that forms the basis of a companionship. That meaning is what the Greek word has, "a joint-participation with someone else in things held in common by both." The English word is sometimes used in this way in academic circles. We speak of the fellows of a college, namely, scholars who reside at the school and participate jointly with the regular teaching faculty. There the idea of joint-participation is prominent. But to have fellowship in any profession or undertaking, or in social intercourse, the participants must have things in common, common likes and dislikes, common skills, a common educational level (in the professions), a common nature or character. Just so, to have fellowship with the Lord Jesus in the sense of companionship, the saint must have common likes and dislikes with the Lord Jesus, he must love what He loves, namely, righteousness, and hate what He hates, namely, sin. He must have a common nature, the divine nature, He must have a common Father, God, our Lord in His deity, the saint as a human being (Heb. 2:11). It is these things held in common on the part of the Lord Jesus and the saint that form the basis of the fellowship and make it possible.

Translation. *That which we have seen with discernment and at present is in our mind's eye, and that which we have heard and at present is ringing in our ears, we are reporting also to you, in order that as for you also, you may participate jointly in common with us. And the fellowship indeed which is ours, is with the Father and with His Son, Jesus Christ.*

(1:4)   The inspired apostle writes that the purpose he had in writing these things is that "your joy may be full." The best texts have "our" not "your," that is, John's joy and that of the recipients, since both will then enjoy that intimate, intelligent fellowship with the Lord Jesus which only comes when the saint sees Him, hears Him speak, and touches Him, through the medium of the Gospel writers and the Holy Spirit as He ministers what they have written about the Lord in their writings. The words "may be full," are what is called in Greek a periphrastic perfect participial construction. The meaning is quite involved. Its richness will appear in the following translation.

Translation. *And these things, as for us, we are writing in order that our joy, having been filled completely full in times past, may persist in that state of fulness through the present time.*

(1:5)   After informing the saints that in order to have an intelligent fellowship with the Lord Jesus they must come to know Him through the portraits painted by the Holy Spirit in the Gospels, John warns them against two heresies which, if followed, would prevent such fellowship. They are included in the heresy called Antinomianism as held by the Nicolaitans. Antinomianism means literally "against law." It is lawlessness. It is disregard for law on the part of the one who professes to be a Christian. That teaching followed out to its logical conclusion results in the two things John is combatting in verses five and six. The first is that there is evil in God. The second is that the person who lives in sin may still have fellowship with Him. Smith's note on this heresy is as follows: "It is said that the Nicolaitans were the followers of Nicolas, one of the seven deacons (Acts 6:5), and this strange story is told of him by Clement of Alexandria: 'He had they say, a beautiful wife, and after the ascension of the Saviour, being taunted by the apostles with jealousy, he brought the woman forward and gave who would permission to marry her. This, they say, is in accordance with that expression of his: *We must abuse the flesh.* And indeed the adherents of his sect follow up the incident and the saying absolutely and unquestioningly and commit fornication without restraint. Clement proceeds to attest the moral purity of Nicolas and explain his action as an inculcation of ascetic self-restraint, but certainly the sect which bore his name was given over to licentiousness. Clement says elsewhere that they were 'dissolute as he-goats,' and others bear like testimony. They were Antinomians, disowning moral obligation. . . . This heresy was rampant among the churches of Asia Minor in St. John's day (cf. Rev. 2:6, 14, 15), and he deals with it in our epistle. See 1:5; 2:6, 15, 17; 3:3-10."

John writes, "There exists this message which we have heard from Him and which at present is ringing in our ears." "Of" is *apo*, not *para* here. The latter word refers to a personal source, the former, to an ultimate source. By using *apo*, John tells his readers that this message was not only heard by him but by others. "Declare" is *anaggellō* "to bring the tidings back to him who receives them."

The message is "God is light" (A.V.). As it stands, the statement is to the effect that God is an abstraction, for light is non-personal and an abstraction. That statement is not true. The word "light" (*phōs*) in the Greek text is without the article. The rule of Greek grammar is that the absence of the definite article shows quality, nature, or essence. What the inspired apostle said was, "God as to His nature, essence, character, is light." That is, "God as a Person has a character or nature that partakes of light." That light, of course, is not physical light, for John in the context is speaking of spiritual things. That light is ethical, spiritual, moral. Then John strengthens his assertion by saying, "And darkness in Him does not exist, not even one bit."

Vincent has an illuminating note: "A statement of the absolute nature of God. Not *a* light, nor *the* light, with reference to created beings, as *the light of men, the light of the world,* but simply and absolutely, *God is light,* in His very nature. . . The expression is not a metaphor. 'All that we are accustomed to term *light* in the domain of the creature, whether with a physical or metaphysical meaning, is only an effluence of that one and only primitive *Light* which appears in the nature of God' (Ebrard). Light is immaterial, diffusive, pure, and glorious. It is the condition of life. Physically, it represents *glory;* intellectually, *truth;* morally, *holiness.* As immaterial it corresponds to God as *spirit;* as diffusive, to God as *love;* as the condition of life, to God as *life;* as pure and illuminating, to God as *holiness* and *truth.* In the Old Testament, light is often the medium of God's visible revelations to men. It was the first manifestation of God in creation. The burning lamp passed between the pieces of the parted victim in God's covenant with Abraham. God went before Israel in a pillar of fire, descended in fire at Sinai, and appeared in a luminous cloud which rested on the mercy-seat in the most holy place."

Again, Vincent says: "No modern writer has developed the idea of God as light with such power and beauty as Dante. His 'Paradise' might truthfully be called a study of light. Light is the only visible expression of God. Radiating from Him, it is diffused through the universe as a principle of life." He quotes a portion:

In presence of that light one such becomes,
That to withdraw therefrom for other prospect
It is impossible he e'er consent:
Because the good, which object is of will,
Is gathered all in this, and out of it.
That is defective which is perfect there.

Translation. *And there exists this message which we have heard from Him and at present is ringing in our ears, and we are bringing back tidings to you, that God as to His nature is light, and darkness in Him does not exist, not even one bit.*

(1:6) John here again deals with the heresy of Antinomianism teaching to the effect that a person may be living in sin and compromising with it, and at the same time have fellowship with God. "If we say" is a deliberative subjunctive, proposing a hypothetical case. John puts the case as a supposition, not an assumed fact. He deals gently and humbly with his readers, including himself in the statement. The claim of this hypothetical person is that he is having fellowship with God. Again, our word "fellowship" (*koinōnian*), has the primary meaning of "to have joint-participation with someone else in things possessed in common by both," and the secondary meaning of "companionship" or "comradeship." This person claims to have things in common with God, common likes and dislikes, a common nature, the divine, which basic things eventuate in a communion of interest and activity which we call fellowship.

This person is said to be walking in the darkness which is not in God, namely, sin. The verb is present subjunctive which speaks of habitual action. Thus, this person is sinning habitually, continuously, which shows that he is an unsaved person. No child of God sins habitually to the exclusion of righteous acts. We learn that from John's use of modes and tenses as we proceed in our exegesis of this epistle. Furthermore, he walks in the darkness. The case of the noun is locative of sphere. He walks, that is, orders his behavior, conducts himself (*peripateō*) in the sphere of the darkness of sin. His actions and words are ensphered by sin. Nothing of God's righteousness or goodness ever enters that circle of sin which surrounds this person. The individual making this claim of fellowship with God while at the same time ordering his behavior within the sphere of sin, is an unsaved person. John says that in making that claim, he is lying, and he is not doing the truth.

Translation. *If we say that fellowship we are having with Him, and in the sphere of the aforementioned darkness are habitually ordering our behavior, we are lying, and we are not doing the truth.*

(1:7) Now John supposes another case, that of a person walking in the sphere of the light which God is and in which He dwells. "Walk" is again present subjunctive, stressing habitual action. It is the habitual actions of a person that are an index to his character. This is a Christian, for only Christians are able to walk in the light that God is and in which He dwells. If we Christians order our behavior within the sphere of the light, John says, "we have fellowship one with another" (A.V.). Now, to whom does the pronoun "we" refer? Does John mean here that we Christians have fellowship with one another, or is it that the Christian and God have fellowship with one another? The theme of the epistle and the immediate context must decide. The theme of First John is "The Saint's Fellowship with God." In verse six, John tells his readers who does not have fellowship with God. In verse seven he tells them who does have fellowship with God. While it is true that when saints order their behavior within the sphere of the light they do have fellowship with one another, yet John is not teaching that here. He is concerned with the heresy of Antinomianism and its relation to the Christian in the latter's relation to God. Thus, those referred to by the pronoun "we" are God and the believer.

The words "one with another" are the translation of a preposition and a reciprocal pronoun in the Greek text. A reciprocal pronoun shows reciprocity. Wonder of wonders, not only do we have fellowship with God, but He reciprocates in having fellowship with us! This fellowship is not a one-sided affair like that of a couple, only one of which is in love with the other.

God condescends to have fellowship with worms of the dust, sinners saved by grace, creatures of His handiwork.

And while we are having this fellowship with Him, the blood of Jesus, His Son, keeps constantly cleansing us from sins of omission, sins of ignorance, sins we know nothing about in our lives and for the reason that we have not grown in grace enough to see that they are sin. These would prevent our fellowship with God if this divine provision of the constant cleansing away of the defilement of sin in our lives was not taken care of by the blood of the Lord Jesus Christ. So holy is the God with whom we have fellowship.

Translation. *But if within the sphere of the light we are habitually ordering our behavior as He Himself is in the light, fellowship we are having with one another. And the blood of Jesus His Son keeps continually cleansing us from every sin.*

(1:8) Here John again combats the Gnostic heresy which held that we do not have any principle of sin within us, since matter is evil and the soul is not contaminated by sinful flesh. Smith, commenting on this verse says: "The heresy of Perfectionism. Some might not say, with the Antinomians, that they were absolved from the obligation of the moral law, but they maintained that they were done with sin, had no more sinful propensities, committed no more sinful acts." Here we have the heresy of the eradication of the totally depraved nature during the earthly life of the Christian. The heresy of perfectionism and of the eradication of the evil nature is the present day form of this problem of the indwelling sinful nature.

"Sin" here is singular in number and is used without the definite article, all pointing to the fact that the nature is referred to, not acts of sin. Here we have the denial of the indwelling, totally depraved nature passed down the race from Adam. John says therefore, "If we say that sin we are not having, ourselves we are deceiving." Notice, if you will, the emphatic position of the pronoun "ourselves." The Christian who believes his evil nature has been completely eradicated is deceiving himself, nobody else. All others can see sin stick out all over his experience. And that sin must come from the indwelling sinful nature.

John says that the truth is not in that person. In the case of the Gnostics, that statement must be taken in an absolute sense. They were unsaved. In the case of a misinformed and mistaken present-day Christian, the statement will have to be qualified to mean that the truth of the indwelling sinful nature is not in him. The context would require this interpretation.

Translation. *If we say that sin we are not having, ourselves we are leading astray, and the truth is not in us.*

(1:9) Now John instructs the saints what to do about sins in their lives. The "we" includes John here, and it would seem that he is speaking of believers, for in other places he gives directions to the unsaved as to what they must do with relation to their sinful state and their sins. The sinner is to *believe* (John 3:16). The saint is to *confess*. The word "confess" is *homologeō*, from *homos*, "the same," and *legō*, "to say," thus, "to say the same thing as another," or, "to agree with another." Confession of sin on the part of the saint means therefore to say the same thing that God does about that sin, to agree with God as to all the implication of that sin as it relates to the Christian who commits it and to a holy God against whom it is committed. That includes the saint's hatred of that sin, his sense of guilt because of it, his contrition because of it, the determination to put it out of his life and never to do that thing again. This is what confession of sin means here. The English word "confess" means "to admit the truth of an accusation, to own up to the fact that one is guilty of having committed the sin." But the Greek word means far more than that, as was shown above. The verb is present subjunctive, speaking of continuous action. This teaches that the constant attitude of the saint toward sin should be one of a contrite heart, ever eager to have any sin in the life discovered for him by the Holy Spirit, and ever eager to confess it and put it out of the life by the power of that same Holy Spirit. David wrote concerning that kind of heart when he penned the words: "The sacrifices of God are a broken spirit: a broken and a contrite heart, O God, thou wilt not despise" (Psalm 51:17).

If we confess our sins, John says, God is *faithful* to forgive them and to cleanse us from all unrighteousness. The word "faithful" is *pistos*. Vincent says of its usage here: "True to his own nature and promises; keeping faith with Himself and with man. The word is applied to God as fulfilling His own promises (Heb. 10:23; 11:11); as fulfilling the purpose for which He called men (I Thess. 5:24; I Cor. 1:9); as responding with guardianship to the trust reposed in Him by men (I Cor. 10:13; I Pet. 4:19). 'He abideth faithful. He cannot deny Himself' (II Tim. 2:13). The same term is applied to Christ (II Thess. 3:3; Heb. 3:2; 2:17). God's faithfulness is here spoken of not only as essential to His own being, but as faithfulness toward us; 'fidelity to that nature of truth and light, related to His own essence, which rules in us as far as we confess our sins' (Ebrard)."

God is also just in forgiving our sins and cleansing us from their defilement. The word "just" is *dikaios*. Vincent has this comment: "Rev. *righteous*. From *dikē*, 'right.' . . . The two words, *faithful* and *righteous*, imply each other. God, who is *absolute rightness*, must be *faithful* to His own nature, and His righteous dealing with men who partake of that nature and walk in fellowship with Him, is simply fidelity to Himself. 'Righteousness is truth passing into action' (Westcott)."

"To forgive" is *hina aphēi*, "in order that He may forgive." *Aphēi* is second aorist subjunctive, speaking, not of a process, but of a single act here. In 1:7 we have durative action, "keeps on continually cleansing," referring to the constant cleansing of the saint from the defilement of sins of ignorance by the blood of Jesus. These are habitual in the life of the believer. But sins we confess, as in 1:9, are not habitual. No child of God knowingly sins habitually. These sins for which confession is required are infrequent, isolated instances in the well-ordered life of a believer. Therefore, the aorist tense is used here, speaking of a single act of forgiveness. The word is the second aorist subjunctive form of *aphiēmi*, "to send away, dismiss," hence of sins, "to remit" as a debt, "to put away." All sin was remitted, paid for, put away on the basis of the satisfaction offered for the demands of God's holy law which sinners broke, when the Lord Jesus died on the Cross. The law was satisfied. All the sins the believer commits, past, those in his unsaved condition, and future, those in his saved state, were put away on a legal basis at the Cross, and are in that sense forgiven the believer the moment he places his faith in the Lord Jesus. But the forgiveness spoken of here has to do, not primarily with the breaking of God's law, for that was taken care of at the Cross and recognized as such at the time the sinner placed his faith in the Saviour. Therefore, sin in a Christian's life is a matter, not between a lawbreaker and a judge, but between a child and his father. It is a matter of grieving the Father's heart when a child of God sins. The putting away of the believer's sin upon confession is therefore a forgiveness granted by the Father and a restoration to the fellowship that was broken by that sin. When the saint confesses immediately after the commission of that sin, fellowship is not broken except for that time in which the sin was committed.

Not only does God forgive the believer, but He cleanses him from the defilement which he incurred in committing that act of sin. Here the verb "to cleanse" is aorist subjunctive, speaking of a single act of cleansing, for known sin in the life of a saint is not habitual, but the out of the ordinary thing.

Translation. *If we continue to confess our sins, faithful is He and righteous to forgive us our sins and to cleanse us from every unrighteousness.*

(1:10) In verse eight, we have the denial of the indwelling sinful nature. In this verse we have the denial of specific acts of sin. The verb is in the perfect tense, which tense in Greek refers to an action completed in past time, having present results. The denial here is of any acts of sin committed in past time with the implication that none are able to be committed at present. This is sinless perfection with a vengeance.

The person who makes that claim, John says, makes God a liar, and does not have the Word of God in him. Smith comments: "Perfectionism has two causes: (1) *The stifling of conscience*: we make Him a liar, i.e., turn a deaf ear to His inward testimony, His voice in our souls. (2) *Ignorance of His Word*: it 'is not in us.' Such a delusion were impossible if we steeped our minds in the Scriptures."

Translation. *If we say that we have not sinned and are not now in such a state that we could sin, a liar we are making Him, and His Word is not in us.*

CHAPTER TWO

(2:1, 2) Smith says: "Observe the sudden change in the apostle's manner. His heart is very tender toward his people, and he adopts an affectionate and personal tone: (1) he passes from the formal 'we' to 'I.' (2) He styles them 'my little children' . . . his favorite appellation (compare 2:12, 28; 3:7, 18; 4:4; 5:21). Not only was it very suitable on the lips of the aged teacher, but it was a phrase of Jesus (John 13:33). St. John had caught the phrase and its spirit. He remembered how the Master had dealt with His disciples, and he would deal with his people after the same fashion and be to them what Jesus had been to himself — as gentle and patient.

"He assumes this tone because he is about to address a warning to them, and he would fain take the sting out of it and disarm opposition. He foresees the possibility of a two-fold perversion of his teaching: (1) 'If we can never in this life be done with sin, why strive after holiness? It is useless; sin is an abiding necessity.' (2) 'If escape be so easy, why dread falling into sin? We may sin with light hearts, since we have the blood of Jesus to cleanse us.' 'No,' he answers, 'I am not writing these things to you either to discourage you in the pursuit of holiness or to embolden you in sinning, but, on the contrary, in order that (hina) ye may not sin.' Compare Augustine: 'Lest perchance he should seem to have given impunity to sins, and men should now say to themselves,' 'Let us sin, let us do securely what we will, Christ cleanses us: He is faithful and righteous, He cleanses us from all iniquity'; 'he takes from thee evil security and implants useful fear. It is an evil wish of thine to be secure; be anxious. For He is faithful and righteous to forgive us our sins, if thou art always displeasing to thyself and being changed until thou be perfected.' As a physician might say to his patient: 'Your trouble is obstinate: the poison is in your blood, and it will take a long time to eradicate it. But I do not tell you this to discourage you or make you careless; no, on the contrary, to make you watchful and diligent in the use of the remedy'; so the apostle says: 'My little children, these things I am writing to you in order that ye may not sin.'

"If, however, we fall into sin, let us not lose heart, for we have an Advocate with the Father . . . Our Advocate does not plead that we are innocent or adduce extenuating circumstances. He acknowledges our guilt and presents His vicarious work as the ground of our acquital. He stands in the Court of Heaven *a Lamb as it had been slain* (Rev. 5:6), and the marks of His sore passion are a mute but eloquent appeal: 'I suffered all this for sinners, and shall it go for naught?' "

The word "advocate" is *paraklētos*, "one called to your side," so, in a forensic sense "one who undertakes and champions your cause." Moulton and Milligan define; "a friend of the accused person, called to speak to his character, or otherwise enlist the sympathy of the judges." This was its use in the secular world of that day.

In the expression, "if any man sin," we have the aorist subjunctive, speaking, not of habitual action, but of a single act. It could better be translated, "if any man commit an act of sin." John regards sin in the believer's life, not as habitual, but as extraordinary, as infrequent. He says, "We have an Advocate with the Father." "With" is *pros*, "facing" the Father. Our Advocate is always in fellowship with the Father in order that if the saint loses fellowship with Him through cherished and unconfessed sin, He might plead our cause on the basis of His precious blood, and bring us back into fellowship again. The word "facing" brings us to this solemn thought, that when we saints sin the Lord Jesus must face the Father with us and our sin. The saint has been saved in His precious blood so that he may be able to keep from sinning, and when he does sin, he wounds the tender heart of the Saviour, and forces Him to face God the Father with that saint whom He has saved in His precious blood. How that should deter us from committing acts of sin!

This Advocate is described by John as "Jesus Christ the righteous." Smith quotes Rothe: "Only the righteous One, the guiltless, the One that is separate from sin, can be the Advocate with God for sinners, in general, the Mediator of salvation, and makes His friendship for us prevalent with God, because only such a one has access to God and fellowship with God (Heb. 7:26; I Peter 3:18; John 16:8, 10)," and Taylor, "What better advocate could we have for us, than He that is appointed to be our Judge."

John further describes Him as "the propitiation for our sins." The word is *hilasmos*. It is from the verb *hilaskomai*. In pagan usage it meant "to appease, to conciliate to one's self, to make a god propitious to one." Herodotus says, "The Parians, having *propitiated* Themistocles with gifts, escaped the visits of the army." However, when the word comes over into New Testament usage, its meaning is radically changed. Canon Westcott says: "The scriptural conception of the verb is not that of appeasing one who is angry with a personal feeling against the offender; but of altering the character of that which, from without, occasions a necessary alienation, and interposes an inevitable obstacle to fellowship. Such phrases as 'propitiating God,' and 'God being reconciled' are foreign to the language of the New Testament."

That from without which occasioned the alienation between God and man, was sin. It was the guilt of sin that separated man from his creator. Our Lord on the Cross assumed that guilt and paid the penalty in His own blood, and thus removed the cause of alienation. Now a holy and righteous God can bestow mercy upon a believing sinner on the basis of justice satisfied. Our Lord provided a satisfaction for the demands of the broken law. That satisfaction is the *hilasmos*. The Greek has it, "He Himself is a satisfaction." The intensive pronoun is used. The point is that the Old Testament priest offered an animal sacrifice, but not himself as the sacrifice. This wonderful New Testament Priest is both the Priest and the Sacrifice.

He is the satisfaction "for our sins, but not only for ours but for the sins of the whole world" (A.V.). Vincent says: *"The sins of* (A.V., italicized) should be omitted; as in Rev., *for the whole world.* Compare I John 4:14; John 4:42; 12:32. 'The propitiation is as wide as the sin' (Bengel). If men do not experience its benefit, the fault is not in its efficacy. Dusterdieck (cited by Huther) says, 'The propitiation has its real efficacy for the whole world; to believers it brings life, to unbelievers, death.' Luther: 'It is a patent fact that thou art a part of the whole world; so that thine heart cannot deceive itself, and think, the Lord died for Peter and Paul, but not for me.'"

Smith comments: "for the *sins* of the whole world." This is grammatically possible (cf. Matt. 5:20), but it misses the point. There are *sins*, special and occasional, in the believer; there is *sin* in the world; it is sinful through and through. The apostle means, 'for our sins and that mass of sin, the world.'"

Translation. *My little children, these things I am writing to you in order that you may not commit an act of sin. And if anyone commit an act of sin, One who pleads our cause we constantly have facing the Father, Jesus Christ the righteous One. And He Himself is a satisfaction for our sins, and not only for ours but also for the whole world.*

(2:3) Smith's comment on verses three to six is helpful: "The apostle foresees the question which may be raised: 'How can I be assured that Christ is all this to *me* — *my* Propitiation, *my* Advocate? And how can I be assured that I have an abiding interest in Him?' He answers: (1) We attain to personal and conscious acquaintance with Christ by observance of His commandments (3-5*a*); (2) we attain to assurance of abiding union with Him by 'walking even as He walked' (5*b*-6). The principle is that it is not enough to understand the theory; we must put it into practice. E.g., what makes an artist? Not merely learning the rules of perspective and mixture of colors, but actually putting one's hand to brush and canvas. First attempts may be unsuccessful, but skill comes by patient practice. Compare Rembrandt's advice to his pupil Hoogstraten, 'Try to put well in practice what you already know; and in doing so you will, in good time, discover the hidden things which you inquire about.' To know about Christ, to understand the doctrine of His person and work is mere theory; we get to know Him and to know that we know Him by practice of His precepts."

"Hereby" is *en toutōi*, literally, "in this." "The expression points to what follows, 'if we keep His commandments,' yet with a covert reference to that idea as generally implied in the previous words concerning fellowship with God and walking with Him in the light" (Vincent). "We do know" is *ginōskō*, "to know by experience" as contrasted to *oida*, "absolute, immediate knowledge of a fact once for all." This knowledge that we know Him is knowledge gained by experience day by day, experiential knowledge gained from the experience of keeping His commandments. "We know Him" is *egnōkamen auton*. The verb is perfect in tense, referring to a past complete act having present results. That is, if we are keeping His commandments, we know that we have in time past come to know Him with the present result that that state of knowing Him is true of us in the present time. "Keep" is *tēreō*, "to attend to carefully, to guard, observe." The word does not merely speak of the act of obeying His commands, but of a solicitous desire that we do not disobey any of them but on the other hand, that we obey them perfectly. It is that holy fear of disobeying God as expressed in the word *phobos* (fear), used in I Peter as defined by Wardlaw: "This fear is self-distrust; it is tenderness of conscience; it is vigilance against temptation; it is the fear which inspiration opposes to highmindedness in the admonition, 'be not highminded but fear.' It is taking heed lest we fall; it is a constant apprehension of the deceitfulness of the heart, and of the insidiousness and power of inward corruption. It is the caution and circumspection which timidly shrinks from whatever would offend and dishonor God and the Saviour." It is the saint's love for God's Word and his guardianship of that Word lest it be dishonored. Alford defines *tēreō,* "to watch, guard" as some precious thing. The verb is present subjunctive, which speaks of continuous action. It is the habitual, moment by moment safeguarding of the Word by the saint lest he violate its precepts. Robertson says that "the Gnostics boasted of their superior knowledge of Christ, and John here challenges their boast by an appeal to experiential knowledge of Christ which is shown by keeping His commandments."

The word "commandments" is not here *nomos,* "law," which John never uses for the rule of Christian obedience, and which is reserved by him for the Mosaic law, John using it 15 times in his Gospel for that purpose (Alford). It is *entolē,* another word meaning "an order, command, charge, precept." The precepts (commandments) are those given by our Lord either personally while on earth or through His apostles in the New Testament Books. Thus, a solicitous guarding of the precepts of Christ, a consumming desire that they be honored, a passionate determination that they always be kept, is a proof gained from experience, that that person has come to an experiential knowledge of the Lord Jesus and is at present in that state of knowing Him. This experiential knowledge is in contrast with and opposed to a mere theoretical knowledge of His Person.

Translation. *And in this we know experientially that we have come to know Him experientially and are in that state at present, if we are continually having a solicitous, watchful care in keeping His precepts.*

(2:4) Here the expanded translation reads, "He who keeps on saying, I have come to know Him experientially with the present result that I am in that state, and His precepts is not habitually guarding with solicitous care, is a liar, and in this one the truth does not exist." Robertson comments: "This is one of the pious platitudes, cheap claptrap of the Gnostics, who would bob up in meetings with such explosions." This person is an unsaved person, for a believer as a habit of life obeys the Word of God.

Translation. *He who keeps on saying, I have come to know Him experientially and as a present result am in that state, and His precepts is not habitually guarding with solicitous care, is a liar, and in this one the truth does not exist.*

(2:5) "Whoso" (*hos d'an*) "whoever," destroys the religious exclusiveness of the Gnostics which limited such a knowledge as is referred to in 2:3, 4 to the intellectual oligarchy, the intelligentsia, and shows that a personal experiential knowledge of the Lord Jesus is open to all true believers. "Keepeth" is present subjunctive, speaking of habitual, continuous action. Thus, whoever keeps on continually keeping (*tēreō*) (having a solicitous, watchful care for the Word so as to guard it from being disobeyed but on the other hand, obeyed) the Word, verily, in him is the love of God perfected. The demonstrative pronoun is used, "in this one truly is the love of God perfected."

As to the meaning of the phrase, "in this one is the love of God perfected," Vincent has a helpful note: "The change in the form of this antithetic clause is striking. He who claims to know God, yet lives in disobedience, is a liar. We should expect as an offset to this: He that keepeth His commandments is *of the truth;* or, *the truth is in him.* Instead, we have, 'In him has the love of God been perfected.' In other words, the obedient child of God is characterized, not by any representative trait or quality of his own personality, but merely as the subject of the work of divine love: as the sphere in which that love accomplishes its perfect work."

As to the phrase "the love of God," Vincent inclines to the view that "the fundamental idea of the love of God as expounded by John is *the love which God has made known and which answers to His nature.*" His reasoning that leads him to this interpretation is as follows: referring to chapter four of this letter he says: "Here we have, verse 9, the *manifestation* of the love of God in us. By our life in Christ and our love to God we are a manifestation of God's love. Directly following this is a definition of the essential nature of love. '*In this* is love; i.e., *herein consists love*: *not that we have loved God, but that He loved us*' (v. 10). Our mutual love is a proof that God dwells in us. God dwelling in us, His love is perfected in us (v. 12). The latter clause, it would seem, must be explained according to verse 10. Then (v. 16), 'We have known and believed the love that God *hath in us.*' 'God is love'; that is His nature, and He imparts this nature to be the sphere in which His children dwell. 'He that dwelleth in love dwelleth in God.' Finally, our love is engendered by His love. 'We love Him because He first loved us' (v. 19).

"In harmony with this is John 15:9, 'As the Father loved Me, I also loved you. Continue ye *in my love.*' *My love* must be explained by *I loved* you. This is the same idea of divine love as the *sphere* or *element* of renewed being; and this idea is placed, as in the passage we are considering, in direct connection with the keeping of the divine commandments. 'If ye keep my commandments ye shall abide in my love.'

"This interpretation does not exclude man's love to God. On the contrary, it includes it. The love which God has, is revealed as the *love* of *God* in the love of His children toward Him, no less than in His manifestations of love to them. The idea of divine love is thus complex. Love, in its very essence, is reciprocal. Its perfect ideal requires two parties. It is not enough to tell us, as a bare, abstract truth, that God is love. The truth must be rounded and filled out for us by the appreciable exertion of divine love upon an object, and by the response of the object. The love of God is *perfected* or *completed* by the perfect establishment of the relation of love between God and man. When man loves perfectly, his love is the love of God shed abroad in his heart. His love owes its origin and its nature to the love of God."

To sum up the matter, we would say that the love of God here is the love that God is in His nature, produced in the believer yielded to the Holy Spirit by the same Holy Spirit, which love causes him to have a solicitous watchful care of His precepts. This love is brought to its completion or perfection in the sense

that it accomplishes that for which it is intended, namely, to cause
the saint to obey God's Word, not because he should, not because
it is right to do so, not in order to escape chastisement should he
disobey it, all of which motives may enter into the subconscious
reasons he may have for obeying it and which in themselves are
proper motives, but he obeys the Word because he loves the
Lord Jesus.   Paul, in Galatians 5:1-26, teaches that the saint is
not under law, and has been put under a superior restraint to
evil and a compelling urge to do right, namely, divine love, produced in the heart by the Holy Spirit.

Translation. *But whoever habitually is with a solicitous care
keeping His Word, truly, in this one the love of God has been
brought to its completion, with the present result that it is in
that state of completion. In this we have an experiential knowledge that in Him we are.*

(2:6) To understand this verse, we will need to study the
Greek word translated "abide," and see how it is used in the
New Testament. It is *menō*. Thayer gives, "to abide, to remain,
to sojourn, tarry." The word refers, in a connection like this,
more than merely to position. It is used very often of persons
abiding in a home, which implies more than mere position, but
rather fellowship, communion, dependence, harmony, friendship.
See, "there abide till ye go thence" (Matt. 10:11); "tarry ye
here and watch with Me" (Matt. 26:38); "Mary abode with
her" (Luke 1:56); "neither abode in (any) house" (Luke 8:27);
"for today I must abide at thy house" (Luke 19:5); "They came
and saw where He dwelt, and abode with Him that day" (John
1:39, 40). These instances could be multiplied. To abide in the
Lord Jesus therefore implies not only position, but relationship.
It implies fellowship. friendship, dependence, harmony, communion. There are three Greek words which give us the three
aspects of a believer's life. The verb of being (*eimi*), refers to
the saint's position in Christ. He has been placed into vital union
with Him by the act of the Holy Spirit baptizing (*baptizō* placing) him in Christ. Our present word, *menō*, refers to the saint's
fellowship with and dependence upon Him, communion, close-

ness of intercourse. The word *peripateō* "to order one's behavior, to conduct one's self," speaks of the saint's manner of life. The first, the saint's position in Christ, makes possible his Christian manner of life. The second, the saint's fellowship with and dependence upon the Lord Jesus, conditions that manner of life, makes it what it should be. The word *peripateō* literally means "to walk around." And since the way a person walks is often a good index as to the kind of person he is, the word not only referred to the physical act of walking, but came to have the idea of the manner of life of the person.

We must look at the Greek word translated "ought." The word is *opheilō*, "to owe, to owe money, be in debt for, to be under obligation, bound by duty or necessity to do something, it behooves one, one ought." It is "used thus of a necessity imposed either by law or duty, or by reason, or by the times, or by the nature of the matter under consideration" (Thayer). Cremer in comparing the synonyms *dei*, "it is a necessity in the nature of the case," and *opheilō*, "to owe," says that the former designates more the necessity, whereas the latter denotes the personal, moral obligation.

"So" is *kathōs*, "according as, just as, even as." "As" is *houtōs*, "in the manner spoken of, in the way described, in this manner, in such a manner, thus, so." "To walk" is a present infinitive in the Greek text emphasizing habitual, continuous action. The Christ-like life here admonished must be the continuous, habitual, moment by moment experience of the believer, no spasmodic, infrequent sort of thing. "Walk" is *peripateō*, "to conduct one's self, to order one's behavior."

Translation. *He who is constantly saying that he as a habit of life is living in close fellowship with and dependence upon Him, is morally obligated just as that One conducted Himself, also himself in the manner spoken of to be conducting himself.*

(2:7) The best manuscripts do not have *adelphoi*, "brethren," but *agapētoi*, "beloved ones." The distinctive word for "love" here is the one used of God's love, as in John 3:16, I John 4:8. It is, "divinely-loved ones," loved by God. The Greek order of

words is, "No new commandment am I writing to you," the
words "no new commandment" being first in the sentence and
thus in the emphatic position. The word "commandment" is
entolē, "a precept" as in 2:4, not in the sense of the Mosaic law
(*nomos* law), but as an exhortation to the Christian, an injunction. The word "new" is *kainos.* There are two words meaning
"new" in the Greek language, *neos,* "new in point of time," and
kainos, "new as pertains to quality, the new as set over against
that which has seen service, the outworn, the effete or marred
through age" (Trench). Thus, John assures his readers that
the commandment or precept he is giving them is nothing new
in quality, but on the other hand, old. The word "old" here is
palaios, in which word "the simple conception of *time* dominates"
(Vincent). "Had" is in the imperfect tense in Greek which
tense speaks of continuous state or action in past time. The
beginning here is the beginning of the Christian experience of
the readers. They had this commandment before them and with
them constantly during their lives as saved individuals. The
words "from the beginning" in the second sentence of this verse
are not found in the best manuscripts. That commandment was
to love one another (John 13:34).

Translation. *Divinely-loved ones, no new commandment am
I writing you, but a commandment, an old one, which you have
had constantly from the beginning. The commandment, the old
one, is the Word which you heard.*

(2:8) Vincent comments: "The commandment of love is
both *old* and *new. Old,* because John's readers have had it from
the beginning of their Christian experience. *New,* because, in
the unfolding of Christian experience, it has developed new
power, meaning, and obligation, and close correspondence 'with
the facts of Christ's life, with the crowning mystery of His passion, and with the facts of the Christian life.'" "Again" is *palin,*
and Smith says: "again, i.e., in another sense, from another
point of view, not in itself but in our recognition of it, 'it is a new
commandment.'"

Robertson says: "Paradox, but truth. Old in teaching (as old as the story of Cain and Abel, 3:11 f.), but new in practice. For this use of *palin* (again) for a new turn see John 16:28. To walk as Christ walked is to put into practice the old commandment and so make it new (ever new and fresh), as love is as old as man and fresh in every new experience."

"Which thing" is *ho,* the neuter relative pronoun. The relative pronoun agrees with its antecedent in gender and number. The word "commandment" is feminine in gender, and therefore it cannot be the antecedent of *ho,* "which thing." Here the relative has no definite antecedent. Being neuter, it refers here to an abstract truth or fact. One would translate, "which fact is true in Him and in you." Now, what is the fact which is thus true in the case of our Lord and in the case of the readers of this epistle? Vincent says that "the fact that the old commandment is new" is the thing referred to by John. Smith says that the fact pointed out is "the paramount necessity of love. This truth, though unperceived, is contained in the revelation of Jesus Christ (in Him) and proved in the experience of believers (in you). It is a fact that hatred of one's brother clouds the soul and shuts out the light. 'I know,' says the Apostle, 'because the darkness is passing away, and the light, the true light, is already shining,' i.e., my eyes are getting accustomed to the light of the gospel-revelation, and I have seen this truth which at first was hidden from me."

"Is past" is *paragetai,* "to pass by, go past," metaphorically, "to pass away, to disappear." The tense is present, speaking here of action going on in present time; "The darkness is passing away." The picture is that of the darkness of sin and unbelief as passing by as a parade goes by on the street. All parades have an end. So will end some day the parade of Satan's hosts. Darkness is *skotia.* Vincent comments: "God is *light;* and whatever is not in fellowship with God is therefore *darkness.* In all cases where the word is not used of physical darkness, it means moral insensibility to divine light; moral blindness or obtuseness."

The word "true" as defining "light" is *alēthinos*. Greek has the synonyms, *alēthēs*, "true," and *alēthinos*, "genuine." Trench says, "God is *alēthēs* (true) and He is *alēthinos*, (genuine): but very different attributes are ascribed to Him by the one epithet, and by the other. He is *alēthēs* (John 3:33; Rom 3:4), inasmuch as He cannot lie, as He is *apseudēs* (without a lie) (Tit. 1:2), the truth-speaking and the truth-loving God. But He is *alēthinos* (I Thess. 1:9; John 17:3; Isaiah 65:16); *very* God, as distinguished from idols and all other false gods, the dreams of the diseased fancy of man, with no substantial existence in the world of realities. . . . This last adjective (*alēthinos*), is particularly applied to express that which is all that it pretends to be; for instance, pure gold as opposed to adulterated metal." The word *alēthinos* as describing "light" here, speaks of the light that God is in His essence, as genuine light is contrasted to a false or spurious light. The false light is Satan who in imitation of God covers himself over with light assumed from the outside, which light does not proceed from nor is it representative of what he is in his inner being, an angel of darkness. This truth is given us in the Greek word *metaschēmatizō*, translated inadequately "transformed" in II Corinthians 11:14 (A.V.). Satan, an angel of darkness, attempts to deceive and attract the human race by disguising himself as an angel of light.

Translation. *Again, a commandment, a new one, I am writing to you, which fact is true in Him and in you, because the darkness is passing away, and the light, the genuine light, already is shining.*

(2:9) Vincent's comment on the expression "hateth his brother" is helpful: "The sharp issue is maintained here as in Christ's words, 'He that is not with Me is against Me' (Luke 11:23). Men fall into two classes, those who are in fellowship with God, and therefore walk in light and love, and those who are not in fellowship with God, and therefore walk in darkness and hatred. 'A direct opposition,' says Bengel; where love is not, there is hatred. 'That heart is not empty.' See John 3:20; 7:7; 15:18; 17:14. The word *hate* is opposed both to the love of

natural affection (*phileō*), and to the more discriminating sentiment — *love founded on a just estimate* (*agapaō*). For the
former see John 12:25; 15:18, 19; compare Luke 14:26. For
the latter, I John 3:14, 15; 4:20; Matt. 5:43; 6:24; Eph. 5:28,
29. 'In the former case, *hatred,* which may become a moral
duty, involves the subjection of an instinct. In the latter case
it expresses a general determination of character' (Westcott)."
The brother here is a fellow-Christian.

As to the words "until now," Vincent remarks, "Though the
light has been increasing, and though he may claim that he has
been in the light from the first."

Translation. *He who is saying that in the light he is, and his
brother he is habitually hating, in the darkness is up to this
moment.*

(2:10) The word "love" here is *agapaō.* To ascertain the
content of this word see Paul's definition of it in I Corinthians
13 (translated there by the word "charity"). See it illustrated
in action in John 3:16. Note how it is produced (Gal. 5:22, 23;
Rom. 5:5). The expression "loveth his brother" must be understood in the light of the above meaning of this word. The essence
of the word is that of a self-sacrificial love that gives of itself for
the happiness and well-being of the fellow-Christian.

The fact that this Christian is habitually loving his brother-
Christian with the above kind of love, is indicative of his close
fellowship with and dependence upon the Lord Jesus, for this
supernaturally-produced love in his heart is present in an overflowing quantity only in the life of a believer who habitually is
abiding in his Lord. The light here is, of course, the Lord Jesus
Himself and all that is written in the Word about Him.

The words, "occasion of stumbling" is *skandalon.* The word
meant, "the movable stick or trigger of a trap; a trap or snare;
any impediment placed in the way and causing one to stumble or
fall; a stumbling-block." Vincent says: "The meaning is not
that he gives no occasion of stumbling to others, but that there
is none in his own way." Smith comments: " 'there is no
occasion of stumbling, nothing to trip him up and make him fall'

— an echo of John 11:9, 10. Another interpretation, less agreeable to the context, but more consonant with the common use of *skandalon* (compare Matt. 13:41; 18:7; Rom. 14:13) is, Because he is winsome and gracious, there is in him no stumbling-block to others, nothing to deter them from accepting the gospel. The love of the primitive Christians impressed the heathen."

Translation. *He who is habitually loving his brother, in the light is abiding, and a stumbling-block in him there is not.*

(2:11) Smith comments: "St. John recognizes no neutral attitude between 'love' and 'hatred.' Love is active benevolence, and less than this is hatred, just as indifference to the gospel-call amounts to rejection of it (compare Matt. 22:5-7). Observe the climax: 'in the darkness is, and in the darkness walketh, and knoweth not where he is going.' The penalty of living in the darkness is not merely that one does not see, but that one goes blind. The neglected faculty is atrophied. Compare the mole, the crustacea in the Mammoth Cave of Kentucky." Commenting on the words "hath blinded," Vincent says: "The aorist tense, *blinded,* indicates a past, definite, decisive act. When the darkness overtook, it blinded. The blindness is no new state into which he has come." This person is, of course, an unsaved person professing Christianity. Habitually conducting one's self in the sphere of darkness is indicative of an unsaved state.

Translation. *But he who as a habit of life hates his brother, in the darkness is, and in the sphere of the darkness is habitually ordering his behavior, and he does not know where he is going, because the darkness blinded his eyes.*

(2:12) "Little children" is *teknion,* "little born ones"; the Scotch, "bairns," fits the meaning very well. "Are forgiven" is *aphiēmi,* "to send from one's self, to send away, to bid go away or depart." God's forgiveness includes the putting away of our sins, their guilt, defilement, and penalty, at the Cross. The verb is in the perfect tense, which tense speaks of a past completed action having present and in some instances, permanent results. Our sins were put away at the Cross, with the result that they are never more remembered against us. Our Lord cried on the

Cross, "It is finished" (A.V.). The perfect tense is used here. The atonement, to which He had reference, was effected at the Cross and became forever the all-sufficient payment for sin. The translation should read, "It stands finished."

The permanent putting away of sin was "for His Name's sake." The words "the Name," are an Old Testament term expressing the sum of the qualities which mark the nature or character of a person, in this case, the Person of God. It refers to all that is true of God in His glory, majesty, and might. The expression here refers to our Lord (2:1), and includes all that He is in His glorious Person. Paul in Philippians 2:9-11 tells us that in view of the self-emptying of our Lord as He chose the Cross rather than remain in Glory ("who instead of the joy then present with Him, endured the Cross" Heb. 12:2), God the Father exalted Him and gave Him "The Name"; placed upon the shoulders of the Man Christ Jesus, all the majesty, glory, and splendor of Deity. Because of what our Lord was in His Person as very God of very God, God the Father put away our sins, recognizing and accepting the atonement He offered on the Cross.

Translation. *I am writing to you, little children, because your sins have been put away for you permanently because of His Name.*

(2:13) "Ye have known" is *egnōkate,* the verb *ginōskō* referring to experiential knowledge, knowledge gained by experience, and it is in the perfect tense. These fathers were the older men, mature in the Christian life, having lived in fellowship with the Lord Jesus for many years, and thus having gained much personal knowledge of Him by experience. The perfect tense shows that this knowledge was a well-rounded matured knowledge, the results of which were a permanent possession of these men grown old in the Christian life.

The young men are said to have overcome the wicked one. The verb is again perfect in tense. As Robertson says, "a permanent victory after conflict." They fought their fight to a finish and were enjoying the fruits of victory, a life lived in the power of the Spirit where their victory over Satan was a consistent one.

"The wicked one" is *ton ponēron*, "the pernicious one." The Greek has two words for the idea of wickedness, *kakos*, "evil in the abstract," and *ponēros*, "evil in active opposition to the good." The *kakos* man is content to perish in his own corruption. The *ponēros* man seeks to drag everyone else down with him into his ultimate downfall. Satan is of the latter character, pernicious.

"Little children" is *paidion*. Vincent says: "Compare *teknia little children* (v. 1), which emphasizes the idea of kinship, while this word emphasizes the idea of *subordination* and consequent *discipline*. Hence, it is the more appropriate word when spoken from the standpoint of authority, than of affection." *Teknia* is related to *tiktō*, "to give birth to," and emphasizes the birth or genital relationship, whereas *paidion* is related to *paideuō*, "to train children." Our word "pedagogue" comes from the latter word. One could translate *paidion*, "little child under instruction."

The first two verbs, "I write," are in the present tense, referring to the apostle's immediate act of writing. The last is in the aorist tense, which in the indicative mode usually refers to a past act. But this verb in that tense and mode and in a context like this is called an epistolary aorist, by which a writer looks at his present act of writing as the recipient of his letter will look at it when he receives it, as a past event. John uses the epistolary aorist twice in verse 14. The words "standing on his neck" in the following translation are used to indicate the present result of the past action of the perfect tense. Ancient kings stood on the necks of the captives whom they conquered as a sign of the victory they gained over them.

Translation. *I am writing to you, fathers, because you have come to know experientially the One who is from the beginning, and as a present result are possessors of that knowledge. I am writing to you, young men, because you have gained the victory over the Pernicious One and as a present result are standing on his neck. I write to you, little children under instruction, because you have come to know the Father experientially, with the present result that you are possessors of that knowledge.*

(2:14) The writer is rendering the epistolary aorist used once in verse 13 and twice in this verse by the present rather than by a past tense, since it is a Greek idiom and not understood by the English reader. A past tense translation would suggest to the English reader a previous letter. John has reference here only to the present letter he is writing.

"Strong" is *ischuros*, which refers to power as an endowment. Strength to overcome Satan is part of the salvation given the believer. It takes the form of the spiritual energy supplied the yielded saint by the Holy Spirit. "Abide" is *menō*, "to dwell in as a home." The word of God, residing in their hearts in an unhindered, welcome state, was that which, together with the power of the Holy Spirit, gave these young men victory over Satan, the Pernicious One, who sought to drag them down with himself into the ruin that some day will be his.

Translation. *I write to you, fathers, because you have come to know experientially the One who is from the beginning, and are as a present result, possessors of that knowledge. I write to you, young men, because you are strong with endowed strength, and the Word of God in you is abiding, and you have gained the victory over the Pernicious One, and as a present result are standing on his neck.*

(2:15-17) The word "world" here is *kosmos* which in its use here is defined by Vincent as follows: "The sum-total of human life in the ordered world, considered apart from, alienated from, and hostile to God, and of the earthly things which seduce from God (John 7:7; 15:18; 17:9, 14; I Cor. 1:20, 21; II Cor. 7:10; James 4:4)." *Kosmos* refers to an ordered system. Here it is the ordered system of which Satan is the head, his fallen angels and demons are his emissaries, and the unsaved of the human race are his subjects, together with those purposes, pursuits, pleasures, practices, and places where God is not wanted. Much in this world-system is religious, cultured, refined, and intellectual. But it is anti-God and anti-Christ.

Trench quotes Bengel as saying that this world of unsaved humanity is inspired by "the spirit of the age," the *Zeitgeist*, which

Trench defines as follows: "All that floating mass of thoughts, opinions, maxims, speculations, hopes, impulses, aims, aspirations, at any time current in the world, which it may be impossible to seize and accurately define, but which constitutes a most real and effective power, being the moral, or immoral atmosphere which at every moment of our lives we inhale, again inevitably to exhale." This is the world-system to which John refers.

The word "love" here is *agapaō,* the word used of God's love for a lost race of sinners, and which is self-sacrificial in its essence (John 3:16), the love which He is by nature (I John 4:8), and the love which is produced in the heart of the yielded saint by the Holy Spirit (Gal. 5:22). The question confronts us now as to how believers can love the sinful world with a love produced in their hearts by the Holy Spirit. The answer is that the Bible writers when taking certain Greek words over into the Bible, poured an additional content of meaning into them, as in this case, but at times use the word, not in its newly-acquired New Testament meaning, but in its purely classical connotation. An example of this is found in the use of *dikaios* (righteous) in Romans 5:7, where the word refers to a righteous man, not in the Bible sense of a justified believing sinner, but in the classical sense, that of a law-abiding, just, and fair individual. Here, *agapaō* is used merely in its classical meaning, that of a love called out of one's heart by the preciousness of the object loved. The word as used here refers to a fondness, an affection, non-ethical in its content, for an object because of its value. It is a love of approbation, of esteem. Demas is said to have loved this present age. He found it precious and thus came to love it.

The verb is a present imperative in a prohibition, which construction in Greek speaks of the act of forbidding the continuance of an action already going on. Some of John's readers were still loving the world-system out from which they had been saved. John says: "Stop loving the world with a love called out of your hearts because of its preciousness."

The expression "if any man love the world" is a hypothetical condition in the subjunctive mode. The verb is in the present tense. John could have used the aorist tense, expressing merely the fact of loving the world. But he goes out of his way to use the present tense, which tense in the subjunctive mode always stresses continuous, habitual action. This marks this hypothetical person as one who loves the world as a habit of life to the exclusion of any love for God. This is an unsaved person.

In this person, the love of the Father does not exist. This is love for the Father as generated in the heart of the yielded believer by the Holy Spirit. And here the word "love" (*agapē*) is used in its New Testament sense.

Vincent, commenting on the words "is not in him," says: "This means more than that he does not love God: rather, that the love of God does not dwell in him as the ruling principle of his life. Westcott cites a parallel from Philo: 'It is impossible for love to the world to coexist with love to God, as it is impossible for light and darkness to coexist.'"

In the phrase, "all that is in the world," the word "all" does not refer to all things severally, but to all that is in the world collectively (Vincent). "Lust" is *epithumia*, "a craving, a passionate desire," good or evil, according to the context. Here it refers to evil cravings. The word "lust" is obsolete today, as it is used here, since the present day usage confines its meaning to an immoral desire. "Flesh" is *sarx* which here refers to the totally depraved nature as governing the individual's reason, will, and emotions. Thus, the lust of the flesh is the passionate desire or the craving that comes from the evil nature. The word "flesh" here has no reference to the physical body except as that body is controlled or energized by the evil nature. The physical body and its members in themselves have no evil desires except as controlled by the totally depraved nature. To say that the physical body of itself has evil desires is Gnosticism, the heresy that matter is inherently evil.

Now, John speaks of one of the manifestations of the evil nature, the lust of the eyes, namely the passionate cravings of the eyes for satisfaction, these cravings finding their source in the evil nature. Another manifestation of the evil nature

is the pride of life. The word is *alazonia,* "vainglory." Vincent
says: "It means, originally, *empty, braggart talk or display;
swagger;* and hence an insolent and vain assurance in one's own
resources, or in the stability of earthly things, which issues in a
contempt of divine laws. The *vainglory of life* is the vainglory
which belongs to the present life." Thayer defines: "an insolent
and empty assurance which trusts in its own power and resources
and shamefully despises and violates divine laws and human
rights." The word "life" here is *bios,* referring to that which
sustains life, namely, food, clothing, and shelter. "Of the Father"
is "out from the Father as a source." "Of the world" is "out from
the world as a source."

"Passeth away" is *paragetai,* "to pass alongside, to pass by."
The verb is in the passive voice. The world is being caused to
pass by. That is, God is causing the world to come to its end.
It is being caused to pass by in a vain (futile) show, this parade
of the world. But, John says, "The one who keeps on habitually
doing the will of God abides forever."

Translation. *Stop considering the world precious with the
result that you love it, and the things in the world. If anyone as
a habit of life is considering the world precious and is therefore
loving it, there does not exist the love possessed by the Father
in him. Because everything which is in the world, the passionate
desire of the flesh, and the passionate desire of the eyes, and
the insolent and empty assurance which trusts in the things that
serve the creature life, is not from the Father as a source but is
from the world as a source. And the world is being caused to
pass away, and its passionate desire. But the one who keeps on
habitually doing the will of God abides forever.*

(2:18) "Time" is *hōra,* "an hour." John says, "It is a last
hour." The article is absent before "hour," and the emphasis
is not therefore upon the fact of a particular, definite time, but
upon the character of that particular, definite time. Vincent
says that John uses the word "hour" as marking a *critical* season.
He says: "The dominant sense of the expression *last days* in
the New Testament is that of a period of suffering and struggle

preceding a divine victory. See Acts 2:17; James 5:3; I Peter 1:20. Hence the phrase here does not refer to the end of the world, but to the period preceding a crisis in the advance of Christ's kingdom, a changeful and troublous period, marked by the appearance of 'many antichrists.' "

As to the term "Antichrist," Vincent says that "the absence of the article shows its currency as a proper name. The distinction between a false Christ (*pseudochristos*) and an antichrist (*antichristos*) is that the former is a pretender to the Messianic office, whereas the latter is against Christ, not pretending to be Christ, but proposing to do the work of Christ."

Trench says of Antichrist, "To me St. John's words seem decisive, that resistance to Christ, and defiance of Him, this, and not any treacherous assumption of his character and offices, is the essential mark of Antichrist; is that which, therefore, we should expect to find embodied in his name; . . . one who shall not pay so much homage to God's Word as to assert its fulfillment in himself, for he shall deny that Word altogether; hating even erroneous worship, because it is worship at all, and everything that is called 'God' (II Thess. 2:4), but hating most of all the Church's worship in spirit and in truth (Dan. 8:11); who, on the destruction of every religion, every acknowledgment that man is submitted to higher powers than his own, shall seek to establish his throne; and, for God's great truth that in Christ God is man, to substitute his own lie, that in him man is God." His word on the subject of a false Christ is as follows: "The *pseudochristos* does not deny the being of a Christ; on the contrary, he builds on the world's expectations of such a person; only, he appropriates these to himself, blasphemously affirms that he is the foretold One, in whom God's promises and men's expectations are fulfilled.

"The distinction, then, is plain. The *antichristos* denies that there is a Christ; the *pseudochristos* affirms himself to be the Christ. Both alike make war against the Christ of God, and would set themselves, though under different pretences, on the throne of His glory. And yet, while the words have this broad distinction between them, while they represent two different manifestations of the kingdom of wickedness, there is a sense in which the final 'Antichrist' will be a 'Pseudochrist' as well; even as it will be the very character of that last revelation of hell to gather up into itself, and to reconcile for one last assault against truth, all anterior and subordinate forms of error. He will not, it is true, call himself the Christ, for he will be filled with deadliest hatred against the name and offices, as against the whole spirit and temper of Jesus of Nazareth, the exalted King of Glory. But, inasmuch as no one can resist the truth by a mere negation, he must offer and oppose something positive in the room of that faith which he will assail and endeavor to utterly abolish. And thus we may certainly conclude that the final Antichrist will reveal himself to the world — for he too will have his *apokalupsis* (revelation) (II Thess. 2:3, 8), his *parousia* (advent) (v. 9) — as, in a sense, the Messiah of God, but still as the world's saviour; as the one who will make the blessedness of as many as obey him, giving them the full enjoyment of a present material earth, instead of a distant, shadowy, and uncertain heaven." This is the personal Antichrist to which John has reference. "Shall come" is present tense in the Greek text. It is the prophetic present, "is about to come."

John asserts that in his time "there are many antichrists." The verb is in the perfect tense, indicating that they have arisen and are on the scene. They have established themselves in the midst of the Church. What will be true of the personal Antichrist when he comes is true of these men in a lesser sense, or in a lesser degree. They are imbued with the spirit that will animate Antichrist. John will have occasion to describe these false teachers as to their attitude towards the Person of the Lord Jesus in succeeding verses (22, 23) of this chapter.

"Whereby" is *hothen*, "for which reason, wherefore." That is, because there were many antichrists in John's time, it follows that it is a last hour. With 1900 years of Church history behind us since John's time, and Modernism sweeping the visible Church, how close must the Rapture and then the Second Advent be. The Church is in its last period, the Laodicean or apostate stage.

Translation. *Little children under instruction, a last hour it is. And even as you heard that Antichrist is coming, even now antichrists, many of them, have arisen, from which (fact) we know by experience that it is a last hour.*

(2:19) The words "out from" and "of" in this verse are the translation of the preposition *ek* which is followed by the ablative case. There are two classifications of the ablative here, ablative of separation and ablative of source. In the statement, "They went out from us," we have the ablative of separation. These false teachers (antichrists) went out from the true believers in the sense that they departed doctrinally from the position of the Church as to the Person of the Lord Jesus, a position which they had held only in an intellectual way. It was a mental assent to the doctrines concerning, not a heart acceptance of, the Person of Christ.

In the words, "They were not of us," we have the ablative of source. That is, the antichrists did not have their source in the Mystical Body of Christ composed only of true believers. They were merely members of the visible, organized church on earth. They did not partake of the divine life animating the members of the Body of Christ, made up of true believers. All of which means that an apostate is an unsaved person who has mentally subscribed to the doctrines of the Christian faith and who then rejects those doctrines while still remaining within the organization of the visible church and posing as a Christian.

John argues that had these antichrists belonged to the Body of Christ, thus possessing divine life in company with true believers, they would in that case have remained with these true believers in matters of doctrine. But, he says, they departed from the doctrinal position of the Church so that it could be shown that they did not belong to the company of the saints. The words of the A.V. are misleading, "that they were not all of us," the implication being left with the reader that some of these antichrists had belonged to the company of the saints. The translation should read, "All were not of us." In the Greek text, the verb separates *not* from *all*. In such cases, according to New Testament usage, the negation is universal. The A.V. *not all* makes it partial (Vincent).

Translation. *Out from us they departed, but they did not belong to us as a source. For if they had belonged to us, they would in that case have remained with us. But (they departed) in order that they might be plainly recognized, that all do not belong to us as a source.*

(2:20) The word "unction" is *chrisma*. The word refers to that with which the anointing is performed, the unguent or ointment. Here it refers to the Holy Spirit with whom the believer is anointed. The two words meaning "to anoint" in the New Testament, *aleiphō* and *chriō*, refer to the act of applying something to something else for a certain purpose. *Aleiphō* was used, for instance, in the papyri of the act of greasing the yoke-band of an ox, namely, the act of applying grease to the yoke-band so that it would not irritate the sleek hide of the ox. *Chriō* was used of the application of a lotion to a sick horse. Thus, the anointing with the Holy Spirit refers to the act of God the Father (applying to the believing sinner) sending the Spirit in answer to the prayer of God the Son to take up His permanent residence in the believer. James 4:5 reads in the Greek text, "Do you think the scripture says in vain, The Spirit who has been caused to take up His permanent residence in us has a passionate longing to the point of envy?" This refers to the initial coming of the Spirit into the heart of the believing sinner at the moment he places his faith in the Saviour. This anointing is never repeated. The Old Testament priests were anointed with oil just once, when they were inducted into their office. The New Testament priest (the believer) is anointed with the Spirit just once, when he is inducted into his office as a priest (when he is saved). This anointing is only potential. That is, in itself it offers no help to the believer. The help the saint receives from the Spirit is through the fullness or control of the Spirit, which control is consequent upon his yieldedness and trust. The anointing is for the purpose of placing the Holy Spirit in a position where He can be of service to the believer, namely, in the saint's inner being. From His position in the believer, the Spirit performs all His office work for him.

One of the ministries of the Spirit consequent upon His indwelling presence is that of enlightening him regarding the meaning of the Word of God. He is the Great Teacher in the Church. As a result of this, John says, "Ye know all things" (A.V.). But the word "all" in the best Greek texts is in the nominative case, which makes it the subject of the verb. The correct translation is, "Ye all know." That is, as a result of the indwelling of the Holy Spirit, the saints are given the ability to know God's truth. The particular word for "know" here is not *ginōskō*, "to know by experience," but *oida*, "to know absolutely and finally." The antichrists, being unsaved and thus devoid of the Holy Spirit, do not have that ability. This ability to know the truth gives the saints the ability also to detect error.

Translation. *But as for you (in contradistinction to the antichrists), an anointing you have from the holy One, and you all know.*

(2:21) "I have not written" is aorist here, but not epistolary aorist. John is referring to the statement he had just made, namely, "You all know," that is, all believers have the ability to know God's Word by reason of the anointing they receive when they are saved, the personal indwelling of the Holy Spirit. "Because" is *hoti*, which could be causal in function (because), or declarative (that). The context decides for the latter use. John had just written that they all knew (v. 20). Now he writes (v. 21) "I did not write to you that you do not know the truth, but that you know it." The word "know" here is again *oida*, referring to an absolute, final, correct knowledge, here of God's Word as understood by the illumination of the Holy Spirit.

Translation. *I did not write to you that you do not know the truth, but that you know it, and that every lie is not out of the truth as a source.*

(2:22) The definite article appears before the word "liar" in the Greek text. It is, "Who is the liar?" Vincent says: "It marks the lively feeling with which the apostle writes. By the definite article, *the* liar, the lie is set forth in its concrete personality: the one who impersonates all that is false, as antichrist represents every form of hostility and opposition to Christ. The denial that Jesus is the Christ is the representative falsehood. He that denies is the representative liar." Commenting on the words, "he that denieth that Jesus is the Christ," Vincent says: "The article with the participle denotes *habitual* denial. Literally, *the one denying,* the one who habitually represents this attitude towards Christ. The words are aimed at the heresy of Cerinthus, a man of Jewish descent and educated at Alexandria. He denied the miraculous conception of Jesus, and taught that, after His baptism, the Christ descended upon Him in the form of a dove, and that He then announced the unknown Father and wrought miracles; but that, towards the end of His ministry, the Christ departed again from Jesus, and Jesus suffered and rose from the dead, while the Christ remained impassible (incapable of suffering) as a spiritual being."

But what is involved in the names "Jesus" and "Christ"? They are more than mere designations of the identity of a certain individual who flourished in the first century. The English name "Jesus" is the transliteration (spelling) of the Greek name *Iēsous,* which in turn is the transliteration of the Hebrew word which in English is spelled "Jehoshua," and which means "Jehovah saves." Thus, in the name "Jesus" there is contained the doctrines of the deity, humanity and vicarious atonement of the Person who bears that name. Only Jehovah could offer a sacrifice which would satisfy the demands of His holy law which the human race broke. But that sacrifice had to include within itself human nature without its sin, for deity in itself could not die, and deity acting as Priest for the sinner must partake of the nature of the individual on whose behalf He officiates.

The name "Christ" is the transliteration of *Christos*, a Greek word meaning "the anointed one," and this is the translation of the Hebrew word from which we get the name "Messiah."

The denial therefore is that the Person called Jesus was neither God nor man, and that on the Cross He did not offer an atonement for sin. Present day Modernism denies the deity of Jesus of Nazareth and the substitutionary atonement He offered on the Cross, while subscribing to His humanity. Modernism is branded here by John as "the liar."

The definite article appears before the word "antichrist." John says, "This one is the antichrist, the one who denies the Father and the Son." Here we have present day Unitarianism with a vengeance. The Jews denied the same thing in the first century. Our Lord asked the Pharisees, "What do you think concerning the Christ (Messiah)? Whose son is He?" They answered, "The son of David." Our Lord asks, "How then does David in (the) Spirit call Him Lord? (*kurios*, "Lord," the Greek word used in the LXX to translate the august title of God, Jehovah). If David therefore calls Him Lord, how is He his son?" Our Lord was pinning down these false teachers, these Unitarians, to an admission of the two Persons of the Trinity, God the Father and God the Son. They believed in the One God who manifested Himself as the Jehovah of the Old Testament, but they refused to believe in the deity of Jesus of Nazareth and His relation to their God as Son of God. Present day Modernism does the same. John brands this denial as partaking of the attitude of Antichrist, and as coming from "the antichrist," not the person of that name yet to come, but the Modernist, whoever he may be who denies the above truth. It is antichrist in spirit, and with a vengeance. Modernism is therefore antichristian in its nature, and does not deserve the name "Christian."

Translation. *Who is the liar if not the one who is denying that Jesus is the Christ? This one is the antichrist, the one who is denying the Father and the Son.*

(2:23) After branding the one who denies the deity of Jesus of Nazareth as seen in His unique sonship in relation to God the

Father as the Antichrist, John proceeds to show his relationship to the God whom he professes to worship. He says: "Everyone who denies the Son, not even does he have the Father." That is, the Modernist who professes to worship the God of the Bible, and who at the same time rejects His Son as very God of very God, does not sustain a saving relationship to the God he professes to worship. He is not His child, not a Christian, but an unsaved individual.

But John says: "The one who confesses the Son, also has the Father." The word "confess" is *homologeō*, "to speak the same thing that another does," hence, "to agree with that person." Thus, the word refers here to the act of a person agreeing with what the Bible teaches regarding the unique sonship of Jesus of Nazareth with respect to God as His Father. The unique sonship of Jesus of Nazareth is clearly brought out in John 5:18 where the first century false teachers accuse Him of claiming to be the unique Son of God. The word "his" of A.V. is the translation of the word *idios* which means "one's own private, personal, unique possession." They saw that if that were true, it would make Him equal with God. And since these Jews were Unitarians, they rejected His claim. But the one who holds the doctrine of the unique sonship of Jesus possesses God the Father also in the sense that he is His child. He is a saved individual. Nestle's Greek text includes the words, "The one who confesses the Son, also the Father he is having."

Translation. *Everyone who denies the Son, not even does he have the Father. The one who confesses the Son, also the Father is he having.*

(2:24-26) The A.V. fails to handle the pronoun used for emphasis at the beginning of this verse. It is, "But as for you," in contradistinction to the aforementioned false teachers, "you let that therefore abide in you which ye heard from the beginning." The point is, they (the false teachers) did not. They at one time subscribed to the true doctrine concerning the Person of the Lord Jesus, but they departed from it (2:19). "Abide" is *menō* "to remain." The exhortation is that the saints should allow the teaching into which they were brought when they were saved to remain in them. They are to continue to hold it fast. They must not allow themselves to become entangled in the Gnostic heresy regarding the Person of the Lord Jesus. But the word *menō* (abide) has in it more than the idea of "to remain." The exhortation includes more than that the saint should allow the basic teaching concerning the Person of our Lord to remain in him. He should have that attitude towards it that it will also feel at home in him, have ready access to every part of his life. In other words, it is the responsibility of the believer to nurture the stability and growth of those doctrines by a holy life and a determination to cling to them and remain true to them. All this is included in the content of meaning of the word *menō*.

John now proposes a hypothetical case. "Shall remain" is aorist subjunctive. The translation reads, "If in you there remains (abides *menō*) that which from the beginning you heard." That is, if the true doctrine relative to the Person of our Lord is abiding in the believer, that is an indication that he is saved and will as a saved person continue to abide both in the Son and in the Father.

Translation. *As for you, that which you heard from the beginning, in you let it be constantly abiding. If in you there abides that which from the beginning you heard, both in the Son and in the Father you will abide. And this is the promise which He Himself promised us, the life, the eternal (life). These things I wrote to you concerning those who are leading you astray.*

(2:27) Again John uses the pronoun in an intensive sense, contrasting his Christian readers with the false teachers. He says, "But as for you, the anointing which you received from Him remains in you," teaching that the Holy Spirit who is that with which the saint is anointed, stays in that person forever. We have the same truth brought out in James 4:5, "The Spirit who has been caused to take up His permanent residence in us." The verb is *katoikizō*, the prefixed preposition *kata*, the root meaning of which is "down," giving permanency to the act of taking up His residence. David could pray, "Take not thy Holy Spirit from me" (Psalm 51:11), since the Spirit came upon an individual in Old Testament times for the period of that person's ministry, and left him when that ministry was over, without affecting his salvation. But in New Testament times, the Spirit is in the believer to stay.

In view of the fact of the indwelling Spirit, the saints, John says, do not have "need that any man teach" them. "Man" is the indefinite pronoun in the Greek text. "Teach" is in the present subjunctive, emphasizing continuous action. The translation reads, "and no need are you constantly having that anyone be constantly teaching you." This does not set aside the usefulness and necessity of God-appointed and equipped teachers in the Church (Eph. 4:11, "teaching pastors," Acts 13:1), but merely means that the saints are not at the mercy of these Gnostic teachers or at the mercy of any teachers, for that matter. No teacher, even a God-appointed one, is the only and ultimate source of the saint's instruction. He has the Holy Spirit and the Word. And in the case of saints who are subjected to the teaching of Modernism, their court of appeal and refuge is the instruction of the Holy Spirit through the Word of God.

John says that the anointing teaches the saints. The act of teaching presupposes a person. This anointing therefore is a Person, the Holy Spirit Himself. The words "ye shall abide" are present imperative in the Greek text. This is not a predictive future, but a command. "Him" refers to the Lord Jesus.

Translation. *But as for you, the anointing which you received from Him remains in you. And no need are you constantly having that anyone be constantly teaching you. But even as His anointing teaches you concerning all things, and is true and is not a lie, and even as He (the Holy Spirit, the anointing) taught you, be constantly abiding in Him.*

(2:28) "When" is *ean,* "if," used with the subjunctive mode, the mode of future probability. The doubt is here, not as to the *fact* of our Lord's coming for His Church, He promised that, but as to the *time* of that coming. One could translate, "whenever

He shall appear." The exhortation, "Be constantly abiding in Him" is given in view of the uncertainty of the time of His coming. The believer must live in close fellowship with His Lord that he may be ready for that coming.

"Appear" is *phaneroō*, in the passive voice as it is here, "to be made manifest or visible." The invisible Lord Jesus will some day be made visible as He comes from heaven into the atmosphere of this earth to catch out His Bride, the Church. For some special work on the subject of the Rapture, see the author's book, *Great Truths To Live By* (pp. 135-143). "Confidence" is *parrēsia*, "freedom in speaking, unreservedness in speech, free and fearless confidence, cheerful courage, boldness, assurance." The word speaks of the heart attitude of a saint who lives so close to the Lord Jesus that there is nothing between him and his Lord when He comes, nothing of known sin in his life when the Rapture occurs. This is the kind of saint that keeps a daily check-up on himself as to sin in his life. He maintains a constant yieldedness to and dependence upon the Holy Spirit to show him sin in his life and give him the grace to judge it and put it out.

"May have" is *schōmen*, the aorist subjunctive, speaking of instantaneous action here. That is, the saint at the time of the Rapture should be living in such close fellowship with his Lord that the sudden appearance of the Saviour merely continues the fellowship that was in progress on earth, like Enoch who walked with God on earth and suddenly was not, for God took him. There is no need for a gradual adjustment to that fellowship into which he is being introduced at the Rapture, because the latter fellowship is just a continuation of the former. It is an instantaneous freedom of speech, of holy boldness, of assurance.

"Be ashamed" is *aischunō*, "to suffuse with shame, make ashamed," in the passive, as it is here, "to be suffused with shame, be made ashamed." The verb is here associated with *ap' autou* "from Him," and could be translated, "in shame shrink from Him." Vincent says: "The fundamental thought is that of *separation* and *shrinking* from God through the shame of conscious guilt."

"Coming" is *parousia*. The word is made up of a participial form of the verb "to be," and a preposition *para*, "beside," and means literally, "to be beside." It speaks of the personal presence of a person. In addition to its meaning of "personal presence beside," it is used to speak of the coming of a person and his arrival or advent.

Translation. *And now, little children, be continually abiding in Him, in order that, whenever He is made visible, we may have instant freedom of speech and not be made to shrink away from Him in shame at His coming and personal presence.*

(2:29) The first "know" is *oida*, "if you know absolutely." The second "know" is *ginōskō*, "to know experientially." Vincent translates, "If ye *know absolutely* that He is righteous, *ye perceive* that every one, etc."

In the clause "is born of Him," the question arises as to whom the pronoun refers, to God or Christ. The context refers the pronoun to the latter. Yet nowhere else in Scripture is it said that believers are born of Christ, but always of God. Vincent quotes Westcott in explanation: "When John thinks of God in relation to men, he never thinks of Him apart from Christ (see I John 5:20); and again, he never thinks of Christ in His human nature without adding the thought of His divine nature. Thus a rapid transition is possible from the one aspect of the Lord's divine-human person to the other."

"Born" is from the perfect participle of *gennaō*. The perfect tense speaks of a past completed action having present results. The expanded translation reads, "having been born with the present result that you are a child (of God) by birth." The relationship between God and the believer as Father and child is a permanent one.

"Doeth" is from the present tense participle of *poieō*. The habitual doing of God's will is in view here. The habitual actions of a person are an index to his character. The habitual actions of righteousness, God's righteousness here as produced by the Holy Spirit (the definite article stands before the word "righteousness" in the Greek text, marking this out as a particular righteousness) is an indication of regeneration.

Translation. *If you know absolutely that He is righteous, you know experientially that every one who habitually does this aforementioned righteousness (which God is), out from Him has been born, with the present result that that one is a born one.*

CHAPTER THREE

(3:1) "Behold" is plural here, literally, "behold ye." The usual form is singular. John is calling upon all the saints to wonder at the particular kind of love God has bestowed upon them. "What manner of" is *potapēn,* "from what country, race or tribe?" The word speaks of something foreign. The translation could read, "Behold, what foreign kind of love the Father has bestowed upon us." The love of God is foreign to the human race. It is not found naturally in humanity. When it exists there, it is in a saved individual, and by reason of the ministry of the Holy Spirit. Smith suggests, "from what far realm? What unearthly love, . . . how other-worldly."

"Hath bestowed" is from *dedōken,* the perfect tense form of *didōmi,* "to give something to some one." The perfect tense is used here to indicate that the gift becomes a permanent possession of the recipient. God has placed His love upon the saints in the sense that they have become the permanent objects of His love. One of the results of this love in action is that we are called sons of God. Smith says: "The purpose of this amazing gift; a wise, holy love, concerned for our highest good, 'not simply that we may be saved from suffering and loss, but in order that we may be styled children of God.' And we have not only the name but the character: 'so we are.'"

The word "sons" (A.V.) is not *huios* (sons), but *teknon,* "born children," (Scotch "bairns"). "Called" is *kaleō,* "named." Vincent says, "The verb (*kaleō*) is never used by John of the divine call." The words "and we are," are "a parenthetical, reflective comment, characteristic of John" (Vincent).

"Knoweth" and "knew" are both *ginōskō,* "to acquire knowledge through the medium of experience." By the world here John means the people of that system spoken of in 2:15-17, the people of the world system of evil. From their experience with us, the people of the world, while recognizing us as Christians, children of God, do not come to an understanding and appreciation of the nature of person we are, since unsaved people never have had a saving relationship with and knowledge of God. Intimate understanding and knowledge of another person is based upon fellowship with him. Since the people of the world have nothing in common with the children of God, they have no fellowship with them, and therefore have no intelligent appreciation and understanding of them. The foreign kind of love produced in us by the Holy Spirit constitutes us a foreign kind of person to the people of this world, and since they do not understand foreigners, people of a different race from themselves, they simply do not understand Christians. Children of God could just as well have come to earth from a strange planet so far as the people of the world are concerned. They are strangers to them.

Translation. *All of you, behold what foreign kind of love the Father has permanently bestowed upon us, to the end that we may be named born-ones of God. And we are. On this account the world does not have an experiential knowledge of us, because it has not come into an experiential knowledge of Him.*

(3:2) Commenting on the words, "Now are we the sons of God," Vincent says: "The two thoughts of the present and future condition of God's children are placed side by side with the simple copula, and, as parts of one thought. Christian condition, now and eternally, centers in the fact of being children of God. In that fact lies the germ of all the possibilities of eternal life."

The verb in the expression "it doth not yet appear" is aorist passive. The correct reading is, "It has not yet been made manifest or visible." Vincent says: "The force of the aorist tense is, *was never manifested on any occasion.*" The word "what" is the interrogative pronoun in the neuter gender in the Greek text. It is used here as in the simple question, "What shall we be?" Bengel comments: "This *what* suggests something unspeakable, contained in the likeness of God."

The verb in the expression "when He shall appear" is *phaneroō*, the same verb used in the case of the previous word "appear" in this verse. It means in the passive, "to be made manifest or visible." Vincent says: "Rev., correctly, *if He* (or *it*) *shall be manifested*. We may render either, 'if *it* shall be manifested,' that is *what we shall be*; or, 'if He,' etc. The preceding *ephanerōthē it is* (not yet) made manifest, must, I think, decide us in favor of the rendering *it*. We are now children of God. It has not been revealed what we shall be, and therefore we do not know. In the absence of such revelation, we know (through our consciousness of childship, through His promise that we behold His glory), that if *what we shall be* were manifested, the essential fact of the glorified condition thus revealed will be likeness to the Lord. This fact we *know* now as a promise, as a general truth of our future state. The condition of *realizing* the fact is the *manifestation* of that glorified state, the revealing of the *what we shall be*; for that manifestation will bring with it the open vision of the Lord. When the *what we shall be* shall be manifest, it will bring us face to face with Him, and we shall be like Him *because* we shall see Him as He is." Thus, the translation so far reads: "Divinely-loved ones, now born ones of God we are. And not yet has it been made visible what we shall be. We know absolutely that when it is made visible, like ones to Him we shall be, because we shall see Him just as He is."

This likeness in this context has to do with a physical likeness, not a spiritual one. Saints are spiritually like the Lord Jesus now in a relative sense, and through the sanctifying work of the Holy Spirit, are being conformed more and more to His spiritual likeness. John is speaking here of the Rapture. Paul in Philippians 3:20 says: "For the commonwealth of which we are citizens has its fixed abode in heaven, out from which also the Saviour, we with our attention withdrawn from all else, are eagerly waiting to welcome, the Lord Jesus Christ, and to receive Him to ourselves; who shall change the outward appearance of the body of our humiliation so as to conform it to an outward expression like to the body of His glory." The word "change" (A.V.) is *metaschēmatizō*, "to change the outward expression by assuming one put on from the outside." The words "be fashioned like," are *summorphon*, "an outward expression which comes from within, and is truly representative of one's inner character." Both words refer to an outward, not an inward change. The Rapture has to do with the glorification of the physical body of the believer, not with a change of his inner spiritual life. While the saint enters heaven in a sinless state, yet he is not catapulted ahead to absolute spiritual maturity in an instant of time. He grows in likeness to the Lord Jesus spiritually through the sanctifying work of the Holy Spirit all through eternity, always approaching that likeness but never equalling it, for finiteness can never equal infinity. The change which comes at the Rapture is therefore a physical one. We shall be like our Lord as to His physical, glorified body. The word *summorphon*, "be fashioned like," speaks of that outer enswathement of glory that now covers the body of the Lord Jesus, and which will at the Rapture, cover ours. Only at the Rapture will we be able to see our Lord as He is now, for physical eyes in a mortal body could not look on that glory, only eyes in glorified bodies. And that is the reason we shall be like Him, for only in that state can we see Him just as He is.

Translation. *Divinely-loved ones, now born-ones of God we are. And not yet has it been made visible what we shall be. We know absolutely that when it is made visible, like ones to Him we shall be, because we shall see Him just as He is.*

(3:3) "Every man who hath," Vincent says is, "a characteristic form of expression with John, containing 'a reference to some who had questioned the application of a general principle in particular cases.' Here to some persons who had denied the practical obligation to moral purity involved in their hope."

The hope here is the Christian hope of some day being like the Lord Jesus in respect to His glorified body. "In" is *epi*, literally, "upon." The idea is, "hope resting upon Him," or "hope set on Him."

The pronoun "Him" refers to the Lord Jesus, not to God the Father, as Smith so clearly brings out when he says: "*hagnos* (pure) also proves that the reference is to Christ. As distinguished from *hagios* (holy), which implies absolute and essential purity, it denotes purity maintained with effort and fearfulness amid defilements and allurements, especially carnal. . . . God is called *hagios* but never *hagnos*. Christ is *hagnos* because of His human experience. The duty of his appearing before God, his presentation to the King, is *hagnizein heauton* (to purify himself), like the worshippers before the Feast (John 11:55), like the people before the Lord's manifestation at Sinai (Ex. 19:10, 11, LXX). It is his own work, not God's, or rather it is his and God's."

As to the expression, "purifieth himself," Alford comments: "These words are not to be taken in any Pelagian sense, as if a man could of himself purify himself: 'apart from Me,' says our Lord, 'ye can do nothing' (John 15:5). The man who purifies himself has this hope resting upon God. This mere fact implies a will to purify himself, not out of, nor independent of, this hope, but ever stirred up by and accompanying it. So that the will is not his own, sprung out of his own nature, but the result of his Christian state, in which God also ministers to him the power to carry out that will in self-purification. . . . The idea of *hagnizein* (to purify) is much the same as that of *katharizein* (to cleanse) (1:9): it is entire purification, not merely from unchastity, but from all defilement of flesh and spirit." Thus, the hope of being like the Lord Jesus arouses the determination to be pure like Him, and this brings into play the will of the Christian to carry that resolve out into action. Thus, in dependence upon the Holy Spirit, the saint puts sin out of his life and keeps it out.

Translation. *And everyone who has this hope continually set on Him is constantly purifying himself, just as that One is pure.*

(3:4, 5) Now John shows the incompatibility of being a child of God and yet continuing in sin. "Committeth" is *poieō*, "to do." Vincent comments: "Rev., better, *every one that doeth sin.* . . . The phrase *to do sin* regards sin as something actually realized in its completeness. He that *does sin* realizes in action *the* sin (note the article *tēn* (the), that which includes and represents the complete ideal of sin." "Transgresseth the law" is literally "doeth (*poieō*) lawlessness." The words, "the transgression of the law" are in the Greek text one word, *anomia,* "lawlessness." It is the word *nomos* "law," with alpha privative put before it which negates the word. The composite word means literally, "no law." The Greek construction makes sin and lawlessness identical.

"Take away" is *airō*, "to lift up and carry away." Smith comments: "atone for sins of the past and prevent sins of the future. *Airō*, properly 'to lift up and carry away' (compare Mark 6:29; John 2:16), but the idea of expiation is involved since it is 'the Lamb of God' that 'taketh away the sins.'"

Translation. *Everyone who habitually does sin, also habitually does lawlessness; and sin is lawlessness. And you know absolutely that that One was manifested in order that He might take away our sins; and sin in Him does not exist.*

(3:6) The words "abideth" and "sinneth" are used here to designate a certain class of individual. Character is shown by one's habitual actions, not the extraordinary ones. The tense of the verbs is present, the kind of action, continuous, habitual. Thus, "every one who habitually is abiding in Him," is a saved person, and, "every one who habitually is sinning," an unsaved person. A Christian as a habit of life is abiding in fellowship with the Lord Jesus. Sin may at times enter his life. But sin is the exception, not the rule. The unsaved person as a habit of life sins continually. "Sinneth" is present in tense, continuous action being indicated. The person who is abiding in Christ is not habitually sinning. The child of God as a habit of life, does righteousness, and sin is not a habit with him. John is not teaching sinless perfection here. Vincent says: "John does not teach that believers do not sin, but is speaking of a character, a habit. Throughout the Epistle, he deals with the ideal reality of life in God, in which the love of God and sin exclude each other as light and darkness." He does not deny that a Christian sins at times. Indeed he admits the possibility of sin in the Christian's life in 1:9, and forbids sin in 2:1. What John denies here is that a Christian sins habitually. He denies that the life of a Christian is wholly turned towards sin as is that of the unsaved person.

He asserts however that "Everyone who keeps on continually sinning, has not seen Him neither known Him." This is an unsaved person. The verbs "seen" and "known" are in the perfect tense, implying that he has neither seen nor known God in times past, with the present result that He is still invisible and unknown to him. The particular word for "see" here means "to see with discernment."

Translation. *Everyone who in Him is constantly abiding is not habitually sinning. Everyone who is constantly sinning has not with discernment seen Him, nor has he known Him, with the result that that condition is true of him at present.*

(3:7) Smith comments: "An affectionate warning against Nicolaitan Antinomianism. The apostle cuts away vain pretences by a sharp principle: a righteous character expresses itself in righteous conduct. Christ (*ekeinos* "that One") is the type. He was 'the Son of God,' and if we are 'children of God,' we must be like Him." "Deceive" is *planaō*, "to lead astray." "Little children" is *teknia*. The verbal form *tiktō* means "to give birth to," thus the noun is "little born ones," "bairns" (Scotch).

Translation. *Little born-ones, stop allowing anyone to be leading you astray. The one who habitually does righteousness is righteous, just as that One is righteous.*

(3:8) "Committeth" is *poieō*, in a present tense participle, "He who is continually doing sin." Smith suggests, "He that makes sin his business or practice." "Of" is *ek*, "out of," used with the ablative case, gives us the ablative of source. He who continually does sin is out of the devil as a source. That is, his sinful propensities, issuing from his totally depraved nature inherited from Adam, find their ultimate source in the devil who brought about the downfall of our first parents. Habitual actions again are an index of character, and here, of source. "Sinneth" is a present of duration which speaks of that which has begun in the past and continues into the present. The translation could read, "The devil has been sinning from the beginning." Vincent says: "He sinned *in* the beginning, and has never ceased to sin *from* the beginning, and still sins." Smith identifies the words "the beginning" as "the beginning of his diabolic career."

"Destroy" is in the Greek text *luō*, "to loosen, dissolve." Westcott comments: "The works of the devil are represented as having a certain consistency and coherence. They show a kind of solid front. But Christ, by His coming, has revealed them in their complete unsubstantiality. He has 'undone' the seeming bonds by which they were held together." But He has done more than that. By the blood of His Cross He has paid for sin, made a way of escape from the arch enemy of men's souls, defeated the purposes of the devil, and will finally bring about his complete downfall.

Translation. *The one who is habitually doing sin is out of the devil as a source, because from the beginning the devil has been sinning. For this purpose there was manifested the Son of God, in order that He might bring to naught the works of the devil.*

(3:9) "Is born" is a perfect participle in the Greek text, speaking of the past completed act of regeneration, namely, the impartation of the divine nature (II Pet. 1:4) or divine life, and the present result, the fact that the person who has been made the recipient of divine life is by nature, and that permanently, a spiritually alive individual. "Commit" is *poieō* in the present tense which always speaks of continuous action unless the context limits it to punctiliar action, namely, the mere mention of the fact of the action, without the mentioning of details. The translation reads, "Every one who has been born out of God, with the present result that he is a born-one (of God), does not habitually do sin." "His seed" refers to the principle of divine life in the believer. It is this principle of divine life that makes it impossible for a Christian to live habitually in sin, for the divine nature causes the child of God to hate sin and love righteousness, and gives him both the desire and the power to do God's will, as Paul says, "God is the One who is constantly putting forth energy in you, giving you both the desire and power to do His good pleasure" (Phil. 2:13). Smith comments: "The reason of the impossibility of a child of God continuing in sin. The germ of the divine life has been implanted in our souls, and it grows — a gradual process and subject to occasional retardations, yet sure, attaining at length to full fruition. The believer's lapses into sin are like the mischances of the weather which hinder the seed's growth. The growth of a living seed may be checked temporarily; if there be no growth, there is no life."

"Cannot sin" is *dunamai*, "I am not able," and the present infinitive of *hamartano*, "to sin." The infinitive in the present tense in Greek always speaks of continuous, habitual action, never the mere fact of the action, since the aorist infinitive which refers to the fact of the action, may be used at will if the writer wishes to speak of the mere fact without reference to details. The translation therefore is, "He is not able to habitually sin." The Greek text here holds no warrant for the erroneous teaching of sinless perfection.

Translation. *Everyone who has been born out of God, with the present result that he is a born-one (of God), does not habitually do sin, because His seed remains in him. And he is not able to habitually sin, because out of God he has been born with the present result that he is a born-one (of God).*

(3:10) The words "in this" point particularly to what follows, although a secondary reference might be to what precedes. "Loveth" is *agapao*, which refers to divine love which is self-sacrificial in its essence, the love produced in the heart of the yielded saint by the Holy Spirit, the love defined by Paul in I Corinthians 13, the love shown by God at Calvary. The brother here is ostensibly a Christian brother. The expression is equivalent to "a fellow-Christian." "Children" is *tekna*, born-ones of the devil in the sense that from Adam they inherit a totally-depraved nature, the same as the devil has.

Translation. *In this is apparent the born-ones of God and the born-ones of the devil. Every one who is not habitually doing righteousness is not of God, also the one who is not habitually loving his brother.*

(3:11, 12) Cain "was of that wicked one." The words "wicked one" are the translation of *ponēros*, "evil in active opposition to the good." The word "pernicious" is a good translation. A *kakos* (evil) man is willing to perish in his own corruption. But a *ponēros* (pernicious) person, seeks to drag every one else down with himself into the corruption and destruction that awaits him. That is Satan.

The word "slew" is *sphazō*, "to slay, slaughter, butcher, by cutting the throat." It was used in classical Greek of slaughtering victims for sacrifice by cutting the throat, also of animals tearing by the throat, of any slaughter by knife or sword. It is used in the LXX (Greek translation of the Old Testament), of the slaying of the Levitical sacrifices (Lev. 1:5). The usual word meaning "to kill" is *apothnēskō*. The inspired writer goes out of his way to use a specialized word to describe the murder of Abel by Cain. The latter cut his brother's throat. God said to Cain, "What hast thou done? The voice of thy brother's blood crieth unto Me from the ground" (Gen. 4:10). The method Cain used to kill his brother was one in which much blood would be shed. The cutting of the jugular vein would fit that description. The human race learned how to kill when it was taught to slay a sacrificial animal as it approached a holy God (Gen. 3:21).

Cain's works are described as evil. The same word (*ponēros*) is used when the devil is spoken of as "that wicked one." His works were pernicious, actively opposed to that which is good.

Translation. *Because this is the message which you heard from the beginning, to the effect that we should habitually be loving one another with a divine love; not even as Cain was out of the Pernicious One, and killed his brother by severing his jugular vein. And on what account did he kill him? Because his works were pernicious and those of his brother, righteous.*

(3:13) "Marvel not" is in a construction in the Greek text which forbids the continuance of an action already going on. It is, "Stop marvelling." John's readers were astounded at the fact that people of the world should hate them because they were children of God. The "if" is *ei*, a particle of a fulfilled condition. It is, "if, as is the case, the world hates you." Smith puts in a word of caution here: "It is no wonder if the world hate us, and its judgment is not decisive. Nevertheless, our business is not to be hated by the world, but to commend Jesus to it and win it. We must not impute to the world's hostility to goodness, the consequences of our own unamiability or tactlessness. 'It is not martyrdom to pay bills that one has run into one's self' (George Eliot)."

Translation. *Stop marvelling, brethren, if, as is the case, the world hates you.*

(3:14) The pronoun is in the emphatic position, "as for us," in contradistinction to the world, "we know that we have passed from death to life." As Smith says: " 'Whatever the world may say, *we* know.' The test is not its hatred but our love." "Have passed" is *metabainō*, "to pass over from one place to another, to migrate." Vincent translates, "have passed over." The verb is in the perfect tense, speaking of a past completed act having in a case like this, permanent results. "We have passed over permanently." The prefixed preposition signifies a change, here, of position or state. "From death" is *ek tou thanatou*, "out of the death." We have here an ablative of separation, "separated from the death." Vincent says that the article before "death" and "life" marks these as the two spheres in which men must be, *death* or *life*. "Know" is *oida*, "to know absolutely." This love for fellow-Christians is that divine love produced in the heart of the yielded believer, the content of which is described in I Corinthians 13 and John 3:16. Evidence of a saved condition is that the person is habitually loving Christians with a love that impels him to deny himself for the benefit of the fellow-Christian.

The individual who does not thus love Christians is abiding in the aforementioned death. This is that condition of the unsaved spoken of in Ephesians 2:1, as "dead in the sphere of trespasses and sins."

Translation. *As for us, we know absolutely that we have passed over permanently out of the sphere of the death into the life, because we are habitually loving the brethren. The one who is not habitually loving is abiding in the sphere of the death.*

(3:15) John says: "Every one who is habitually hating his brother is a manslayer." How are we to understand this? Is he an actual murderer without committing the act of killing another? Alford has an illuminating note: "The living spirit of man being incapable of a state of indifference; that he who banished brotherly love has in fact abandoned himself to the rule of the opposite state. In the ethical depth of the apostle's view, love and hate, like light and darkness, life and death, necessarily replace, as well as necessarily exclude, one another. He who has not the one, of necessity has the other in each case. He who hates his brother is stated to be a manslayer. The example given (v. 12) showed the true and normal result of hate, and again in the apostle's ethical depth of view, as in our Lord's own (Matt. 5:21, 27), he who falls under a state, falls under the normal results of that state carried out to its issue." All of which means that the one who habitually hates his fellow-man to the exclusion, of course, of any good attitude towards him, is a potential murderer. Should occasion arise, his hate would issue in action like that of Cain. A person like that, John says, does not have eternal life abiding in him. In short, he is unsaved.

Translation. *Every one who habitually is hating his brother is a manslayer. And you know absolutely that every manslayer does not have life eternal abiding in him.*

(3:16) "Hereby" is *en toutōi*, "in this." "Perceive" is *ginōskō* in the perfect tense. The word speaks of knowledge gained by experience. The saints have experienced the love of God in that He laid down His life for them, and in that they have become the recipients of salvation. This knowledge is a permanent possession. "Life" is *psuchē*, "soul." Our Lord's death on the Cross involved not only His physical death, but abandonment from God because of human sin laid on Him. It was this that touched His soul and caused Him to cry out, "My God, My God, why hast thou forsaken me?" "Ought" is *opheilō*, speaking of a moral obligation. "Lives" again is *psuchē*, "soul." The ego must be crucified. Self must be denied for the benefit of one's brother. It must be kept in mind that our Lord's death had atoning value, whereas our laying down our lives in glad service to our fellow man does not.

Translation. *In this we have come to know by experience that love, because that One on behalf of us laid down His soul. And, as for us, we have a moral obligation on behalf of our brethren to lay down our souls.*

(3:17) "Good" is *bios*, "the necessaries of life" such as food, clothing, and shelter. "World" here is not used in the bad ethical sense but refers to this mundane sphere of life on earth. "Has" is present subjunctive, speaking of habitual possession. The verb speaks of a person who regularly has the necessities of life. "Seeth" is *theōreō*, "to look with interest and purpose." Vincent translates, "deliberately contemplates." The verb speaks of continuous action. This person deliberately contemplates over a protracted space of time. This is not a hasty glance. It is seeing a Christian in need of the necessities of life over a long period.

"Shutteth up" is *kleiō*, "to shut up," and in the aorist subjunctive, speaking merely of the fact of an action. The word could be used of the slamming of a door, the snapping of a lock. It speaks here of this person who snaps shut the door of his heart against any compassionate feelings toward his needy brother and against any merciful actions. "Bowels" is *splagchna*, the oriental metaphor for what we speak of as the heart. "How" is *pōs*, "how is it possible?" Smith says: "Love must be practical. It is easy to 'lay down one's life': martyrdom is heroic and exhilarating; the difficulty lies in doing the little things, facing day by day the petty sacrifices and self-denials which no one notices and no one applauds."

Translation. *But whoever has as a constant possession the necessities of life, and deliberately keeps on contemplating his brother constantly having need, and snaps shut his heart from him, how is it possible that the love of God is abiding in him?*

(3:18) Robertson comments: "What John means is, 'not merely by word or by the tongue.' He does not condemn kind words which are comforting and cheering, but warm words should be accompanied by warm deeds to make real 'in deed and in truth.' Here is a case where actions speak louder than mere words." Smith quotes Sheridan: "He appears to have as much speculative benevolence as any private gentleman in the kingdom, though he is seldom so sensual as to indulge himself in the exercise of it."

Translation. *Little born-ones, let us not be loving in the sphere of word nor even in the sphere of the tongue, but in the sphere of deed and truth.*

(3:19, 20) Smith is helpful here. "The foregoing exhortation may have awakened a misgiving in our minds: 'Am I as loving as I ought?' Our failures in duty and service rise up before us, and 'our heart condemns us.' So the apostle furnishes a grand reassurance: 'Herein shall we get to know that we are of the truth, and in His presence shall assure our heart, whereinsoever our heart condemn us, because, etc.' The reassurance is two-fold: (1) The worst that is in us is known to God, and still He cares for us and desires us. Our discovery has been an open secret to Him all along. (2) He 'readeth everything' — sees the deepest things, and these are the real things. This is the true test of a man: Is the deepest that is in him the best? Is he better than he seems? His failures lie on the surface: is there a desire for goodness deep down in his soul? Is he glad to escape from superficial judgments and be judged by God who 'readeth everything?' who sees 'with larger eyes than ours,' to make allowance for us all?" David was a man after God's own heart because the general tenor of his life was habitually Godward. The Psalms give the real David.

"Assure" is *peithō*, "to persuade"; Thayer on this word offers, "to tranquilize." Smith translates, "to pacify, win with confidence, soothe the alarm" of our heart. "Before" is *emprosthen*, "in the presence of." The translation reads so far: "In this we shall know experientially that out of the truth we are, and in His presence shall tranquilize our hearts." Vincent quotes the Revision, "whereinsoever our heart condemn us, because God is greater than our heart." The sense of the whole passage is therefore, "In this we shall know experientially that out of the truth we are, and in His presence shall tranquilize our heart in whatever our heart condemns us, because God is greater than our hearts and knows all things."

Vincent's note is valuable: "Is this superior greatness to be regarded as related to God's *judgment* or to His *compassion?* If to His *judgment,* the sense is: God who is greater than our heart and knows all things, must not only *endorse* but *emphasize* our self-accusation. If our *heart* condemn, how much more *God,* who is greater than our heart. If to His *compassion,* the sense is: when our heart condemns us we shall quiet it with the assurance that we are in the hands of a God who is greater than our heart — who surpasses man in love and compassion no less than in knowledge. This latter sense better suits the whole drift of the discussion."

Translation. *In this we shall know experientially that we are out of the truth, and in His presence shall tranquilize our hearts in whatever our heart condemns us, because greater is God than our hearts and knows all things.*

(3:21, 22) The words, "If our heart condemn us not," do not claim sinless perfection, but represent the heart attitude of a saint that so far as he knows has no unconfessed sin in his life, has nothing between himself and the Lord Jesus, a saint who is yielded habitually to the Holy Spirit and living in close fellowship with his Lord. "Confidence" is *parrēsia,* "freedom in speaking, unreservedness in speech, free and fearless confidence, cheerful courage, boldness, assurance." "Toward" is *pros,* "facing, toward," thus, "face to face" with God, "facing" God. The article appears before "God" here, thus referring the word "God" to God the Father.

"Ask" is *aiteō*, "to ask for," and in the present subjunctive, speaking of continuous action. It is, "whatever we keep on asking for," speaking of repeated and continuous praying, day after day. The prerequisites for answered prayer are an uncondemning heart, the habitual keeping of God's commandments, and the habitual doing of those things which please Him. "Sight" is *enōpion*, from *ōp*, "to see," and *en*, "in," thus, "a penetrating gaze."

Translation. *Divinely-loved ones, if our heart is not condemning us, a fearless confidence we constantly have facing God (the Father), and whatever we are habitually asking, we keep on receiving from Him, because His commandments we are habitually keeping with solicitous care, and the things which are pleasing in His penetrating gaze we are habitually doing.*

(3:23) "Should believe" is aorist subjunctive, its classification, constative aorist, viewing the entire course of a Christian's life in one panoramic view. That is, the whole tenor of a saint's life should be Christward. "The Name" is dative case. Saints have already believed *on* the name of Jesus Christ for their entrance into salvation. Now, in their saved state, they are to believe the Name of Jesus Christ. The word "Name" stands for all that the Son of God is in His wonderful Person. Robertson quotes Westcott, "a compressed creed." This belief is an intellectual assent to all that the Bible states is true of our Lord and a heart submission to Him personally. "Love" here is again the divine, supernatural love produced in the heart of the yielded saint.

Translation. *And this is His commandment, to the effect that we should believe the Name of His Son Jesus Christ, and that we should be habitually loving one another even as He gave a commandment to us.*

(3:24) Vincent quotes Bede, "Therefore let God be a home to thee, and be thou the home of God: abide in God, and let God abide in thee." Paul prays in Ephesians 3:16, 17 that the saints might "be strengthened with might through His Spirit in the inner man in order that the Christ might finally settle down and feel completely at home" in their hearts.

The knowledge of the fact that God is abiding in the saint comes from the Holy Spirit. He bears witness in connection with our human spirit as energized by Him, that we are born-ones of God (Rom. 8:16).

Translation. *And the one who as a habit of life exercises a solicitous care in keeping His commandments, in Him is abiding, and He Himself (is abiding) in him. And in this we know experientially that He is abiding in us, from the Spirit as a source whom He gave to us.*

CHAPTER FOUR

(4:1) Smith introduces this important section with the following comment: "The apostle has just said that the Spirit begets in us the assurance that God abideth in us. And this suggests a warning. The Cerinthian heresy also had much to say about 'the spirit.' It boasted a larger spirituality. Starting with the philosophical postulate of an irreconcilable antagonism between matter and spirit, it denied the possibility of the incarnation and drew a distinction between Jesus and the Christ. Its spirit was not 'the Spirit of Truth' but 'a spirit of error,' and thus the necessity arises of 'proving the spirits.' "

"Believe not" is in a construction in the Greek text which forbids the continuation of an action already going on. It is, "Stop believing every spirit." The fact is that some were being carried away with the errors of the Gnostics. The word "spirit" is *pneuma*. The word as used here refers to "one in whom a spirit is manifest or embodied, hence one actuated by a spirit, whether divine or demonical" (Thayer). Paul finds the source of false doctrine in demons who actuate the false teachers who propound heresy (I Tim. 4:1 "devils" should be "demons" *daimonion*). Thus these spirits are human beings actuated either by demons or the Holy Spirit. In this case they would be the teachers, pastors, and evangelists who circulated around the local churches.

The exhortation is to try these individuals to see whether they are of God or not. The word "try" is *dokimazō*, "to put to the test for the purpose of approving, and finding that the person put to the test meets the specifications laid down, to put one's approval upon him." Thus, the teacher, for instance, was not to be put to the test for the purpose of condemning him, but with

the intent to approve him. The brother was not to be treated
as a heretic before he had shown himself to be one.

The reason for putting visiting teachers to such a test was that
many false prophets "are gone out into the world." The verb
is perfect in tense. They have gone out and they are as a present
result in the world of mankind, and they have established themselves amongst the people.

Translation. *Divinely-loved ones, stop believing every spirit.
But put the spirits to the test for the purpose of approving them,
and finding that they meet the specifications laid down, put your
approval upon them, because many false prophets are gone out
into the world.*

(4:2, 3) John now gives the test which will prove that the
Holy Spirit is actuating a teacher. If that teacher confesses that
Jesus Christ is come in the flesh, that is a proof of the fact that
he is a true believer and is actuated by the Holy Spirit. The
word "confess" is *homologeō,* from *homos,* "the same," and *legō,*
"to speak," thus, "to speak the same thing as another," thus "to
agree with another" on some particular thing. Therefore,
every teacher who is in agreement with the Bible "that Jesus
Christ is come in the flesh" is of God.

Now, what is involved in the statement, "Jesus Christ is come
in the flesh"? The name "Jesus" is the English form of the
Greek *Iēsous,* and this is the Greek form of the Hebrew name
"Jehoshua" which means "Jehovah saves." "Christ" is from
christos, "the Anointed One." The words "is come" are in the
perfect tense in the Greek text. From the foregoing it follows
that the statement speaks of the God of the Old Testament who
in the Person of His Son became incarnate in human flesh without its sin, died on the Cross to satisfy the just demands of His
law which man broke, and raised Himself from the dead in the
body in which He died, to become the living Saviour of the
sinner who places his faith in Him in view of what He did for
him on Calvary's Cross. The person who teaches that, John
says, is actuated by the Holy Spirit. Likewise, the teacher who
does not agree to that doctrine is not of God. He is actuated

by the spirit of Antichrist who denies and is against all that the Bible teaches regarding the person and work of the Lord Jesus. *This is Modernism.*

Translation. *In this you know experientially the Spirit of God. Every spirit who agrees that Jesus Christ in the sphere of flesh is come, is of God; and every spirit who does not confess this aforementioned Jesus (agree to the above teaching concerning Him), is not of God. And this is the (spirit) of the Antichrist which you have heard that it comes, and now in the world already is.*

(4:4) The intensive use of the personal pronoun gives us, "as for you, little born-ones (in contradistinction to the anti-Christian teachers), you are of God." John states that the saints to whom he is writing have overcome these false teachers. The verb is perfect in tense, speaking of a past completed victory, and a present state of being a conqueror. That is, the saints to whom John refers were not taken in by the heresies of the false teachers, and were in a settled state of victory over them. They were confirmed in their attitude against heresy and had their eyes wide open to its source and nature.

The reason why they thus gained a complete victory over the false teachers and their heresies is that God the Holy Spirit who indwelt them is greater than that fallen angel Satan who is in the world system of evil.

Translation. *As for you, out of God you are, little born-ones, and you have gained a complete victory over them, because greater is He who is in you than he who is in the world.*

(4:5) The personal pronoun is intensive here. It is, "They themselves are of the world." We have here ablative of source. These false teachers have their source in the world system of evil, this present pernicious age. "Speak they of the world" could mean, "speak they concerning the world." But the Greek is clear here. It is, "out of the world as a source they speak." The source of their false doctrines is the world. The demons of Satan are part of this world system, and the source of all heresy.

The world of sinners accepts their teaching, for it recognizes its own language.

Translation. *They themselves are out of the world as a source. On this account out of the world as a source they are constantly speaking. And the world listens to them.*

(4:6) The intensive pronoun is used. "As for us (in contradistinction to the false teachers), out of God we are." "He that knoweth" is present tense, progressive action, speaking, not of a complete knowledge, but a progressive, experiential knowledge. It is the growing saint to whom reference is made. Vincent says: "he who is habitually and evermore clearly perceiving and recognizing God as his Christian life unfolds. The knowledge is regarded as progressive and not complete." "Hereby" is *ek toutou.* "Not the same as the common *en toutōi* (in this) (v. 2). It occurs only here in this Epistle. *En toutōi* is *in this*: *ek toutou, from this.* The former marks the *residing* or *consisting* of the essence or truth of a thing in something the apprehension of which conveys to us the essential nature of the thing itself. The latter marks the *inference* or *deduction* of the truth from something, as contrasted with its immediate perception in that something. Rev., *by this*" (Vincent).

Smith comments: "Men's attitude to the message of the incarnate Saviour ranks them on this side or on that — on God's side or the world's. Of course St. John does not ignore St. Paul's "speaking the truth in love" (Eph. 4:15). The message may be the truth and be rejected, not because of the hearer's worldliness, but because it is wrongly delivered — not graciously and winsomely. Compare Rowland Hill's anecdote of the preaching barber who had made a wig for one of his hearers — badly made and nearly double the price. When anything particularly profitable escaped the lips of the preacher, the hearer would observe to himself, 'Excellent. This should touch my heart; but oh, the wig.'" Robertson says: "John had felt the cold, indifferent, and hostile stare of the worldling as he preached Jesus." He quotes Westcott, "The power of recognition (*ginōskomen,* we know by experience) belongs to all believers. Alford says that "the spirit of truth" is the Holy Spirit who teaches the truth, and "the spirit of error" is the spirit who comes from the devil, teaching lies and seducing men into error. The spirit that comes from the devil teaching heresy, Paul declares to be a demon (I Tim. 4:1).

Translation. *As for us, out of God we are. The one who is knowing God is hearing us. He who is not out of God is not hearing us. From this we know the Spirit of the truth and the spirit of the error.*

(4:7, 8) "Beloved" is *agapētoi,* "divinely-loved ones," that is, "beloved ones, loved by God." Those who are loved by God should love one another. The love with which children of God should love one another is the *agapē* love which God is in His nature, the love which is produced by the Holy Spirit in the heart of the yielded saint, the love which was seen in action at the Cross, and the love whose constituent elements are defined for us in I Corinthians 13. The exhortation is in the present subjunctive which speaks of continuous action. The translation reads, "Let us be habitually loving one another." The words "one another" are a reciprocal pronoun in the Greek text. There should be reciprocity in the exercise of this love. Everyone who habitually loves "is born of God." "Is born" is perfect tense in the Greek text, literally "has been begotten with the present result that that person is a child" of God. The new-birth is a permanent thing. A child of God remains a child of God forever.

The one who is not habitually loving "knoweth not God." "Knoweth" is aorist tense in the Greek text, literally, "did not know God." Vincent says, "He never knew." Smith translates, "did not get to know." The verb is ingressive aorist, referring to entrance into a new condition.

As to the statement, "God is love," we would suggest that that simply is not true. God is not an abstraction. The word "God" has the article, the word "love" does not, which construction in Greek means that the two words are not interchangeable. The absence of the article emphasizes nature, essence, character. The translation should read, "God as to His nature is love." That is, God is a loving God. It is His nature to be loving.

Translation. *Divinely-loved ones, let us be habitually loving one another, because this aforementioned love is out of God as a source; and everyone who is habitually loving, out of God has been born with the present result that he is regenerated and knows God in an experiential way. The one who is not habitually loving has not come to know God, because God as to His nature is love.*

(4:9) "Toward us" is *en hēmin*, "in our case." "Only begotten" is *monogenēs*, "single of its kind, only." Thayer says: "Used of Christ, denotes *the only Son of God* or one who in the sense in which He Himself is the Son of God has no brethren." Our Lord is the uniquely begotten Son of God in the sense that He proceeds by eternal generation from God the Father as God the Son in a birth that never took place because it always was, possessing co-eternally with God the Father and God the Spirit, the essence of Deity.

"Sent" is *apostellō*, "to send on a commission as an envoy, with credentials (the miracles), to perform certain duties," here, to die for sinners, providing a salvation to be offered on the basis of justice satisfied to the one who places his faith in Him as Saviour. The verb is in the perfect tense speaking of a past complete action having present results. The prefixed preposition is *apo*, "off." He has sent off the Son with the result that a salvation has been provided for sinful man.

Translation. *In this was clearly shown the love of God in our case, because His Son, the only begotten One, God sent off into the world in order that we may live through Him.*

(4:10) In the expression, "Herein is love," the definite article appears before the word "love," not any kind of love, but the particular love that inheres in God's nature, divine love. "We loved" is perfect in tense. The human race has not loved God with the present result that it does not possess any love for Him. "He loved" is constative aorist, giving a panoramic view of God's love for the human race. God has always loved sinners. "Sent" is also aorist, marking the Incarnation as an historic event. "Propitiation" is *hilasmos*. The English word "propitiate" means "to appease and render favorable." That was the pagan meaning of the Greek word. The pagan worshipper brought gifts to his god to appease the god's wrath and make him favorable in his attitude towards him. But the God of Christianity needs no gifts to appease His wrath and make Him favorable towards the human race. Divine love springs spontaneously from His heart. His wrath against sin cannot be placated by good works. Only the infliction of the penalty of sin, death, will satisfy the just demands of His holy law which the human race violated, maintain His government, and provide the proper basis for His bestowal of mercy, namely, divine justice satisfied. This is the *hilasmos,* that sacrifice which fully satisfies the demands of the broken law. It was our Lord's death on Calvary's Cross. Thus does this pagan word accrue to itself a new meaning as it enters the doctrinal atmosphere of the New Testament.

Translation. *In this is the love, not that we have loved God with the present result that we possess love (for Him), but that He Himself loved us, and sent off His Son, a satisfaction concerning our sins.*

(4:11) "So" is *houtōs,* and refers back to the act of God sending off His Son to become the expiatory sacrifice for our sins. It was an act of infinite love and infinite sacrifice, not only on the part of the Son on the Cross, but on the part of the Father who sent the Son, for the heart of the Father was pierced when sin was laid on the Son at the Cross and His holiness demanded that He abandon the Son (Zech. 12:10). In the same manner, to the same extent, John says that the saints have a moral obligation to be constantly loving one another. The infinitive "to love" is present tense in Greek, speaking of continuous action. The "if" is a particle of a fulfilled condition, and should be "since" or "in view of the fact." "Ought" is *opheilō* which speaks of a moral obligation.

Translation. *Divinely-loved ones, since in that manner and to that extent did God love us, also, as for us, we are under moral obligation to be constantly loving one another.*

(4:12) The word "God" is in the emphatic position, coming first in the Greek sentence, namely, "God no one ever yet has seen." The word "God" is without the article, indicating that character, essence, or nature is stressed. "Deity in its essence" no one has ever yet seen. The particular word for "see" here is *theaomai*, "to behold, look upon, view attentively, contemplate." The verb is in the perfect tense. The expanded translation reads, "Deity in its essence no one has ever yet beheld, with the present result that no one has the capacity of beholding Him."

The words "His love" do not refer to our love for Him, nor to His love for us, but to the love which is peculiarly His own, which answers to His nature (Vincent). "Is perfected" is *teleioō*, "to bring to completion, to accomplish, finish." If saints have this *agapē* love habitually for one another, that shows that this love which God is in His nature, has accomplished its purpose in their lives. It has made us loving and self-sacrificial in our characters. This love has been brought to its human fulness in the lives of the saints. The verb "is perfected" is perfect in tense, speaking of a past completed act having present results.

Translation. *God in His essence no one has ever yet beheld, with the result that no one has the capacity to behold (Him). If we habitually are loving one another, God in us is abiding, and His love has been brought to its fulness in us, and exists in that state of fulness.*

(4:13) Alford comments: "nearly repeated from 3:24. But why introduced here? In the former verse, the *fact* of His abiding in us was assured to us, if we love one another. Of this fact, when thus loving, we need a token. Him we cannot see: has He given us any testimony of His presence in us? He has given us such a testimony, in making us partakers of His Spirit. This fact it is to which the Apostle calls our attention, as proving not the external fact of the sending of the Son (v. 14), but one within ourselves, the indwelling of God in us, and our abiding in Him." "Know" is *ginōskō*, "to know by experience." That is, the saint experiences the work of the Holy Spirit in him, and from that experience, he deduces the fact that the Holy Spirit is in him, a gift of God. This experiential knowledge confirms the fact that the saint dwells in God and God in him. "Dwells" is *menō*, which is used often in the Gospel narratives of one person dwelling in the home of another. The word speaks of fellowship between two or more individuals. The pronoun is used intensively here, namely, "He (God) Himself in us." "Hath given" is perfect tense in the Greek text. The Spirit was given the saints as a permanent gift. He is in us to stay, as James says (4:5), "The Spirit who has been caused to take up His permanent residence in us."

"Of His Spirit" is *ek tou pneumatos autou*, literally, "out of His Spirit." Paul's words in I Corinthians 12:4-11 are of help here. John in using *ek*, "out of," does not mean to infer that the individual saint receives only part of the Holy Spirit, for a person cannot be divided and parcelled out in parts. Each saint receives the Holy Spirit Himself in His entirety. John is here referring to that which the saint experiences of the indwelling Holy Spirit, namely, the operation of the spiritual gifts. No saint is given all of them. The individual saint who is the recipient of these spiritual gifts of the Spirit receives certain ones (*ek*) out of the total number. But the presence of these gifts in him, shown by their outworking in his life, is also an evidence of the presence of the Spirit in him, and this latter, a proof of the fact that God dwells in that saint and that saint dwells in God.

Translation. *In this we know experientially that in Him we are dwelling and He Himself in us, because He has given us out of His Spirit as a permanent gift.*

(4:14) The pronoun appears in its intensive use in the Greek text. It is, "as for us (in contradistinction to certain others), we have seen." The verb is *theaomai*, "to steadfastly and deliberately contemplate." The verb is in the perfect tense, speaking of a past complete action with its present existing results. The act of viewing was not a mere momentary thing. It consisted of a process, which process was a completed one, one in which an assured result would be obtained. Furthermore, that result was an abiding fact.

"Sent" is perfect in tense, and the preposition *apo* is prefixed, all of which gives us, "has sent off." The expression, "the Saviour of the world" has a reference to the fact that the Roman emperor was called *sōtēr tou kosmou,* "Saviour of the world." The Samaritan men also have the above in mind when they say to the woman, "We have heard Him ourselves, and know that this is the Christ, the Saviour of the world" (John 4:42). Emperor worship was the state religion of the Roman Empire, and the binding factor that united its far-flung, heterogeneous subject-peoples together in a union stronger than that of any military force. To recognize our Lord as the Saviour of the world instead of the Emperor was a capital offence, for such recognition was a blow at the very vitals of the Empire. That was the quarrel which Rome had against Christianity, and that was the reason for the bloody persecutions.

Translation.   *And as for us, we have deliberately and stead-fastly contemplated, and we are testifying that the Father has sent off the Son as Saviour of the world.*

(4:15) "Confess" is *homologeō,* "to speak the same thing that another speaks," thus, "to agree with someone as to a certain proposition." The word therefore implies a statement with which one is in agreement, that statement formulated by someone else, here, the doctrine concerning our Lord. The verb is in the aorist tense, making the act of confession a definite one, and the classification, constative aorist, speaking of the fact that that confession is a life-time confession, and represents the sustained attitude of the heart. The confession is that Jesus is the Son of God, thus, God the Son, thus very God of very God. Robertson says, "This confession of the deity of Jesus Christ implies surrender and obedience also, not mere lip service (cf. I Cor. 12:3; Rom. 10:6-12)."

Translation.   *Whoever confesses that Jesus is the Son of God, God in him dwells and he himself in God.*

(4:16) The pronoun is used in an intensive sense, "As for us, we have known and believed." Both verbs are in the perfect tense, emphasizing not only a past completed act but abiding results in present time. "To us" is *en hēmin*, "in us," that is, "in our sphere, in our case," speaking of the sphere in which God's love operates.

Translation. *And as for us, we have known the love which God has in our case, and have that knowledge at present, and we have believed and at present maintain that attitude; God is as to His nature, love, and he who dwells in the aforementioned love, in God is dwelling, and God in him is dwelling.*

(4:17) "Is made perfect" is perfect tense, "has been made perfect or complete, and exists in its finished results." This represents a past fact in the saint's life and a present reality. "Our love" is literally "the love with us." This is not primarily God's love for us or our love for Him, but the love which God is in His nature, produced in our hearts by the Holy Spirit. The saint who in the future Rapture of the Church will approach the Judgment Seat of Christ with boldness (*parrēsia*, freedom of speech) is the saint who in his earthly life has had the love that God is in His nature brought to its full capacity of operation by the Holy Spirit in his life. That fullness of love results in a life devoted entirely to the Lord Jesus. The word speaks of unreservedness of speech, a free and fearless confidence, with nothing to hide or be ashamed of. In that kind of life, the saint has nothing of which to be ashamed at the judgment of his works. That kind of life is a Christ-like life, and that makes the saint as he dwells in the midst of a world of sinful people, like Christ. And the Lord Jesus will not at the Judgment Seat of Christ condemn those who while they lived on earth, were like Him.

Translation. *In this has been brought to completion the aforementioned love with us, which love exists in its completed state, in order that we may be having unreservedness of speech at the day of judgment, because just as that One is, also, as for us, we are in this world.*

(4:18) The fear spoken of here is not a godly fear or filial reverence, a holy fear of displeasing the Father through sin (I Peter 1:17, Heb. 12:28), but as the context indicates ("fear hath torment"), a slavish fear of a slave for a master, or of a criminal

before a judge. The divine love produced in the heart of the
yielded saint includes the former but not the latter. "Torment"
is *kolasis*, " 'correction, punishment, penalty,' and brings with it
or has connected with it the thought of punishment" (Thayer).
Thus, the saint who has experienced the fulness of this divine
love in his earthly life, will have no fear of correction or penalty
(loss of reward) at the Judgment Seat of Christ. The word
"perfect" is *teleios*, "that which is complete, brought to its
fulness." The saint who approaches that tribunal in a spirit of
fear is the saint who has not experienced the fulness of this love,
and for the reason that he did not maintain a Spirit-filled life
during his earthly sojourn.

Translation. *Fear does not exist in the sphere of the aforementioned love. Certainly, this aforementioned, completed love
throws fear outside, because this fear has a penalty, and the one
who fears has not been brought to completion in the sphere of
this love, and is not in that state at present.*

(4:19-21) The word "Him" is not in the best Greek texts,
and the word "love" is not indicative in mode but subjunctive,
expressing an exhortation. The Greek has it, "As for us, let
us be loving, because He Himself first loved us." Smith says:
"The thought is that the amazing love of God in Christ is the
inspiration of all the love that stirs in our hearts. It awakens
within us an answering love — a grateful love for Him mani-
festing itself in love for our brethren (cf. v. 11)."

The expanded Greek translation of verse 20 reads as follows:
"If anyone says, I am constantly loving God with a divine love,
and his brother is as constantly hating, he is a liar. For the
one who is not constantly loving with a divine love his brother
whom he has seen with discernment and has still within the
range of his vision, God whom he has not seen with discernment
and does not have within the range of his vision, he is not able
to be loving."

The love here is as before, *agapē*, divine love, self-sacrificial in
its essence. The brother is of course a fellow-Christian. The
perfect tense is used in the case of the verbs meaning "to see."

This was no passing glance, but a completed act having abiding results.

Translation. *As for us, let us be constantly loving, because He Himself first loved us. If anyone says: I am constantly loving God, and his brother is as constantly hating, he is a liar. For the one who is not constantly loving his brother whom he has seen with discernment and at present has within the range of his vision, God whom he has not seen with discernment and at present does not have within the range of his vision, he is not able to be loving. And this commandment we have from Him; the one who is constantly loving God, should constantly be loving also his brother.*

CHAPTER FIVE

(5:1) The Cerinthian Gnostics denied the identity of Jesus and the Christ. That is, they denied that the individual whom the Christian Church knew by the name "Jesus" was also the Christ. The word "Christ" is the English spelling of the Greek word *christos* which means "the anointed one." But the predicted Anointed One was to be God-incarnate, virgin-born into the human race. Thus, the incarnation is in view here. But this belief is not a mere intellectual assent to the fact of the incarnation, but a heart acceptance of all that it implied in its purpose, the substitutionary death of the Incarnate One for sinners, thus making a way of salvation in which God could bestow mercy on the basis of justice satisfied. That person, John says, and he uses the perfect tense here, has been born of God and as a result is a child of God. "Him that begat" is God. "Him that is begotten of Him" is the child of God. John says therefore that the person who loves God as his Father also loves God's children because of the fact of the family relationship, that of having a common Father and that of sustaining the relationship with other believers, that of children in the same family.

Translation. *Everyone who believes that Jesus is the Christ, out from God has been born and as a result is His child. And everyone who loves the One who begot, loves the one who has been begotten out from Him.*

(5:2) "By this" is *en toutōi*, literally, "in this." Vincent says, "Not *by* this or *from* this, as an *inference*, but *in* the very exercise of the sentiment toward God, we perceive." "When" is *hotan*, "more strictly, *whenever*. Our perception of the existence of love to our brethren is developed *on every occasion* when we exercise love and obedience toward God" (Vincent). Love (*agapē*, divine love) on the part of a saint for his brother in

172

Christ is shown when that saint observes the commandments of
God, for obedience to the commandments puts that saint in right
relationship to his brother Christian, which relationship results
in his acting in a loving manner toward that Christian. The con-
verse also is true, namely, when a saint disobeys God's commandments, he is acting in an unloving way toward his fellow-saint.
The word "keep" is *tēreō*, "to attend to carefully, to take care
of, to guard, observe." The word in this connection speaks of a
watchful, solicitous guarding and care of God's commandments
lest we disobey them, with the thought that we are concerned
with His honor and glory and our Christian testimony to the
same. It is a jealous safe-keeping of His commandments lest
they be violated. The words "love" (second occurrence) and
"keep" are in the present subjunctive, speaking of continuous
action. "Know" is *ginōskō*, "to know by experience."

Translation. *In this we know experientially that we are
habitually loving the born-ones of God, whenever God we are
habitually loving and His commandments are habitually guarding
and observing with solicitous care.*

(5:3) In the expression "the love of God," we have the
objective genitive, in which the noun in the genitive case (God),
receives the action of the noun of action (love). Thus, we are
to understand that John means "the love for God." That is, the
saint's love for God is shown by his keeping His commandments.
This should be the motivating factor in our keeping God's Word,
our love for Him. This love is *agapē*, that divine love produced
in the heart of the yielded saint by the Holy Spirit, which love
impels us to obey Him. "Grievous" is "heavy." The word
speaks of that which is burdensome, severe, stern, violent, cruel,
unsparing. Love for God makes the keeping of His commandments a delight rather than a burden.

Translation. *For this is the love for God, namely, that we are
habitually and with solicitous care guarding and observing His
commandments. And His commandments are not burdensome.*

(5:4, 5) The reason why God's commandments are not burdensome is that obedience to them enables the saint to overcome

the world. "Whatsoever" is neuter in gender, the comprehensive, categorical neuter, expressing the universality of the principle, and refers to persons, those persons born of God. "Born" is again perfect in tense, referring to a past completed act of regeneration with the present result that that regenerated individual has been made a partaker of the divine nature and as such is a child of God (II Peter 1:4, John 1:12 "sons," *tekna*, "bairns," born-ones). "Overcometh" is *nikaō*, "to carry off the victory, come off victorious." The verb implies a battle. Here the forces of the world-system of evil, the flesh (totally depraved nature), the devil, and the pernicious age-system (*zeitgeist* German) with which the saint is surrounded, are all engaged in a battle against the saint, carrying on an incessant warfare, the purpose of which is to ruin his Christian life and testimony. The verb is in the present tense, "is constantly overcoming the world." It is a habit of life with the saint to gain victory over the world. To go down in defeat is the exception, not the rule.

In the expression, "This is the victory that overcometh," the verbal form is an aorist participle, literally, "This is the victory that overcame the world"; as Smith says, "St. John says first, 'is conquering,' because the fight is in progress, then 'that conquered' because the triumph is assured." The same authority says, " 'Our faith' conquers the world by clinging to the eternal realities." Vincent says, "*Our faith* is embraced in the confession that Jesus is the Christ, the Son of God." This is brought out in v. 5, in the question, "Who is he who is constantly conquering the world but the one who believes that Jesus is the Son of God?" A heart belief in the incarnation with all that that implies results in an individual who gains the victory over the world. Unitarianism was clearly one of the most wide-spread heresies of the early Church, for John over and over again in this epistle writes against it.

Translation. *Because everything born of God is constantly coming off victorious over the world. And this is the victory that has come off victorious over the world, our faith. Who is he who is constantly coming off victorious over the world but the one who believes that Jesus is the Son of God?*

(5:6) "Came" is an aorist participle in the Greek text, referring to a definite fact in history, the first Advent of the Son of God embracing human nature without its sin through virgin birth. "By" is *dia*, the preposition of intermediate agency, speaking here of accompaniment and instrumentality. His coming to make an atonement for sin was accompanied by and made effective through water and blood. Vincent says, "*Water* refers to Christ's baptism at the beginning of His Messianic work, through which He declared His purpose to fulfil all righteousness (Matt. 3:15). *Blood* refers to His bloody death upon the Cross for the sin of the world." Robertson says, "These two incidents in the Incarnation are singled out because at the baptism Jesus was formally set apart to His Messianic work by the coming of the Holy Spirit upon Him and by the Father's audible witness, and because at the Cross His work reached its culmination ('It is finished,' Jesus said)."

The combination "Jesus Christ," used together by John to designate one individual, is a refutation of the Cerinthian Gnostic heresy to the effect that Jesus was the person, only human, not deity, and that the Christ or divine element came upon Him at His baptism and left Him before His death on the Cross.

In the words, "not by water only, but by water and blood," John changes from the preposition *dia* to *en*. It is locative of sphere, "not in the sphere of the water only but in the sphere of the water and the blood." *Dia* presents the medium through which, and *en*, the sphere or element in which Jesus Christ came to offer Himself as the atonement for sin.

It is the Holy Spirit who is the third witness to the Incarnation, the water and the blood being the other two. John writes, "And the Spirit is the One who is constantly bearing witness, because the Spirit is the truth." This latter statement does not take away from the conception of the Holy Spirit as one of the Persons of the Trinity, for the Lord Jesus referred to Himself as the truth (John 15:26). The idea is that it is the Holy Spirit whose characteristic is truth, to whom John refers.

Translation. *This is the One who came through water and blood, Jesus Christ; not in the sphere of the water only, but in the sphere of the water and the blood. And the Spirit is the One who is constantly bearing witness, because the Spirit is the truth.*

(5:7) There is general agreement among textual critics that the contents of this verse are spurious, and do not belong to the original text. "The fact and the doctrine of the Trinity do not depend upon this spurious addition" (Robertson).

(5:8) The words "in earth" are not found in the best manuscripts. The same three witnesses of verse 6 are repeated. The expression "these three agree in one" is literally in the Greek text, "are to the one thing"; that is, in the words of Vincent, "they converge upon the one truth, Jesus Christ, the Son of God, come in the flesh." Alford translates, "Concur in the one, contribute to one and the same result, namely, the truth that Jesus is the Christ, and that we have life in Him."

Translation. *Because three there are that are constantly bearing testimony, the Spirit and the water and the blood. And the three concur in the one thing.*

(5:9) The word "if" here is not *ean*, a conditional particle of an unfulfilled condition, but *ei*, the conditional particle of a fulfilled condition. It is used with the indicative mode, and assumes the reception of the witness of men to be a fact. The idea is, "In view of the fact that we receive the witness or testimony (*marturia*) of men." "Receive" is *lambanō*, "to take, appropriate, receive." The reception of testimony is therefore the act of appropriating it to ourselves as something to be depended upon as the truth. John's thought is here, "Since we are in the habit of receiving the testimony of men, the testimony of God is greater, *and therefore should be received."*

"For" is *hoti* "because." Vincent says, "Not explaining *why it is greater,* but why the principle of the superior greatness of divine testimony should apply and be appealed to in this case. Supply mentally, *and this applies in the case before us,* for etc." "Which" is not *hēn* but *hoti* in the best texts. John's thought is as follows: "Since we are in the habit of receiving the testimony of men, the testimony of God is greater (and therefore should be received); because this is the testimony of God (and this applies in the case before us) that God has borne testimony concerning His Son with the present result that that testimony is on record." That is, we receive testimony from our fellow-man. But God's testimony is greater than man's testimony. God testifies of the fact that He has borne testimony concerning His Son, and since He is the One who has borne this testimony, not man, that testimony should be received. The verb is in the perfect tense, speaking of a past act of bearing testimony with the result that the testimony is on record at the present time.

Translation. *Since the testimony of men we are habitually receiving, the testimony of God is greater, because this is the testimony of God, that He has borne testimony concerning His Son, and this testimony is on record.*

(5:10, 11) Smith has a most helpful note here: "A subtle and profound analysis of the exercise of soul which issues in assured faith. Three stages, 'believe God,' . . . accept His testimony concerning His Son, *i.e.,* not simply His testimony at the Baptism (Matt. 3:17), but the historic manifestation of God in Christ, the Incarnation. God speaks not by words but by acts, and to set aside His supreme act, and all the forces which it has set in operation is to 'make Him a liar' by treating His historic testimony as unworthy of credit. (2) 'Believe in the Son,' . . . make the believing, self-surrender, which is the reasonable and inevitable consequence of contemplating the Incarnation and recognizing the wonder of it. (3) The Inward Testimony . . . The love of Jesus satisfies the deepest need of our nature. When He is welcomed, the soul rises up and greets Him as 'all its salvation and all its desire' and the testimony is no longer external in history but an inward experience, and therefore indubitable."

"Witness" is *martus.* It is used of a witness, "one who avers, or can aver, what he himself has seen or heard or knows by any other means" (Thayer). It is used of one who testifies to what he has seen or heard, for instance, a witness in a court of law. Thus, the one who believes on the Son of God has the testimony in him to the effect that he thus believes. Paul in Romans 8:16 tells us that the Holy Spirit bears testimony in connection with our human spirits as energized by the Holy Spirit that we are children of God. That is, our human spirit, energized by the Holy Spirit, gives us the consciousness that we as believers are children of God. The Holy Spirit testifies to us that that same thing is true. The following verbs, "hath made, believeth, gave record" are in the perfect tense, and as Vincent says, the act perpetuates itself in the present condition of the person acting in the verb. In verse 11 we have the simple aorist in the verb "hath given," marking the giving of His Son at the Cross as an historic fact.

Translation. *The one who believes on the Son of God has the testimony in himself. The one who does not believe God has made Him a liar, and as a result considers Him to be such, because he has not believed the testimony which God has given concerning His Son, which testimony is on record, with the result that he is in a settled state of unbelief. And this is the testimony, that life eternal God gave us.*

(5:12) The definite article appears before the word "life," pointing out a particular life, that life which God is and which He gives sinners who place their faith in the Son. The first mention of the Son is without the qualifying words, "of God," the second has them. Bengel remarks: "The verse has two clauses: in the former, *of God* is not added, because believers know *the Son;* in the other it is added, that unbelievers may know at length how serious it is not to have Him."

Translation. *The one who has the Son, has the life. The one who does not have the Son of God, the life he does not have.*

(5:13) Smith comments: "The purpose for which St. John wrote his Gospel was that we might believe in the Incarnation, and so have eternal life (20:31); the purpose of the Epistle is not merely that we may have eternal life by believing, but that we may *know that we have it.* The Gospel exhibits the Son of God, the Epistle commends Him. It is a supplement to the Gospel, a personal application and appeal."

"I have written" is an epistolary aorist, a courtesy extended the reader by the writer of a letter in which the latter puts himself at the viewpoint of the reader when he receives the letter, looking at the letter which he is writing as a past event, although it is a present one with him. John refers here, therefore, not to a previous letter, but to the one he is writing. "Know" is *oida*, speaking, not of experiential knowledge, but of absolute, beyond the peradventure of a doubt knowledge, a positive knowledge. The words, "and that ye may believe on the name of the Son of God," are not found in the best texts. The words, "unto you that believe on the name of the Son of God," appear after the words, "that ye may know that ye have eternal life," in the Greek text.

Translation. *These things I write to you in order that you may know with an absolute knowledge that life you are having, eternal (life), to you who believe on the name of the Son of God.*

(5:14, 15) "Confidence" is *parrēsia*, "free and fearless confidence, cheerful courage, boldness, assurance." "In Him" is *pros auton*. The preposition *pros* means "toward," speaking of the saint's attitude towards a prayer-hearing and a prayer-answering God. "Ask" is *aiteō*, "to ask for something to be given." It is in the middle voice in which the person acting in the verb does so in his own interest. It is in the present subjunctive, which speaks of continuous action. Thus, the total idea is, "if we keep on asking for something for ourselves." "Will" is *thelēma*, a desire which springs from the emotions. Smith suggests: "A large assurance: our prayers are always heard, never unanswered. Observe two limitations, (1) *according to His will* which does not mean that we should first ascertain His will and then pray, but that we should pray with the proviso, express or implicit, 'If it be thy will.' Matthew 26:39 is the model prayer. (2) The promise is not 'He granteth it' but 'He hearkeneth to us.' He answers in His own way. Verse 15. An amplification of the second limitation. 'We have our requests' not always as we pray but as we would pray were we wiser. God gives us not what we ask but what we really need." Said

Shakespeare, "We, ignorant of ourselves, beg often our own harms, which the wise powers deny us for our good; so find we profit by losing of our prayers."

Translation. *And this is the assurance which we are having toward Him, that whatever we keep on asking for ourselves according to His will, He hears us. And if we know with an absolute knowledge that He hears us, whatever we are asking for ourselves, we know with an absolute knowledge that we have the things which we have asked from Him.*

(5:16, 17) For the exposition of this difficult verse, we turn to Alford, and his canons or rules of interpretation. He says: "Our first canon of interpretation of 'the sin unto death' and 'not unto death' is this, that the 'death' and the 'life' must correspond. The former cannot be bodily death, while the latter is eternal and spiritual life. This clears away at once all those commentators who understand the sin unto death to be one for which bodily death is the punishment, either by human law generally, . . . or by sickness inflicted by God.

"Our second canon will be, that this sin unto death being thus a sin leading to eternal death, being further explained to the readers here, must be presumed as *meant to be understood by what the Evangelist has elsewhere laid down* concerning the possession of life and death. Now we have from him a definition immediately preceding this, in verse 12, 'The one who has the Son has the life. The one who does not have the Son of God, the life does not have.' And we may safely say that the words 'unto death' here are to be understood as meaning 'involving the loss of *this life* which men have only by union with the Son of God.' And this meaning they must have, not by implication only, which would be the case if any obstinate and determined sin were meant, which would be a *sign* of the fact of severance from the life which is in Christ (see 3:14, 15, where the inference is of this kind), but directly and essentially, *i.e.,* in respect of that very sin which is pointed at by them. Now against this canon are all those interpretations far too numerous to mention, which make *any* atrocious and obstinate sin to be that intended.

THE EXEGESIS OF I JOHN

181

It is obvious that our limits are thus confined to *abnegation of Christ,* not as inferred by its fruits otherwise shown, but as the act of sin itself.

"Our third canon will help us decide, within the above limits, which especial sin is intended. And it is, that by the very analogy of the context, it must be *not a state of sin, but an appreciable* ACT *of sin,* seeing that that which is opposed to it *in the same kind,* as being not unto death, is described by 'if anyone see his brother sinning.' (The verb "see" is aorist subjunctive, speaking of a single act of seeing. K.S.W.)

"In enquiring what this is, we must be guided by the analogy of what St. John says elsewhere. *Our* state being that of life in Christ Jesus, there are those who have gone out from us, not being of us (2:19), who are called antichrists, who not only 'have not' Christ, but are Christ's enemies, denying the Father and the Son (2:22), whom we are not even to receive into our houses nor to greet (II John 10, 11). These seem to be the persons pointed out here, and this is the sin, namely, the denial that Jesus is the Christ, the incarnate Son of God. This alone of all sins bears upon it the stamp of severance from Him who is the Life itself. As the confession of Christ, with the mouth and in the heart, is salvation unto life (Rom. 10:9), so denial of Christ with the mouth and in the heart, is sin unto death."

From the above we are led to the conclusion that "the sin unto death" refers in the context in which John is writing, to the denial of the Incarnation, and that it would be committed by those whom John designates as antichrists, who did not belong to the true Christian body of believers, but were unsaved. In view of the foregoing interpretation which is based upon the historical background and the context in which John is writing, we can now proceed with the exegesis of this verse. We will look at the Greek text itself. "See" is aorist subjunctive, speaking of a single act, not a continuous viewing. The sin in question here therefore is not an habitual one but a single act. The word "unto" is *pros,* "near, facing." Vincent says: "describing the nature of the sin. The preposition unto (*pros*) signifies *tendency toward,* not necessarily *involving death.*" "He shall ask" is *aiteō*, in future tense, the imperative future. Vincent suggests: "In prayer. The future tense expresses not merely *permission* (it shall be permitted him to ask), but the certainty that, as a Christian brother, he will ask. An *injunction* to that effect is implied." "For it," referring to "the sin unto death," is *ekeinos*, the pronoun of the remote person or thing. Vincent says in this connection. "Note the sharp distinctness with which *that* terrible sin is thrown out by the pronoun of remote reference and its emphatic position in the sentence." "Pray" is *erōtaō*, used of one on equal terms with another making request. Vincent suggests that "it may mark a request based upon fellowship with God through Christ, or it may hint at an element of presumption in a prayer for a sin unto death." The present writer confesses his utter inability to understand this verse except that the sin unto death is the denial of the incarnation, and that it is committed by an unsaved person who professes to be a Christian. The rest of the verse is an enigma to him, and he will not attempt to offer even a suggestion as to its possible interpretation.

Translation. *If anyone sees his brother sinning a sin which is not in its tendency towards death, he should ask, and He will give him life, to those who are sinning not with a tendency towards death. There is a sin which tends towards death. Not concerning that one do I say that he should ask. Every unrighteousness is sin. And there is a sin which does not tend towards death.*

(5:18) "We know" is *oida*, "to have positive, absolute knowledge." "Is born" is in the perfect tense, and speaks of a past complete act of regeneration with the present result that the believing sinner is a born-one of God. "Is begotten" is aorist tense and speaks of the Son of God, Son of God by eternal generation from God the Father in a birth that never took place because it always was. "Sinneth" is present tense, continuous action. The one born of God does not keep on habitually sinning. "Keepeth" is *tēreō*, "to take care of, to guard." The word expresses watchful care. "Wicked one" is *ponēros*, "evil in active opposition to the good, pernicious." The word refers to Satan who is not content to perish in his own corruption, but seeks to drag everyone else down with himself to his final doom. "Toucheth" is *haptō,* in the middle and passive voice, "to grasp, to lay hold of." "Himself" is *autos,* the pronoun of the third person, and should be rendered "him." As Smith says, "There is no comfort in the thought that we are in our own keeping; our security is not in our grip on Christ but His grip on us."

Translation. *We know absolutely that everyone who has been born out of God and as a result is a regenerated individual, does not keep on habitually sinning. But He who was born out of God maintains a watchful guardianship over him, and the Pernicious One does not lay hold of him.*

(5:19) "Lieth" is *keimai.* Vincent comments: "The word is stronger than *esti,* 'is,' indicating the passive, unprogressive state in the sphere of Satan's influence. 'While we are *from* God, implying a birth and a proceeding forth, and a change of state, the *kosmos* (the world), all the rest of mankind, remains in the hand of the evil one' (Alford)." "Wickedness" is *ponēros,* the word translated "wicked one" in verse 19, and refers again to Satan. "World" is *kosmos,* the world-system of evil of which all the unsaved are a part.

Translation. *We know with an absolute knowledge that out of God we are, and the whole world in the Pernicious One is lying.*

(5:20) Smith, commenting on this verse, says: "The assurance and guarantee of it all — the incarnation, an overwhelming demonstration of God's interest in us and His concern for our highest good. Not simply a historic fact but an abiding operation — not 'came' (*ēlthe*) but 'hath come and hath given us.' Our faith is not a matter of intellectual theory but of personal and growing acquaintance with God through the enlightenment of Christ's Spirit."

"Is come" is *hēkō,* "to have come, have arrived, be present." John does not use *erchomai* here, a verb which speaks only of the act of coming, but *hēkō,* which includes in the idea of coming, the fact of arrival and personal presence. It is, "the Son of God

has come (in incarnation), has arrived and is here." While He
departed in His glorified body to Heaven, yet He is here in His
presence in the Church. His coming was not like that of a
meteor, flashing across the sky and then gone. He remains in
His followers on earth. "Hath given" is perfect in tense, "has
given with the result that the gift is in the permanent possession
of the recipient."

"True" is not *alēthēs*, "true," that is, veracious, but *alēthinos*
"genuine" as opposed to the false and counterfeit, here, the genuine God as opposed to the false God of the heretics.

Translation. *We know with an absolute knowledge that the
Son of God has come and is here, and that He has given us a
permanent understanding in order that we may be knowing in
an experiential way the One who is genuine. And we are in
the Genuine One, in His Son, Jesus Christ. This is the genuine
God and life eternal.*

(5:21) "Little children" is *teknia,* a tender word, "little born-
ones." "Keep" is *phulassō,* "to guard, to watch, to keep watch."
It is used of the garrison of a city guarding it against attack from
without. Smith says, "The heart is a cidatel, and it must be
guarded against insidious assailants from without." The verb
here is not in the present tense imperative, commanding an
habitual guarding, but in the aorist, which marks a crisis. "The
Cerinthian heresy was a desperate assault demanding a decisive
repulse" (Smith).

"Idols" is *eidōlon,* "an image, likeness, idol." Smith says,
"St. John is thinking, not of the heathen worship of Ephesus —
Artemis and her Temple, but of the heretical substitutes for the
Christian conception of God." He had just written concerning
the genuine God of the Bible. Now he warns against the false,
counterfeit gods of paganism. Vincent suggests that the command, however, has apparently the wider Pauline sense, to guard
against everything which occupies the place of God.

Translation. *Little children, guard yourselves from the idols.*

THE
EXPANDED TRANSLATION
OF
FIRST JOHN

Read this through at a single sitting. In that way you will grasp the full sweep of John's letter. Repeated readings unhindered by chapter and verse divisions will merge its various parts into one harmonious and connected whole.

THE EXPANDED TRANSLATION
OF
FIRST JOHN

*That which was from the beginning, that which we have heard
with the present result that it is ringing in our ears, that which
we have discerningly seen with our eyes, with the present result
that it is in our mind's eye, that which we gazed upon as a
spectacle, and our hands handled with a view to investigation,
concerning the Word of the life. And this aforementioned life
was made visible, and we have seen (it) with discernment and
have (it) in our mind's eye, and are bearing witness to and bringing back to you a message concerning this life, the eternal, which
is of such a nature as to have been in fellowship with the Father
and was made visible to us. That which we have seen with
discernment and at present is in our mind's eye, and that which
we have heard and at present is ringing in our ears, we are
reporting also to you, in order that as for you also, you may
participate jointly in common with us. And the fellowship
indeed which is ours, is with the Father and with His Son, Jesus
Christ. And these things, as for us, we are writing in order
that our joy, having been filled completely full in times past, may
persist in that state of fulness through present time.*

*And there exists this message which we have heard from Him
and at present is ringing in our ears, and we are bringing back
tidings to you, that God as to His nature is light, and darkness
in Him does not exist, not even one bit. If we say that fellowship
we are having with Him, and in the sphere of the aforementioned
darkness are habitually ordering our behavior, we are lying, and
we are not doing the truth. But if within the sphere of the light*

we are habitually ordering our behavior as He Himself is in the light, fellowship we are having with one another. And the blood of Jesus His Son keeps continually cleansing us from every sin.

If we say that sin we are not having, ourselves we are leading astray, and the truth is not in us. If we continue to confess our sins, faithful is He and righteous to forgive us our sins and to cleanse us from every unrighteousness. If we say that we have not sinned and are not now in such a state that we could sin, a liar we are making Him, and His Word is not in us.

My little children, these things I am writing to you in order that you may not commit an act of sin. And if anyone commit an act of sin, One who pleads our cause we constantly have facing the Father, Jesus Christ the righteous One. And He Himself is a satisfaction for our sins, and not only for ours but also for the whole world.

And in this we know experientially that we have come to know Him experientially and are in that state at present, if we are continually having a solicitous, watchful care in keeping His precepts. He who keeps on saying, I have come to know Him experientially and as a present result am in that state, and His precepts is not habitually guarding with solicitous care, is a liar, and in this one the truth does not exist. But whoever habitually is with a solicitous care keeping His Word, truly, in this one the love of God has been brought to its completion, with the present result that it is in that state of completion. In this we have an experiential knowledge that in Him we are. He who is constantly saying that he as a habit of life is living in close fellowship with and dependence upon Him, is morally obligated just as that One conducted Himself, also himself in the manner spoken of to be conducting himself.

Divinely-loved ones, no new commandment am I writing to you, but a commandment, an old one, which you have had constantly from the beginning. The commandment, the old one, is the Word which you heard. Again, a commandment, a new one, I am writing to you, which fact is true in Him and in you, because the darkness is passing away, and the light, the genuine light, already is shining.

He who is saying that in the light he is, and his brother he is habitually hating, in the darkness is up to this moment. He who is habitually loving his brother, in the light is abiding, and a stumbling block in him there is not. But he who as a habit of life hates his brother, in the darkness is, and in the sphere of the darkness is habitually ordering his behavior, and he does not know where he is going, because the darkness blinded his eyes.

I am writing to you, little children, because your sins have been put away for you permanently because of His Name. I am writing to you, fathers, because you have come to know experientially the One who is from the beginning, and as a present result are possessors of that knowledge. I am writing to you, young men, because you have gained the victory over the Pernicious One and as a present result are standing on his neck. I write to you, little children under instruction, because you have come to know the Father experientially, with the present result that you are possessors of that knowledge. I write to you, fathers, because you have come to know experientially the One who is from the beginning, and are as a present result, possessors of that knowledge. I write to you, young men, because you are strong with endowed strength, and the Word of God in you is abiding, and you have gained the victory over the Pernicious One, and as a present result are standing on his neck.

Stop considering the world precious with the result that you love it, and the things in the world. If anyone as a habit of life is considering the world precious and is therefore loving it, there does not exist the love possessed by the Father in him. Because everything which is in the world, the passionate desire of the flesh, and the passionate desire of the eyes, and the insolent and empty assurance which trusts in the things that serve the creature life, is not from the Father as a source but is from the world as a source. And the world is being caused to pass away, and its passionate desire. But the one who keeps on habitually doing the will of God abides forever.

Little children under instruction, a last hour it is. And even as you heard that Antichrist is coming, even now antichrists, many of them, have arisen, from which (fact) we know by experience that it is a last hour. Out from us they departed, but they did not belong to us as a source. For if they had belonged to us, they would in that case have remained with us. But (they departed) in order that they might be plainly recognized, that all do not belong to us as a source.

But as for you (in contradistinction to the antichrists), an anointing you have from the holy One, and you all know. I did not write to you that you do not know the truth, but that you know it, and that every lie is not out of the truth as a source.

Who is the liar if not the one who is denying that Jesus is the Christ? This one is the antichrist, the one who is denying the Father and the Son. Everyone who denies the Son, not even does he have the Father. The one who confesses the Son, also the Father is he having.

As for you, that which you heard from the beginning, in you let it be constantly abiding. If in you there abides that which from the beginning you heard, both in the Son and in the Father you will abide. And this is the promise which He Himself promised us, the life, the eternal (life). These things I wrote to you concerning those who are leading you astray. But as for you, the anointing which you received from Him remains in you. And no need are you constantly having that anyone be constantly teaching you. But even as His anointing teaches you concerning all things, and is true and is not a lie, and even as He (the Holy Spirit, the anointing) taught you, be constantly abiding in Him.

And now, little children, be continually abiding in Him, in order that, whenever He is made visible, we may have instant freedom of speech and not be made to shrink away from Him in shame at His coming and personal presence. If you know absolutely that He is righteous, you know experientially that every one who habitually does this aforementioned righteousness (which God is), out from Him has been born, with the present result that that one is a born one.

All of you, behold what foreign kind of love the Father has permanently bestowed upon us, to the end that we may be named born-ones of God. And we are. On this account the world does not have an experiential knowledge of us, because it has not come into an experiential knowledge of Him. Divinely-loved ones, now born-ones of God we are. And not yet has it been made visible what we shall be. We know absolutely that when it is made visible, like ones to Him we shall be, because we shall see Him just as He is. And everyone who has this hope continually set on Him is constantly purifying himself just as that One is pure.

Everyone who habitually does sin, also habitually does lawlessness; and sin is lawlessness. And you know absolutely that that One was manifested in order that He might take away our sins; and sin in Him does not exist. Everyone who in Him is constantly abiding is not habitually sinning. Everyone who is constantly sinning has not with discernment seen Him, nor has he known Him, with the result that that condition is true of him at present. Little born-ones, stop allowing anyone to be leading you astray. The one who habitually does righteousness is righteous, just as that One is righteous. The one who is habitually doing sin is out of the devil as a source, because from the beginning the devil has been sinning. For this purpose there was manifested the Son of God, in order that He might bring to naught the works of the devil. Everyone who has been born out of God, with the present result that he is a born-one (of God) does not habitually do sin, because His seed remains in him. And he is not able to habitually sin, because out of God he has been born with the present result that he is a born-one (of God). In this is apparent the born-ones of God and the born-ones of the devil. Everyone who is not habitually doing righteousness is not of God, also the one who is not habitually loving his brother.

Because this is the message which you heard from the beginning, to the effect that we should habitually be loving one another with a divine love; not even as Cain was out of the Pernicious

*One, and killed his brother by severing his jugular vein. And
on what account did he kill him? Because his works were pernicious and those of his brother righteous. Stop marvelling,
brethren, if, as is the case, the world hates you. As for us, we
know absolutely that we have passed over permanently out of
the sphere of the death into the life, because we are habitually
loving the brethren. The one who is not habitually loving is
abiding in the sphere of the death. Everyone who habitually is
hating his brother is a manslayer. And you know absolutely
that every manslayer does not have life eternal abiding in him.*

*In this we have come to know by experience that love, because
that One on behalf of us laid down His soul. And, as for us, we
have a moral obligation on behalf of our brethren to lay down
our souls. But whoever has as a constant possession the necessities of life, and deliberately keeps on contemplating his brother
constantly having need, and snaps shut his heart from him, how
is it possible that the love of God is abiding in him? Little born-
ones, let us not be loving in the sphere of word nor even in the
sphere of the tongue, but in the sphere of deed and truth. In this
we shall know experientially that we are out of the truth, and in
His presence shall tranquilize our hearts in whatever our heart
condemns us, because greater is God than our hearts and knows
all things. Divinely-loved ones, if our heart is not condemning
us, a fearless confidence we constantly have facing God (the
Father), and whatever we are habitually asking, we keep on
receiving from Him, because His commandments we are habitually keeping with solicitous care, and the things which are
pleasing in His penetrating gaze we are habitually doing.*

*And this is His commandment, to the effect that we should
believe the Name of His Son Jesus Christ, and that we should
be habitually loving one another even as He gave a commandment to us. And the one who as a habit of life exercises a solicitous care in keeping His commandments, in Him is abiding, and
He Himself (is abiding) in him. And in this we know experientially that He is abiding in us, from the Spirit as a source whom
He gave to us.*

Divinely-loved ones, stop believing every spirit. But put the spirits to the test for the purpose of approving them, and finding that they meet the specifications laid down, put your approval upon them, because many false prophets are gone out into the world. In this you know experientially the Spirit of God. Every spirit who agrees that Jesus Christ in the sphere of flesh is come, is of God; and every spirit who does not confess this aforementioned Jesus (agree to the above teaching concerning Him), is not of God. And this is the (spirit) of the Antichrist which you have heard that it comes, and now in the world already is. As for you, out of God you are, little born-ones, and you have gained a complete victory over them, because greater is He who is in you than he who is in the world. They themselves are out of the world as a source. On this account out of the world as a source they are constantly speaking. And the world listens to them. As for us, out of God we are. The one who is knowing God is hearing us. He who is not out of God is not hearing us. From this we know the Spirit of the truth and the spirit of the error.

Divinely-loved ones, let us be habitually loving one another, because this aforementioned love is out of God as a source; and everyone who is habitually loving, out of God has been born with the present result that he is regenerated and knows God in an experiential way. The one who is not habitually loving has not come to know God, because God as to His nature is love. In this was clearly shown the love of God in our case, because His Son, the only begotten One, God sent off into the world in order that we may live through Him. In this is the love, not that we have loved God with the present result that we possess love (for Him), but that He Himself loved us, and sent off His Son, a satisfaction concerning our sins.

Divinely-loved ones, since in that manner and to that extent did God love us, also, as for us, we are under moral obligation to be constantly loving one another. God in His essence no one has ever yet beheld, with the result that no one has the capacity to behold (Him). If we habitually are loving one another, God in us is abiding, and His love has been brought to its fulness in us, and exists in that state of fulness. In this we know experientially that in Him we are dwelling and He Himself in us, because He has given us out of His Spirit as a permanent gift. And as for us, we have deliberately and steadfastly contemplated, and we are testifying that the Father has sent off the Son as Saviour of the world. Whoever confesses that Jesus is the Son of God, God in him dwells and he himself in God. And as for us, we have known the love which God has in our case, and have that knowledge at present, and we have believed and at present maintain that attitude; God is as to His nature, love, and he who dwells in the aforementioned love, in God is dwelling, and God in him is dwelling.

In this has been brought to completion the aforementioned love with us, which love exists in its completed state, in order that we may be having unreservedness of speech at the day of judgment, because just as that One is, also, as for us, we are in this world. Fear does not exist in the sphere of the aforementioned love. Certainly, this aforementioned, completed love throws fear outside, because this fear has a penalty, and the one who fears has not been brought to completion in the sphere of this love, and is not in that state at present. As for us, let us be constantly loving, because He Himself first loved us. If anyone says, I am constantly loving God, and his brother is as constantly hating, he is a liar. For the one who is not constantly loving his brother whom he has seen with discernment and at present has within the range of his vision, God whom he has not seen with discernment and at present does not have within the range of his vision, he is not able to be loving. And this commandment we have from Him; the one who is constantly loving God, should constantly be loving also his brother.

Everyone who believes that Jesus is the Christ, out from God has been born and as a result is His child. And everyone who loves the One who begot, loves the one who has been begotten out from Him. In this we know experientially that we are habitually loving the born-ones of God, whenever God we are habitually loving and His commandments are habitually guarding and observing with solicitous care. For this is the love for God, namely, that we are habitually and with solicitous care guarding and observing His commandments. And His commandments are not burdensome. Because everything born of God is constantly coming off victorious over the world. And this is the victory that has come off victorious over the world, our faith. Who is he who is constantly coming off victorious over the world but the one who believes that Jesus is the Son of God?

This is the One who came through water and blood, Jesus Christ; not in the sphere of the water only, but in the sphere of the water and the blood. And the Spirit is the One who is constantly bearing witness, because the Spirit is the truth. Because three there are that are constantly bearing testimony, the Spirit and the water and the blood. And the three concur in the one thing.

Since the testimony of men we are habitually receiving, the testimony of God is greater, because this is the testimony of God, that He has borne testimony concerning His Son, and this testimony is on record. The one who believes on the Son of God has the testimony in himself. The one who does not believe God has made Him a liar, and as a result considers Him to be such, because he has not believed the testimony which God has given concerning His Son, which testimony is on record, with the result that he is in a settled state of unbelief. And this is the testimony, that life eternal God gave us. The one who has the Son, has the life. The one who does not have the Son of God, the life he does not have.

These things I write to you in order that you may know with an absolute knowledge that life you are having, eternal (life), to you who believe on the name of the Son of God. And this is the assurance which we are having toward Him, that whatever we keep on asking for ourselves according to His will, He hears us. And if we know with an absolute knowledge that He hears us, whatever we are asking for ourselves, we know with an absolute knowledge that we have the things which we have asked from Him.

If anyone sees his brother sinning a sin which is not in its tendency towards death, he should ask, and He will give him life, to those who are sinning not with a tendency towards death. There is a sin which tends towards death. Not concerning that one do I say that he should ask. Every unrighteousness is sin. And there is a sin which does not tend towards death. We know absolutely that everyone who has been born out of God and as a result is a regenerated individual, does not keep on habitually sinning. But He who was born out of God maintains a watchful guardianship over him, and the Pernicious One does not lay hold of him. We know with an absolute knowledge that out of God we are, and the whole world in the Pernicious One is lying. We know with an absolute knowledge that the Son of God has come and is here, and that He has given us a permanent understanding in order that we may be knowing in an experiential way the One who is genuine. And we are in the Genuine One, in His Son, Jesus Christ. This is the genuine God and life eternal. Little children, guard yourselves from the idols.

THE
EXEGESIS
OF
SECOND JOHN

In order to reap the most benefit from his study, the student is urged to work through John's letter verse by verse, with his Bible and this exegesis before him, seeking to understand the meaning of the Word in the light of the word studies, interpretations, and expanded translation.

SECOND JOHN

(1, 2) John calls himself "the elder." The Greek word is *presbuteros*. It was used originally in secular life of an older man, afterwards as a term of rank or office. The members of the Sanhedrin were called *presbuteros* (elders). In the Christian Church, the men who had attained to a well-proved, mature Christian experience were designated as elders. From the ranks of these the bishops were chosen. For a discussion of the latter subject, see the author's book, *The Pastoral Epistles in the Greek New Testament* (p. 77). John is writing as one of these men grown old in the Christian Faith. And yet, an examination of the two letters, II and III John, discloses the fact that he was exercising authoritative supervision over a wide circle of churches, he was corresponding with and visiting them, interfering with their disputes and settling these by his personal and solitary arbitrament, and sending deputies and receiving them (Smith). This indicates that he was also acting in an official capacity as an elder.

He writes to "the elect lady." The following considerations point to the interpretation that this was a Christian woman of some prominence in the Church. The apostle addresses his letter to her and her children, and mentions the fact that in his travels he met others of her children, and reports that they were ordering their behavior in the sphere of the truth. He also sends greetings from the children of this elect lady's sister. The word "lady" is *kuria*. It is the feminine form of *kurios*, which means "lord, master." It was a common name in those days. It is the Greek form of the name "Martha" which means "mistress." She was a devout Christian who lived near Ephesus. Women occupied a prominent place among the Greeks at this time, which fact, together with her character as a Christian, would account for the fact that she was so well-known in the first-century Church. Her home was the meeting-place of the local assembly, there being no church buildings in those days. "Elect" is *eklektos*, "one picked out, chosen." The reference is to the fact that this lady was one of the elect of God, one of the chosen-out ones of God, chosen-out from among mankind by the sovereign grace of God for salvation.

"Children" is *teknon*, "born-ones," Scotch, "bairns." "Whom" is in the masculine gender, referring to both sons and daughters, and to the Lady herself.

The aged apostle writes that he loves this elect Lady and her children. The particular word he chooses is *agapaō*, not *phileō*. Had he used the latter word, he would have been expressing a human fondness for her, which would have been a grave mistake in a man of John's position in the Church. He tells her that he loves her and her children with a Christian love, a love produced in his heart by the Holy Spirit, a pure, self-sacrificial, heavenly, non-human love devoid of any sex relation. It is as if he said, "I love you in the Lord." But he is not satisfied with thus carefully delineating his love for her by the use of *agapaō*. He adds the qualifying phrase, "in the truth." It is locative of sphere. That is, the love with which he loved this well-known woman of position in the Church was circumscribed by the truth as it is in Christ Jesus. It was in connection with the Word of God that he loved her. His love for her had to do with Christian relationships in the Church life and work. The example of John in all this could well be emulated in these days. He uses the pronoun in an intensive way, "whom, as for myself, I love in the sphere of the truth." But not only does John especially love her, but all those who have come to know experientially the truth and as a result have it in their knowledge, also love her.

John and all those who have come to know the truth, love her "for the truth's sake." "For" is *dia*, a preposition which means, "for the sake of, because of." That is, they loved her because of her Christian character which exemplified the truth as it is found in the Word of God. This truth, John describes as "abiding in us." Smith says, "not merely apprehended by the intellect but welcomed by the heart." The word is *menō*, which is used often in the Gospels of one living as a guest in the home of another. Thus the truth is a welcome guest in the heart of the Christian. This truth, John says, "shall be with us forever." Smith adds "as our guest and companion."

Translation. *The Elder, to the chosen-out Lady, and to her born-ones, whom, as for myself, I love in the sphere of the truth, and not only I, but also all who have come to know experientially the truth and at present possess a knowledge of it, because of the truth which is continuously dwelling in us, and with us it shall be forever.*

(3) The Greek text has, "There shall be with us grace, mercy, peace." For an extended treatment of the word "grace," please see the author's book, *Treasures from the Greek New Testament* (pp. 15-19). Briefly, in the ethical terminology of the pagan Greeks, *charis* (grace) referred to a favor conferred freely, with no expectation of return, and finding its only motive in the bounty and free-heartedness of the giver. Of course, this favor was always done for a friend, never for an enemy. When *charis* is taken into the New Testament, it leaps an infinite distance forward, for the "favor" God did at Calvary in becoming sin for man and paying the penalty instead of man, was done for a race that bitterly hated Him, a race, unlovely, and humanly speaking, unlovable. Mercy (*eleos*) is God's "kindness and goodwill toward the miserable and afflicted, joined with a desire to relieve them" (Vincent). Grace meets man's need in respect to his guilt and lost condition; mercy, with reference to his suffering as a result of that sin. Trench says: "In the divine mind, and in the order of our salvation as conceived therein, the *mercy* precedes the *grace*, God so loved the world with a pitying love (therein was the *mercy*), that He *gave* His only-begotten Son (herein the *grace*), that the world through Him might be saved. But in the order of the manifestation of God's purpose of salvation, the grace must go before the mercy and make way for it. It is true that the same persons are the subjects of both, being at once the guilty and the miserable; yet the righteousness

of God, which it is quite as necessary should be maintained as His love, demands that the guilt should be done away before the misery can be assuaged; only the forgiven may be blessed. He must pardon before He can heal . . . From this it follows that in each of the apostolic salutations where these words occur, grace precedes mercy."

Peace is *eirēnē*. The verb is *eirō*, "to bind together." Thus, our Lord made peace through the blood of His Cross when He made it possible for a holy God in perfect justice and holiness to bind together a believing sinner and Himself in an indissoluble, living union.

Grace for daily living as the Holy Spirit ministers to the spiritual needs of the yielded saint, mercy in the form of God's care over the physical needs of the saint, and peace in the form of heart tranquility, shall be with us, John says.

These come from the presence of God the Father and from the presence of Jesus Christ, the Son of the Father. The Greek preposition translated "from" is not *apo,* speaking of ultimate source, but *para,* referring to immediate, personal source. Of course all these find their ultimate source in Deity, but the personal, immediate source is emphasized here by John. This preposition "from" is repeated with the words, "Jesus Christ." Westcott says that "it serves to bring out distinctly the twofold personal relation of man to the Father and the Son." Brooke comments: "The Fatherhood of God, as revealed by one who being His Son *can* reveal the Father, and who as man (Jesus) can make Him known to men." "The Son has interpreted the Father to man, 'not merely in truth,' enlightening the intellect, but 'in love,' engaging the heart" (Smith).

Translation. *There shall be with us grace, mercy, peace, from the presence of God the Father, and from the presence of Jesus Christ, the Son of the Father, in the sphere of truth and love.*

(4) "I rejoiced" is *chairō,* expressing a glad surprise. John had often been disappointed in the kind of lives some of the young people of the early Church were living. But when he met some of this elect Lady's children, he experienced a glad surprise.

"I found" is perfect tense, "I have found." He sits down and writes this Lady at once, telling her of the good news. The character of the lives which these children were living demonstated to John that this was no spasmodic thing, but a practice with them, for the present results of the perfect tense are not lost sight of here. Evidently he had had contact with them for some time.

The expression, "found of thy children" is literally, "found some out of thy children." The indefinite pronoun is understood here. John ran across some of this Lady's children in his preaching and administrative itineraries. They were "walking in truth." "Walking" is *peripateō*, "to order one's behavior, to conduct one's self." "In truth" is the locative of sphere. Her children were conducting themselves in the sphere of the truth as it is in Christ Jesus. That is, their actions and words were circumscribed by the Word of God. Their conduct was governed by the Word of God. This truth is further defined by John as being the commandment received from God as to how a Christian should conduct himself. John uses the word *teknon*, born-ones, Scotch "bairns," a most tender word.

Translation. *I rejoiced greatly that I have found some of your born-ones conducting themselves in the sphere of the truth, even as a commandment we received from the presence of the Father.*

(5) "Beseech" is *erōtaō*, "to request, entreat, beg, beseech." "Had" is imperfect tense, "which we were constantly having." The commandment was always with the Christian Church ever since its beginning, and was with the individual saint from the beginning of his Christian experience. The commandment was to the effect that Christians should love one another. The verb is in the present subjunctive, stressing continuous action. The distinctive word for "love" here is *agapaō*. This love with which saints are to love one another needs to be defined. The English word "love" may mean any one of a dozen kinds of love. There are as many meanings to it as there are persons in a preacher's audience, for a speaker is understood in the definition his audience puts upon a word, unless he defines it himself. Wise is the

preacher who defines it for his people. This love with which a saint should love another saint is produced by the Holy Spirit in the heart of the saint, and its amount and intensity are determined by the degree of yieldedness on the part of that saint. It is self-sacrificial in its essence (John 3:16). It is longsuffering in its character, kind, self-abasing, humble, well-behaved, altruistic, is not provoked, thinks no evil, does not rejoice in iniquity, rejoices in the truth, bears all things, believes all things, hopes all things, endures all things, never fails (I Cor. 13:4-8). The words "one another" are a reciprocal pronoun in the Greek text. That is, there must be reciprocity among the saints as to this love. A saint must reciprocate the love shown him by a fellow-saint.

Translation. *And now I entreat you, Lady, not as writing a commandment to you which is new, but that (commandment) which we have been having continually from the beginning, that we should be habitually loving one another with a divine love.*

(6) "Love" has the definite article. It was the love just referred to in the commandment, namely, "And this is the aforementioned love." John defines it as walking according to God's commandments. "According to" is *kata,* the local meaning of which is "down," thus suggesting domination. We are to order our behavior, conduct ourselves, dominated by the commandments of God. They are to be the dominating factor in our behavior. In the clause, "ye should walk in it," the word "it" refers to "love," not "commandment." We should conduct ourselves in the sphere of love. Divine love, produced in the heart by the Holy Spirit, is the motivating factor that impels saints to observe the commandments of God.

Translation. *And this is the aforementioned love, that we should order our behavior dominated by His commandments. This is the commandment, just as you heard from the beginning, that in its sphere we should be ordering our behavior.*

(7) And now John gives his reason for his urgent entreaty that the saints conduct themselves in the sphere of God's commandment to love one another. It is the presence of heretics and

their heresies in the visible Church. "Deceivers" is *planos,* "wandering, roving, misleading, leading into error, a vagabond, tramp, impostor, a corrupter, deceiver," thus, a false teacher who leads others into heresies.

"Are entered into," is *exēlthon, "went forth* into" the world. The verb is aorist, speaking here of a particular crisis in the first-century Church when these false teachers suddenly broke with the saints in matters of doctrine, and went forth teaching heresy. "World" here is *kosmos,* the world of unsaved humanity. These, John says, "confess not that Jesus Christ is come in the flesh." "Confess" is *homologeō,* "to agree with" someone as to a certain teaching. These teachers were not in agreement with the doctrines of the Church. They not only did not admit them to be true but differed with them by teaching heresy.

"Is come" is a present participle in the Greek text. There is no article before the word "flesh." The emphasis is upon character or manner. The prepositional phrase qualifies the coming as a flesh-coming. The word "flesh" refers, not to the totally-depraved nature, but to the physical body and human life with its human limitations. The denial here is that of the incarnation, not specifically of the First and Second Advent, although both are included in the apostle's thought, but of the *fact* of an Advent of Deity at all, of an incorporation by Deity of human nature. Here we have Unitarianism with a vengeance again.

John says that this is "the deceiver and the antichrist," the definite article appearing with both nouns. "This" is *houtos,* the demonstrative pronoun in the masculine gender, referring here to personality. That is, the teacher who denies the fact of an incarnation is a deceiver and an anti-christ, and as Alford says, a representative and precursor of Antichrist himself.

Translation. *Because many deceivers went forth into the world, those who do not agree that Jesus Christ comes in the sphere of flesh. This one is the deceiver and the antichrist.*

(8) "Look to yourselves" is literally, "ever keep a watchful eye upon yourselves" (*blepō*). The best texts have, not, "we

lose not," but, "ye lose not." "Lose" is *apollumi*, "to destroy, ruin, lose." "We receive" is in the best texts, "ye receive."

Smith explains: "We have worked together: see that you do not forfeit the reward of your labor. Get a full wage. Be not like workmen who toward the close of the day fall off, doing their work badly or losing time, and get less than a day's pay. . . . We have been fellow-workers thus far, and I mean to be faithful to the last: see that you also be so." He adds, "Their danger lay in taking up with false teaching and losing the comfort of the gospel in its simplicity and fulness."

Translation. *Ever be keeping a watchful eye upon yourselves in order that you do not lose the things we accomplished, but that you receive a full reward.*

(9) "Transgresseth" is *proagō*, "to lead forward, to go before," in a bad sense, "to go further than is right or proper," in this context, "to go beyond" the limits of true doctrine.

"Doctrine" is *didachē*, "teaching," namely, that which is taught. Smith says that it is the teaching which recognizes Jesus as the Christ, the Messiah, the Saviour. We have a genitive of reference, "teaching with reference to Christ." "The Cerinthian Gnostics boasted of their enlightenment. They were 'progressives,' advanced 'thinkers' " (Smith). Robertson says: "These Gnostics claimed to be the progressives, the advanced thinkers, and were anxious to relegate Christ to the past in their onward march. This struggle goes on always among those who approach the study of Christ. Is He a 'landmark' merely or is He our goal and pattern? Progress we all desire, but progress toward Christ, not away from Him." In the second instance of the use of the expression, "in the doctrine of Christ," the words "of Christ" are not found in the best texts. The person therefore, who goes beyond the teaching of the incarnation of the Son in human flesh, thus denying the incarnation, does not possess God in a saving relationship. That person is Unitarian in doctrine and a Modernist or Liberal, an unsaved person who has no right to the name "Christian."

Translation. *Everyone who goes ahead and does not remain in the teaching with reference to Christ, does not have God. The one who remains in the aforementioned teaching, this one has both the Father and the Son.*

(10, 11) The "if" is the particle of a fulfilled condition. There were such teachers circulating around the local churches who were Unitarians. These visitors to whom John has reference were not ordinary guests needing hospitality, but teachers, as is shown by the words "bring not this doctrine." John forbids her to show them hospitality. Since the local church held its meetings, not in a building designated for that purpose, but in the homes of its members, it is very possible that the local church of her community met for worship in her home, since she was a woman of outstanding prominence. If this was the case, the command of John would extend to the responsibility of the local church of today to exclude Modernists from occupying its pulpit.

She is forbidden to bid these false teachers "godspeed." The Greek is, "and say not to him 'greeting.'" The Greek word is *chairein,* "rejoice, hail." The word was used for a greeting or farewell. The context speaks of the coming of the false teacher and the necessity of barring his entrance to the home, either with respect to general hospitality, or if the home was the meeting place of the local church, with reference to his teaching at the worship service. It would seem therefore that the reference here is to the greeting, not the farewell. The words "receive not" and "neither bid godspeed" are in a Greek construction which forbids the continuance of an act already going on. This Lady had received such false teachers and had given them greeting, of course, innocently. John exhorts her to stop doing so.

The reason for the prohibition of hospitality and greeting in the case of false teachers, here, the Gnostics, was that the Christian who did offer both, became a sharer or partner of the false teachers in the disseminating of heresy. The word "partaker" is *koinōnia,* "a partner, one who cooperates with another." Robertson says: "It is to be borne in mind that the churches often met in private homes (Rom. 16:5; Col. 4:15), and if these travelling deceivers were allowed to spread their doctrines in these homes and then sent on with endorsement as Apollos was from Ephesus and Corinth (Acts 18:27), there was no way of escaping responsibility for the harm wrought by these propagandists of evil. It is not a case of mere hospitality to strangers."

Translation. *If, as is the case, a certain one comes to you, and this teaching is not bearing, stop receiving him into (your) home. And stop giving him greeting. For the one who gives him greeting is a partner in his works which are pernicious.*

(12) "Would" is *boulomai*, "a desire which comes from one's reason." John had considered the matter carefully and had come to the conclusion that it would be wiser to wait until he saw this Lady again to talk things over with her rather than include them in this letter. Smith has a most helpful note in this connection: "Why would he not write all that was in his mind? It was a deliberate decision ere he took pen in hand: This is the force of 'I would not.' His heart was full, and writing was a poor medium of communication. . . . he was an old man, and writing was fatiguing to him (Plummer). The reason is deeper. The 'many things' which he had in mind, were hard things like his warning against intercourse with heretics, and he would not write at a distance but would wait till he was on the spot and had personal knowledge. It is easy to lay down general principles, but this application to particular cases is a delicate task, demanding knowledge, sympathy, charity. (1) The sight of peoples' faces appeals to one's heart and softens one's speech. (2) When one meets with people and talks with them, one's judgment of them and their opinions is often modified. Writing from Ephesus, St. John might have condemned a teacher in a neighboring town whose teaching he knew only by report; but perhaps if he met the man and heard what he had to say, he might discover that there was nothing amiss, at all events, nothing which called for excommunication. Dr. Dale of Birmingham was at first inclined to look with disfavor on Mr. Moody. He went to hear him, and his opinion was altered. He regarded him ever after with profound respect, and considered that he had a right to preach the

gospel, 'because he could never speak of a lost soul without tears in his eyes.' St. John shrank from hasty condemnation that there might be no after-regret."

"Paper" is *chartēs*. The reference is to the Egyptian papyrus, the form of paper used at that time. It was made of a tall, smooth reed which had a triangular stalk. This contained the pith from which the paper was made. The paper was made by arranging the pith in strips, laying other strips crosswise, uniting these two layers with a paste, and putting all under a heavy pressure. This was papyrus, writing material of the ancients. "Ink" is *melanos*, "that which is black." Ancient ink was prepared from soot, vegetable, or mineral substances. Gum and vitriol were used also. Colored inks, red and gold, were used (Vincent). "Would" is an epistolary aorist and can best be rendered by the present tense in English. The writer puts himself at the viewpoint of the recipient, and views an act that is present with him as a past event.

"Might be full" is a periphrastic construction which totals up to the following: "in order that our joy, having been filled completely full, might persist in that state of fulness through present time."

Translation. *Having many things to be writing to you, I do not, after giving the matter mature consideration, desire to do so with pen and ink, but I am hoping to be present with you and to speak face to face, in order that our joy, having been filled completely full, might persist in that state of fulness through present time.*

(13) John closes this rather informal yet divinely-inspired letter by relaying greetings from the children of the sister of this elect Lady. This sister was a Christian as seen in the word "elect."

Translation. *There greet you the children of your sister, the chosen-out one.*

THE
EXPANDED TRANSLATION
OF
SECOND JOHN

Read this letter through as the elect Lady
did, in one continuous reading. Read it repeatedly to grasp its richness.

THE EXPANDED TRANSLATION
OF
SECOND JOHN

The Elder, to the chosen-out Lady, and to her born-ones, whom, as for myself, I love in the sphere of the truth, and not only I, but also all who have come to know experientially the truth and at present possess a knowledge of it, because of the truth which is continuously dwelling in us, and with us it shall be forever. There shall be with us grace, mercy, peace, from the presence of God the Father, and from the presence of Jesus Christ, the Son of the Father, in the sphere of truth and love.

I rejoiced greatly that I have found some of your born-ones conducting themselves in the sphere of the truth, even as a commandment we received from the presence of the Father. And now I entreat you, Lady, not as writing a commandment to you which is new, but that (commandment) which we have been having continually from the beginning, that we should be habitually loving one another with a divine love. And this is the aforementioned love, that we should order our behavior dominated by His commandments. This is the commandment, just as you heard from the beginning, that in its sphere we should be ordering our behavior. Because many deceivers went forth into the world, those who do not agree that Jesus Christ comes in the sphere of flesh. This one is the deceiver and the antichrist.

Ever be keeping a watchful eye upon yourselves in order that you do not lose the things we accomplished, but that you receive a full reward. Everyone who goes ahead and does not remain in the teaching with reference to Christ, does not have God. The one who remains in the aforementioned teaching, this one has both the Father and the Son. If, as is the case, a certain one comes to you, and this teaching is not bearing, stop receiving him into (your) home. And stop giving him greeting. For the one who gives him greeting is a partner in his works which are pernicious.

Having many things to be writing to you, I do not, after giving the matter mature consideration, desire to do so with pen and ink, but I am hoping to be present with you and to speak face to face, in order that our joy, having been filled completely full, might persist in that state of fulness through present time. There greet you the children of your sister, the chosen-out one.

THE
EXEGESIS
OF
THIRD JOHN

In order to reap the most benefit from his study, the student is urged to work through John's letter verse by verse, with his Bible and this exegesis before him, seeking to understand the meaning of the Word in the light of the word studies, interpretations, and expanded translation.

THIRD JOHN

(1)   The Greek order of words is, "The elder to Gaius, the beloved." John calls him "beloved," four times in this brief letter, here, and in verses 2, 5, and 11. The adjective describes this man as being well-beloved by his fellow-saints, an outstanding member of the local church to which he belonged. The word "beloved" is *agapētos,* the word used of divine love. For the significance of the term "elder" see notes on II John 1.

Translation. *The Elder, to Gaius, the beloved, whom, as for myself, I love in the sphere of the truth.*

(2)   Regarding the contents of this verse, Adolph Deissmann in his monumental work, *Light from the Ancient East,* shows that the words "I pray that in all things thou mayest prosper and be in health," are found frequently in letters of that day. He presents a letter, "Apion to Epimachus his father and lord, many greetings. Before all things I pray that thou art in health, and that thou dost prosper and fare well continually." In another letter we have, "Antonius Maximus to Sabina his sister, many greetings. Before all things I pray that thou art in health." Here is a letter from a prodigal son to his mother, "Antonus Longus to Nilus his mother, greetings. And continually do I pray that thou art in health. I make intercession for thee day by day to the lord Serapis." Deissmann appends this note: "Misunderstanding this formula, many commentators on the Third Epistle of St. John have assumed that Gaius, the addressee, had been ill immediately before." It is therefore not necessary to suppose that Gaius was ill.

The letters from which the above excerpts were taken were written by pagans. The reader will note the first-century custom of a letter-writer in writing his name first and then that of the person to whom it was addressed, also the custom of these pagan peoples to pray to their gods even about such a mundane matter as the health of a loved-one. John adds to the formula by praying that the physical health of Gaius may equal the health of his soul, which latter health was robust. If the physical health of some saints equalled the health of their souls, they would be persons of the stature of an Atlas or a Hercules, while in the case of others they would be physical dwarfs, emaciated and weak. How often great spiritual vitality is found in saints of infirm health and broken bodies.

The word "soul" is *psuchē*. Vincent defines it as follows: "The *soul* is the principle of individuality, the seat of personal impressions. It has a side in contact with both the material and the spiritual element of humanity, and is thus the mediating organ between body and spirit. Its meaning, therefore, constantly rises above *life* or the *living individual,* and takes color from its relation to either the emotional or the spiritual side of life, from the fact of its being the seat of the feelings, desires, affections, aversions, and the bearer and manifester of the divine life-principle (*pneuma*). Consequently *psuchē* (soul) is often used in our sense of *heart* (Luke 1:46; John 10:24; Acts 14:2); and the meanings of *psuchē* (soul), and *pneuma* (spirit), occasionally approach each other very closely."

It was the inner heart-life of Gaius that John said was in a prosperous condition. The word "prospereth" is *euodoō*. The word is made up of *hodos* "a road," and *eu,* "good," thus, "a good road, or a good journey." The verb is used of the granting of a prosperous and expeditious journey, and means, "to cause to prosper." The words "above all things" are the A.V. translation of *peri pantōn,* which Vincent says is wrong. "This sense of *peri* is contrary to New Testament usage. The preposition means *concerning.* So Rev., 'I pray that *in all* things thou mayest prosper.'"

Translation. *Beloved, in all things I am praying that you will be prospering, and that you will be continually having good health just as your soul is prospering.*

(3) John now discloses the source of his information regarding the properous condition of the inner heart-life of Gaius. Christian workers were always going out from Ephesus on preaching and teaching missions, and bringing back to John, reports from the various churches. "Came" is a present participle in the Greek text, and speaks of continuous action. The brethren were constantly coming back from these missions and bringing John glowing reports of the truth of God in the heart of Gaius and of the out-working of that truth in his life. The words "the truth that is in thee" are literally "your truth," that is "your share of that truth in which you walk" (Alford).

Translation. *For I rejoiced greatly when brethren were constantly coming and constantly bearing witness of your truth, just as, as for you, in the sphere of the truth you are conducting yourself.*

(4) The Greek reads, "Greater joy than this I do not have." "Children" is *teknon*. The verbal form is *tiktō*, "to give birth to"; thus a *teknon* is a child as it is seen in relation to its parents. The use of this word and the fact that "my" is not the personal pronoun in the genitive case in the Greek text but a possessive adjective, literally, "my own," would seem to indicate that Gaius was a convert of John.

Translation. *Greater joy than this I do not have, namely, that I am hearing that my own children are habitually ordering their behavior in the sphere of the truth.*

(5-7) For, "thou doest faithfully," Vincent offers, quoting the Rev., "thou doest a faithful work," and Smith, "a work of faith." The hospitality of Gaius was not merely a kind and generous act, but he considered it a religious or spiritual service. That is, the hospitality he afforded travelling preachers and teachers, he considered a definite piece of work for the Lord Jesus, as Christian service. The verb here is *poieō*, "to do." The second occurrence of the word "doest" is *ergazomai*, "to labor, be active, to perform." It emphasizes the process rather than the end of the action, and includes the ideas of continuity and repetition. Gaius was continually engaged in caring for the needs of the servants of the Lord who were ministering the Word from place to place. "And to strangers" is literally in the Greek text, "and this to strangers." That is, those who were the recipients of the hospitality of Gaius were for the most part, not his friends, but those with whom he was not acquainted.

The word "charity" is today an unfortunate translation. The word is *agapē,* the particular word for the divine love which is produced in the heart of the yielded saint by the Holy Spirit, a love which is self-sacrificial in its essence, always giving of itself for the benefit of others. "Church" is *ekklēsia,* "a called-out body of people," thus, "an assembly," here referring to the local church or assembly at Ephesus. These testified to the loving hospitality of Gaius in the assembly of the saints when they were visiting the church at Ephesus.

"Bring forward on their journey" is *propempō,* "to send forward, bring on the way, accompany or escort." Robertson says: "From Homer's time . . . it was customary to speed the parting guest, sometimes accompanying him, sometimes providing money and food. Rabbis were so escorted, and Paul alludes to the same gracious custom in Romans 15:24 and Titus 3:13."

"After a godly sort" is *axios tou theou,* "worthily of God," that is, as God would have treated them.

"For His Name's sake" is literally "for the sake of the Name." It is for the sake of the Name of Jesus that these missionaries went forth. The word "Name" is here used absolutely, and does not refer to "Jesus" as a name or designation of an individual. Paul uses it in Philippians 2:10 in the same way. It is at the Name conferred upon Jesus at His exaltation consequent upon His humiliation, that every knee shall bow. "The Name" is an Old Testament expression speaking of all that God is in His glorious attributes. It refers here and in Philippians to all that the Lord Jesus is in His glorious attributes. The word is used in the sense of reputation, of what a person is in character and stands for. For instance, we say, "That man has a name for absolute honesty." Thus, these first-century missionaries went from place to place preaching the gospel and teaching the Word for the sake of all that Jesus was in His glorious Person and what He meant to them in that respect.

"Gentiles" is *ethnikos*. Here it refers to the pagan world of that time. These itinerant missionaries would accept no support from the pagans to whom they went, and rightly so, lest they be accused of commercializing their ministry.

Translation. *Beloved, you are doing a work of faith, whatever you are performing for the brethren, and this to strangers, those who bore testimony of your love before the assembly, whom you are doing well to send forward on their journey in a manner worthy of God; because, for the sake of the Name they went forth, taking not even one thing from the pagans.*

(8) The pronoun is used in an intensive way here. It is, "As for us, in contradistinction to the pagans." "Ought" is *opheilō*, "to have a moral obligation." "Receive" is *hupolambanō*, made up of *hupo*, "under," and *lambanō*, "to take," thus, "to catch hold from underneath and lift up," thus, in the language of today, "to underwrite," that is, assume responsibility for the expenses of someone. "Might be" is *ginomai*, "to become." "Fellow-helpers" is *sunergos*, "a companion in work, a fellow-worker." "To the truth" is either dative case, "for the truth," or associative-instrumental, "with the truth."

Translation. *Therefore, as for us, we ought as a moral obligation to underwrite such as these, in order that we may become fellow-workers with the truth.*

(9) The A.V. does not take notice of the indefinite pronoun *ti*, "somewhat, something," in the statement, "I wrote to the church." The reference is to a letter which John had written to the local church of which Gaius was a member. Smith suggests that it was a brief letter of commendation (II Cor. 3:1), introducing and authorizing a company of itinerant brethren, probably those referred to in verse 5. The use of the indefinite pronoun *ti*, Vincent suggests, indicated that "the apostle did not regard the communication as specially important."

The name "Diotrephes" is the English spelling of the Greek *diotrephēs*. The word is made up of *Dios* (*of Zeus*) (Jove), and *trephō*, "to nourish," and it means, "Zeus-nursed." Zeus was the chief of the gods in the Greek pantheon. The custom in the early Church was for a Christian Greek to discard his pagan name and take a Christian name at his baptism, the Christian name often being descriptive of his Christian character, such as is seen in the case of Epaphroditus, whose name means "charming." He was a charming Christian. Diotrephes had never changed his name, although he was a professing Christian, and a member of the local church of which Gaius was a member. Robertson calls him an "ambitious leader and sympathizer with the Gnostics." Since he was of Gnostic leanings in his doctrine, he opposed John and any letters of commendation he had sent. John warns Gaius against him. He says that Diotrephes would not receive him. The word is *epidechomai*, "to receive hospitably." He refused to accept John's authority and any teachers John would send.

The apostle describes him as one "who loveth to have the preeminence." The word is made up of *phileō*, "to be fond of," and *prōtos*, "first," thus, "to be fond of being first." Smith remarks that *"proagein* (transgresseth) of II John 9, and *philoproteuein* (fond of being first) of III John 9, denote two tempers which disturbed the Christian life of Asia Minor — intellectual arrogance and personal aggrandisement." He evidently was not satisfied with the official position he held and its scope of power, but desired to rule the entire church. Robertson, in connection with his discussion of this man's character, says that he wrote an article for a denominational paper on Diotrephes, and the editor told him that twenty-five deacons stopped the paper to show their resentment against being personally attacked.

Translation. *I wrote somewhat to the church. But the one who is fond of being the first one of them, Diotrephes, is not accepting us.*

(10) "If I come" is *ean elthō*, an hypothetical case. Smith says, "the aged apostle with his failing strength can only 'hope' (cf. verse 14) to undertake the journey." On the words, "remember his deeds," the same authority says, "not 'remind him

of his works' . . . but 'bring his works to remembrance' by reciting them at the meeting of the church. St. John does not threaten excommunication or any sort of discipline, but simply will state the facts and let them speak for themselves."

"Prating" is *phluo*, "to bubble up or boil over." The word is used to describe talk which is both fluent and empty. "Malicious" is *poneros*, "pernicious." Not content with undercutting John with pernicious words, Diotrephes refuses to accept the itinerant Bible teachers whom John had commended to the church, and prevents (*koluo*, hinders, prevents, forbids) those who after mature consideration (*boulomai* "would" A.V.) desired to welcome them, and excommunicates (*ekballo* "to cast out") them. Alford says, "The present tense indicates his habit. He was evidently one in high power, and able to forbid, and to punish, the reception of the travelling brethren."

Translation. *On this account, if I should come, I shall bring to remembrance his works which he has been constantly doing, prating against us with pernicious words, and not being content with these things, neither does he himself accept the brethren; and those who after mature consideration desired to do so, he prevents, and out of the church he throws them.*

(11) "Follow" is *mimeomai*, "to imitate." Our word "mimick" comes from this word. The verb is present-imperative in a prohibition, and Robertson translates here, "do not have the habit of imitating." The usual meaning of this Greek construction is that of forbidding the continuance of an action already going on (Dana and Mantey, *A Manual Grammar of the Greek New Testament*). But Gaius, because of his exceptionally excellent Christian testimony, can hardly be accused of imitating that which is evil.

Translation. *Beloved, do not have the habit of imitating the evil, but the good. The one who is in the habit of doing good, out of God is. The one who is in the habit of doing evil has not seen God and at present as a result has no vision of Him.*

(12) Demetrius was probably the bearer of this letter to Gaius. He was a stranger to the members of the local church of which

Gaius was a member, and needed a word of commendation from the apostle. John writes, "to Demetrius there has been borne testimony." He uses the perfect tense, which means that the testimony to the Christian character of Demetrius that was given in the past, stood at the same level at the time of the writing and sending of this letter as it did when it was first spoken. John reports that this testimony came from three sources in the city of Ephesus, the community as a whole ("of all"), the truth itself, and from John himself and his colleagues ("we bear record").

Translation. *To Demetrius there has been borne testimony by all, and by the truth itself. And, as for us, moreover, we are bearing testimony. And you know positively that our testimony is true.*

(13, 14) "Had" is imperfect in tense, literally, "I was having" many things to write to you when I began this letter. "Pen" is *kalamos,* a reed-pen, as distinguished from a sharp stylus used for writing on waxed tablets. John asked Gaius to greet the members of the church by name. John, like a true shepherd of God's flock, knew them all by name.

Translation. *I was having many things to write to you, but I do not desire to be writing to you with ink and pen. But I am hoping shortly to see you, and face to face we shall speak. Peace be to you. The friends send greeting to you. Be greeting the friends by name.*

THE
EXPANDED TRANSLATION
OF
THIRD JOHN

Read this letter through as you would an
ordinary letter, delighting in its informality,
but ever remembering the fact of its inspiration by God.

THE EXPANDED TRANSLATION
OF
THIRD JOHN

The Elder, to Gaius, the beloved, whom, as for myself, I love in the sphere of the truth. Beloved, in all things I am praying that you will be prospering, and that you will be continually having good health just as your soul is prospering. For I rejoiced greatly when brethren were constantly coming and constantly bearing witness of your truth, just as, as for you, in the sphere of the truth you are conducting yourself. Greater joy than this I do not have, namely, that I am hearing that my own children are habitually ordering their behavior in the sphere of the truth.

Beloved, you are doing a work of faith, whatever you are performing for the brethren, and this to strangers, those who bore testimony of your love before the assembly, whom you are doing well to send forward on their journey in a manner worthy of God; because, for the sake of the Name they went forth, taking not even one thing from the pagans. Therefore, as for us, we ought as a moral obligation to underwrite such as these, in order that we may become fellow-workers with the truth.

I wrote somewhat to the church. But the one who is fond of being the first one of them, Diotrephes, is not accepting us. On this account, if I should come, I shall bring to remembrance his works which he has been constantly doing, prating against us with pernicious words, and not being content with these things, neither does he himself accept the brethren; and those who after mature consideration desired to do so, he prevents, and out of the church he throws them. Beloved, do not have the habit of imitating the evil, but the good. The one who is in the habit of doing good, out of God is. The one who is in the habit of doing evil has not seen God and at present as a result has no vision of Him.

To Demetrius there has been borne testimony by all, and by the truth itself. And, as for us, moreover, we are bearing testimony. And I know positively that our testimony is true. I was having many things to write to you, but I do not desire to be writing to you with ink and pen. But I am hoping shortly to see you, and face to face we shall speak. Peace to you. The friends send greeting to you. Be greeting the friends by name.

THE
EXEGESIS
OF
JUDE

In order to reap the most benefit from his
study, the student is urged to work through
Jude's letter verse by verse, with his Bible
and this exegesis before him, seeking to understand the meaning of the Word in the
light of the word studies, interpretations, and
expanded translation.

JUDE

(1) The author's name in Greek appears as "Judas." This Judas was a brother of James, the superintendent of the Church at Jerusalem, and is named among the brethren of the Lord (Matt. 13:55; Mk. 6:3). It was a very common name in Israel. "Servant" is *doulos,* "a bondslave." Vincent says, "He does not call himself an apostle, as Paul and Peter in their introductions, and seems to distinguish himself from the apostles in vv. 17, 18, 'The apostles of our Lord Jesus Christ, how that they said, etc.' We are told that Christ's brethren did not believe on Him (John 7:5); and in Acts 1:14, the brethren of Jesus are mentioned in a way which seems to separate them from the apostles." Alford says: "a servant of Jesus Christ, probably not here in the wider sense in which all Christians are servants of Christ, but in that special sense in which those were bound to His service who were employed in the preaching and disseminating of His word."

The author calls himself "brother of James." This makes him a brother of the Lord Jesus in the family of Joseph and Mary. Vincent comments: "That Jude does not allude to his relationship to the Lord may be explained by the fact that the natural relationship in his mind would be subordinate to the spiritual (see Luke 11:27, 28), and that such a designation would, as Dean Alford remarks, 'have been in harmony with those later and superstitious feelings with which the next and following ages regarded our Lord's earthly relatives.' He would shrink from emphasizing a distinction to which none of the other disciples or apostles could have a claim, the more so because of his former unbelief in Christ's authority and mission. It is noticeable that James likewise avoids such a designation."

Both the Nestle and the Westcott and Hort texts have *agapaō,* "to love," instead of *hagiazō,* "to sanctify." The participle is in the perfect tense, speaking of a past complete act having present, and in a context like this, permanent results. The distinctive word for "love" here is the word for God's self-sacrificial love which was shown at Calvary. This love here is the outgoing of God's love for the saints in which He gives of Himself for their good. He will do anything within His good will for the saints. He went all the way to Calvary for them when they were unlovely and naturally unlovable. He will do as much and more for His saints who in Christ are looked upon by God the Father with all the love with which He loves His Son. The perfect tense speaks here of the fact that the saints are the permanent objects of God's love. Jude is therefore writing to those who have been loved by God the Father with the present result that they are in a state of being the objects of His permanent love, and that love extends not merely through the brief span of this life, but throughout eternity. And then some dear children of God fear that they might be lost. "Preserved" is *tēreō*, "to guard, to hold firmly, to watch or keep," expresses watchful care, and is suggestive of present possession. Here again Jude uses the perfect participle. The saints have been kept guarded by God the Father with the present, and here, permanent result that they are the objects of His permanent, watchful care. The words "Jesus Christ" are in the simple dative case. God the Father is keeping them guarded *for* Jesus Christ. Our Lord prayed (John 17:11), "Holy Father, keep (*tēreō*, same word) through thine own name those whom thou hast given Me, that they may be one as we are." Our Lord committed the saints into the watchful care of God the Father, and He is keeping them *for* Jesus Christ, not in the sense that the Father is keeping the saints in lieu of His Son keeping them, but in the sense that the Father is keeping them so that they might continue to be forever the possession of the Lord Jesus.

"Called" is *klētos*, placed at the end of the sentence for emphasis. It is an adjective used to describe those who were called in the sense of being invited, for instance, to a banquet. The word here speaks of that effectual call of God whereby the sinner called to salvation is constituted willing to receive that which he by nature rejects, namely, salvation, this being the pre-salvation work of the Holy Spirit in which He brings the sinner to the place of repentence and the act of faith in the Lord Jesus as Saviour.

Translation. *Jude, a bondslave of Jesus Christ and brother of James, to those who by God the Father have been loved and are in a state of being the permanent objects of His love, and who for Jesus Christ have been guarded and are in a permanent state of being carefully watched, to those who are called ones.*

(2) "Mercy" is *eleos*. Trench when comparing *charis* (grace) with *eleos* (mercy) says: "While *charis* has thus reference to the *sins* of men, and is that glorious attribute of God which these sins call out and display, His *free gift* in their forgiveness, *eleos*, has special and immediate regard to the *misery* which is the consequence of these sins, being the tender sense of this misery displaying itself in the effort, which only the continued perverseness of man can hinder or defeat, to assuage and entirely remove it. . . . In the divine mind, and in the order of our salvation as conceived therein, the *eleos* (mercy) precedes the *charis* (grace). God so loved the world with a pitying love (herein was the *eleos*), that He *gave* His only begotten Son (herein the *charis*), that the world through Him might be saved (compare Eph. 2:4; Luke 1:78, 79). But in the order of the manifestation of God's purposes of salvation the grace must go before the mercy, the *charis* must go before and make way for the *eleos*. It is true that the same persons are the subjects of both, being at once the guilty and the miserable; yet the righteousness of God, which it is quite necessary should be maintained as His love, demands that the guilt should be done away before the misery can be assuaged; only the forgiven can be blessed. And as the righteousness of God absolutely and in itself requires this, so no less that righteousness as it has expressed itself in the moral constitution of man, linking as it there has done misery with guilt, and making the first the inseparable companion of the second."

"Peace" is *eirēnē,* the verbal form being *eirō,* "to join." To make peace is therefore to join together that which has been separated. Our Lord through the blood of His Cross has made peace between a holy God and sinful man in the sense that He has joined together those who were by sin separated, God and the believing sinner. This is justifying peace. Jude, writing to the saints, is speaking here of sanctifying peace, that state of tranquillity which is the result of the *eleos* (mercy) of God assuaging the evil results of sin.

"Love" here is *agapē,* that divine love which God is and which is shed abroad in the heart of the yielded saint. Mayor says: "The divine love is infused into them, so that it is their own, and becomes in them the source of a divine life (Rom. 13:10). In virtue of this gift they are inspired with a love which is like the love of God, and by this they truly claim the title of children of God as partakers of His nature (I John 4:7, 10)." Jude prays that mercy, peace, and love may be in them in an increasing abundance.

Translation.   *Mercy to you, peace, and love be multiplied.*

(3) "Beloved" is *agapētoi,* a plural adjective, "beloved ones," that is, "divinely-loved ones," loved by God, God's beloved ones. "Gave all diligence" is literally, "making all diligence." The latter word is *spoudē,* the verbal form being *speudō,* "to hasten, desire earnestly." Alford says: "It implies more than mere earnest desire; a man's *spoudē* is necessarily action as well as wish. 'Giving diligence' seems the exact idea required." The participle is present in tense, the action simultaneous with the infinitive. The translation reads, "when giving all diligence to be writing to you." The word "common" is *koinos,* the verbal form being *koinōneō,* "to become a sharer, a partner." Thus, the idea is of "a common salvation" possessed in common with others. The best texts add *hēmōn,* "our salvation held in common by all of us."

"It was needful" is *anagkēn eschon,* literally, "I had need." The verbal form of *anagkē* is *anagkazō,* "to necessitate, compel, drive to, constrain," whether by force, threats, persuasion, entreaties. The noun means "necessity" either imposed by external conditions, or by the law of duty. Alford translates, "I found it necessary." The Revision renders it, "I was constrained." The compulsion to exhort the saints to contend for the faith found its source in the Holy Spirit. The first infinitive "to write" is in the present tense, speaking of continuous action. The second is in the aorist tense, implying an act performed at once. Mayor comments, "The aorist, contrasted with the preceding present, implies that the new epistle had to be written at once and could not be prepared for at leisure, like the one he had previously contemplated. It was no welcome task: 'necessity was laid upon him.'" Jude had originally intended writing a letter containing a positive presentation of the doctrines of the Christian faith. The Holy Spirit laid upon his heart the necessity of writing in defence of the faith.

The exhortation was to earnestly contend for the faith. The faith here is not faith as exercised by the individual, but Christianity itself in its historic doctrines and life-giving salvation. "Earnestly contend" is *epagonizomai,* found only here in the New Testament. The simple verb was used of athletes contending in the athletic contests. The word speaks of a vigorous, intense, determined struggle to defeat the opposition. Our word "agony" is the English spelling of the noun form of this word. The Greek athletes exerted themselves to the point of agony in an effort to win the contest. With such intense effort does Jude say that saints should defend the doctrines of Christianity. Peter, in his first epistle (3:15), tells us how we are to do so. He says that we should "be ready always to give an answer" to the opposition. The words "give an answer" are in the Greek a technical term of the law courts, speaking of the attorney for the defence "presenting a verbal defence" for his client. This is part of the ministry of every pastor. He must guard the flock of God under his charge from the inroads of Modernism by presenting evidences of the divine source of Christianity and the falsity of the modernistic position. The intensity of the defence must be adjusted to the intensity of the opposition which comes from Satan through

Modernism. The word "once" is *hapax*, "once for all." Vincent says, "Not *formerly*, but *once for all.*" He quotes Bengel, "No other faith will be given." "Delivered" is *paradidōmi*, "*to give over into* (one's) *power* or *use*, *to deliver to one something* to keep, use, take care of, manage." The idea is that God gave the Christian doctrines to the saints as a deposit of truth to be guarded. "Saints" is *hagios*, "a set-apart person, set apart for the worship and service of God," namely, a believer, a Christian.

Translation. *Divinely-loved ones, when giving all diligence to be writing to you concerning the salvation possessed in common by all of us, I had constraint laid upon me to write to you, beseeching (you) to contend with intensity and determination for the Faith once for all entrusted into the safe-keeping of the saints.*

(4) Now Jude gives the reason why the saints should contend for the faith. False teachers crept into the Church. The words "crept in" are *pareisdunō, dunō*, "to enter," *eis*, "into," *para*, "beside," thus, "to enter alongside." Vincent translates, "*to get in by the side*, to slip in a side-door." These are the tactics of Modernism, slipping into orthodox pulpits by stealth and dishonesty.

There is a Greek word in II Corinthians 11:13-15 which admirably describes the methods of the Modernist, who takes after his father, the Devil. It is *metaschēmatizō*, translated "transformed" in A.V. It refers to the act of an individual changing his outward expression by assuming an expression put on from the outside, an expression that does not come from nor is it representative of what he is in his inner character. Lucifer did that after he struck at God's throne and became the fallen angel, Satan. As a fallen angel he gave expression to his sin-darkened heart. But he knew that he could not attract the human race that way. He must impersonate God if he expected to be worshipped as God. He therefore assumed an outward expression of light, put on from the outside and not representative of his inner sinful being. He disguised himself as an angel of light. His ministers, (servants), Modernistic preachers, have done the same (v. 15). Using evangelical terms such as "salvation, faith, regeneration, atonement, resurrection," they put their own private meanings upon them (which negate the orthodox view), and pose as orthodox exponents of Christianity. Reader, do not trust a Modernist any farther than you would a rattlesnake. A rattlesnake will give you warning before it strikes, but not a Modernist. The eternal welfare of your soul depends upon what you believe regarding the person and work of our Lord on the Cross.

Jude says these false teachers were "ordained to this condemnation." The word "ordained" would indicate that it was the decree of God that these men should be false teachers. However, the word in the Greek text has quite a different connotation. It is *prographō,* "to write beforehand."

Mayor translates, "to designate." The reference is to the prophecy of Enoch with regard to these false teachers (v. 14). The word "to" is *eis,* and should be translated here "with reference to." "Condemnation" is *krima,* in this context, "judgment," in the sense of the condemnation of wrong, the decision which one passes on the faults of others. Enoch wrote beforehand (prophesied) concerning the fact of the stealthy entrance of these men into the midst of the people of God and true doctrine, the word "this" referring to their creeping in unawares, the word "condemnation" (judgment) speaking of the estimation of their activities as being wrong.

These men are called ungodly. The word is *asebēs,* "destitute of reverential awe toward God, impious." "Turning" is *metatithēmi,* "to transpose" two things, one of which is put in place of the other. Thus, these false teachers put lasciviousness in the place of the grace of God. "Lasciviousness" is *aselgeia.* The *aselgeia* person is he who in the words of Trench "acknowledges no restraints, who dares whatever his caprice and wanton petulance may suggest." The word "wantonness" best translates it. The meaning of the word partakes of the spirit of anarchy. That is the spirit of Modernism which refuses to acknowledge the authority of God's Word, and itself sits in judgment upon it.

Now, what is involved in their act of "denying the only Lord God and our Lord Jesus Christ"? The word "deny" is *arneomai*, "to deny, disown." It is used of followers of Jesus who, for fear of death or persecution, deny that Jesus is their Master, and desert His cause; also of those who deny God and Christ, who by cherishing and disseminating pernicious opinions and immorality, are adjudged to have apostatized from God and Christ (Thayer).

The word "God" is not found in the best texts. "Lord" is not *kurios* in the Greek text, the usual word for "lord," but *despotēs*, which speaks of one who is the absolute owner, and has uncontrolled power over another. The word *despotēs* is always used of God the Father in the Greek N. T., except in II Peter 2:1, and the adjective "only" is used elsewhere of the Father only. It would seem therefore that God the Father is in view here, and God the Son in the words "our Lord Jesus Christ." Mayor suggests that the two Persons of the Godhead are presented here to combat the Gnostic denial of the union of the divine and human in one Person.

This authority says that "Westcott notes that a common Gnostic theory was that 'the Aeon Christ' descended upon the man Jesus at His baptism and left Him before His passion. Those who held such a doctrine denied . . . the union of the divine and human in one Person . . . and this denial involves the ideas of sonship and fatherhood as correlative, but because . . . it is only in the Son that we have the full revelation of God as Father." Modernism is Unitarian in its theology, and this description of a false teacher of the first century fits the Modernist of the twentieth.

Translation. *For certain men entered surreptitiously who were of old predicted with reference to this judgment, (men) destitute of reverential awe towards God, putting anarchy in the place of the grace of God, and denying the only absolute Master and our Lord Jesus Christ.*

(5) After referring to the occasion of his letter, namely, the presence of apostate teachers in the visible organized church on

earth (vv. 3, 4), Jude speaks of apostasy in Israel and among the angels, and the sins of Sodom and Gomorrha (vv. 5-7).

"I will" is *boulomai,* "a desire which springs from the reasoning faculties." The words "though ye once knew this," are an inadequate rendering of the Greek text here. The translation of the best Greek reading here, *eidotas hapax panta* is, "knowing once for all, all things," that is, all things which pertain to the context in which Jude is speaking. Mayor, commenting on the use of *hapax* (once for all), says, "it suggests something of anxiety and upbraiding, which may be compared to the tone of St. Paul in writing Galatians."

The instance to which Jude has reference is that of the Jews, after having been convinced by the spies of the truth of God's assertion that the land of Canaan was a land flowing with milk and honey, most productive as proved by the grapes they brought out, yet refused to enter it, not trusting God to give them the land as He said He would do. This was apostasy, sinning with the eyes wide open, and could only be dealt with by the infliction of the death penalty. That generation died a physical death in the wilderness.

Translation. *Moreover, after mature consideration, I desire to remind you, (who) know all things once for all, that the Lord, having saved the people out of Egypt, then destroyed those who did not believe.*

(6) From the apostasy of Israel, Jude turns to the sin of the angels. He describes them as those who "kept not their first estate." The word "estate" is the A.V. translation of *archē.* The word means first of all, "beginning." Thus does the A.V. understand it. The angels left their first or original status as angels, their original position, to violate the laws of God which kept them separate from the human race, members of which latter race occupy a different category among the created intelligences than that of angels. Angels are a host. They do not reproduce themselves. There are the same number of angels today as there were when they were created. The human race reproduces

itself. From a beginning of two individuals the race has grown to the proportions it is today.

The second meaning of *archē* is derived from the first, namely, "sovereignty, dominion, magistracy," the beginning or first place of power. The word is translated "principalities" in Ephesians 6:12, and refers to demons there. Thus, this meaning of *archē* teaches that these angels left their original dignity and high positions. *Archē* is used in the Book of Enoch (12:4) of the Watchers (Angels) who have *abandoned the high heaven and the holy eternal place* and defiled themselves with women (Mayor).

This original state of high dignity which these angels possessed, Jude says, they did not keep. The verb is *tēreō*, "to guard." The verb expresses the act of watchful care. That is, these angels did not fulfil their obligation of carefully guarding and maintaining their original position in which they were created, but transgressed those limits to invade territory which was foreign to them, namely, the human race.

They left their own habitation. "Habitation" is *oikētērion*, "a dwelling-place," here, heaven. "Their own" is *idion*, "one's own private, personal, unique possession," indicating here that heaven is the peculiar, private abode of the angels. Heaven was made for the angels, not for man. It is the temporary abode of the departed saints until the new heavens and new earth are brought into being, but man's eternal dwelling-place will be on the perfect earth (Rev. 21:1-3). "Left" is *apoleipō*. The simple verb *leipō* means "to leave." The prefixed preposition *apo* makes the compound verb mean "to leave behind." These angels left heaven behind. That is, they had abandoned heaven. They were done with it forever. The verb is aorist in tense which refers to a once-for-all act. This was apostasy with a vengeance. They had, so to speak, burnt their bridges behind them, and had descended to a new sphere, the earth, and into a foreign relationship, that with the human race, foreign, because the latter belongs to a different category of created intelligences than they.

These angels are reserved in everlasting chains under darkness. "Reserved" is *tēreō*, and is in the perfect tense. That is, they have been placed under a complete and careful guard, with the result that they are in a state of being under this complete and careful guard continually.

These angels are carefully guarded in everlasting chains. "Chains" is *desmos,* "a band or bond." The word does not indicate that the angels are chained, but that they are in custody, detained in a certain place. The custody is everlasting. The Greek word is *aidios,* "everlasting." "Darkness" is *zophos,* "darkness, blackness," used of the darkness of the nether world. "Unto" is *eis* which can very well be translated here, "with a view to." That is, these angels are in the custody of God, carefully guarded with a view to "the judgment of the great day." That day will be the Day of the Lord, more specifically, the time of the Great White Throne Judgment (Rev. 20:11-15). Peter in his second epistle (2:4), tells us that the place of their present incarceration is Tartarus, the prison house of fallen angels. He mentions them again in his first epistle (3:19, 20), and the fact that our Lord, between His death and resurrection, went there and made a proclamation to them. Please see treatment of this subject in the author's book, *First Peter in the Greek New Testament*, pp. 97-106.

Translation. *And angels who did not carefully guard their original position of preeminent dignity, but abandoned once for all their own private dwelling-place, with a view to the judgment of the great day, in everlasting bonds under darkness, He has put under careful guard.*

(7) This verse begins with *hōs,* an adverb of comparison having the meanings of "in the same manner as, after the fashion of, as, just as." Here it introduces a comparison showing a likeness between the angels of verse 6 and the cities of Sodom and Gomorrha of this verse. But the likeness between them lies deeper than the fact that both were guilty of committing sin. It extends to the fact that both were guilty of the same identical sin.

The punctuation of the A.V. is misleading, as an examination of Greek text discloses.

The A.V. punctuation gives the reader the impression that Sodom and Gomorrha committed fornication and that the cities about them committed fornication in like manner to the two cities named. The phrase "in like manner" is according to the punctuation construed with the words "the cities about them." A rule of Greek grammar comes into play here. The word "cities" is in the nominative case. The words "in like manner" are in the accusative case and are classified as an adverbial accusative by Dana and Mantey in their *Manual Grammar of the Greek New Testament* (pp. 91, 93). This latter construction is related syntactically, not with a word in the nominative case but with the verbal form in the sentence. All of which means that the words "in like manner" are related to the verbal forms, "giving themselves over to fornication" and "going after strange flesh." In addition to all this, the Greek text has *toutois,* "to these." Thus, the translation should read, "just as Sodom and Gomorrha and the cities about them, in like manner to these, having given themselves over to fornication and having gone after strange flesh." The sense of the entire passage (vv. 6, 7) is that the cities of Sodom and Gomorrha and the cities about them, in like manner to these (the angels), have given themselves over to fornication and have gone after strange flesh. That means that the sin of the fallen angels was fornication. This sin on the part of the angels is described in the words, "going after strange flesh." The word "strange" is *heteros,* "another of a different kind." That is, these angels transgressed the limits of their own natures to invade a realm of created beings of a different nature. This invasion took the form of fornication, a cohabitation with beings of a different nature from theirs. This takes us back to Genesis 6:1-4 where we have the account of the sons of God (here, fallen angels), cohabiting with women of the human race. For a discussion of this subject, the reader is referred to the author's volumes, *First Peter in the Greek New*

Testament (pp. 97-107), and *The Practical use of the Greek New Testament* (pp. 31-35).

The words describing both the sin of the angels and of the inhabitants of Sodom and Gomorrha, "giving themselves over to fornication" are the translation of *ekporneuō*. The prefixed preposition *ek* indicates in the usage of the word a lust that gluts itself, satisfies itself completely. The force of *ek* which itself means "out," is "out and out." It signifies a giving of one's self utterly. The words "strange flesh," that is, flesh of a different and in this case an opposite (diametrically opposed) nature, speak of the angels' intercourse with women, the latter being forbidden flesh. The sin of the angels was against nature. In the case of the cities mentioned, it was the sin which Paul mentions in Romans 1:27, a departure from the natural use and against nature.

Just as the incarceration of the fallen angels is an example of God's judgment upon sin, so the cities of Sodom and Gomorrha, "are set forth as an example, suffering the vengeance of eternal fire." "Are set forth" is *prokeimai*. The verb means "to lie exposed," and is used in classical writings of food on the table ready for the guests, and of a corpse laid out for burial. The word "example" is *deigma*, from the verb *deiknumi*, "to display or exhibit." The noun therefore refers to something which is held up to view as a warning.

"Suffering" is *hupechō*, "to hold under, to put under," metaphorically, "to sustain, undergo." Vincent says, "The participle is present, indicating that they are suffering to this day the punishment which came upon them in Lot's time." The reference to these cities is not therefore limited to the ruins of the literal cities, but to the inhabitants who right now are suffering in Hades. The rich man in Hades (Luke 16:22-24) is another instance of the lost who are now in conscious suffering, awaiting the Great White Throne Judgment and everlasting suffering in hell. For a discussion of Hell, Hades, and Tartarus, consult the author's book, *Treasures in the Greek New Testament* (pp. 44-46).

"Vengeance" is *dikē*, "justice, a judicial decision, especially, a sentence of condemnation, execution of sentence, punishment." Vincent suggests "punishment" rather than "vengeance" as the most appropriate word. The same authority states that the best modern expositors render, "are set forth as an example of eternal fire, suffering punishment." He quotes Lumby as saying, "A destruction so utter and so permanent as theirs has been, is the nearest approach that can be found in this world to the destruction which awaits those who are kept under darkness to the judgment of the great day." "Eternal" is *aiōnios*, here better rendered "everlasting" rather than "eternal" since the suffering has a beginning but no ending.

Translation. *Just as Sodom and Gomorrha and the cities about them, in like manner to these, having given themselves out and out to fornication and having gone off to a different kind of flesh, are set forth as an exhibit, undergoing the punishment of everlasting fire.*

(8) "Likewise" is *homoios*, "in the same way." The A.V. takes no notice of *mentoi*, a particle of affirmation and often of opposition, meaning "but yet, nevertheless." Vincent says the word expresses the fact "that though they have these fearful examples before them, *yet* they persist in their sin."

"These dreamers" ("filthy" is not in the original) is a demonstrative pronoun and a present participle. The verb is *enupniazō*, "to dream." It is used of divinely suggested dreams. Thayer gives its metaphorical use here as follows; "to be beguiled with sensual images and carried away to an impious course of conduct." "Defile" is *minainō*, "to defile, pollute, sully, contaminate, soil." Thayer says it is used here in a physical and moral sense, the word "flesh" here speaking of literal flesh, and thus suggesting the sin of licentiousness. Immorality is thus in view here.

"Despise" is *atheteō*, "to do away with something laid down, prescribed, established." It means also "to thwart the efficacy of anything, nullify, make void, frustrate." "Dominion" is *kuriotēs*, "one who possesses dominion." The word *kurios*, "lord," speaks of one who is lord or master over another. *Kuriotēs* is used of angels in Ephesians 1:21, Colossians 1:16, and II Peter 2:10. Mayor says: "On first reading one is inclined to take the words "dominion" and "dignities" simply as abstractions. The result of indulgence in degrading lusts is the loss of reverence, the inability to recognize true greatness and due degrees of honor. . . . When we examine however the use of the word *kuriotēs* and the patristic comments, and when we consider the reference to the archangel's behavior towards Satan, . . . we seem to require a more pointed and definite meaning, not simply 'majesty,' but 'the divine majesty,' not simply 'dignities' but 'the angelic orders.' . . . We have then to consider how it can be said that the libertines (these filthy dreamers) 'despise authority' in like manner to the above-mentioned offenders. For the former we may refer to verse 4 (denying our Lord), for the latter, to the contempt shown by the Israelites towards the commandments of God. So the desertion of their appointed station and abode by the angels showed their disregard for the divine ordinance, and the behavior of the men of Sodom combined with the vilest lusts, an impious irreverance towards God's representatives, the angels (Gen. 19:5)." Thus, these false teachers refuse to show proper reverence for the angelic beings.

"Dignities" is *doxa,* "splendor, brightness, dignity, preeminence, magnificence, excellence." The word is used, Mayor says, in the singular of the Shekinah, which would suggest that Clement may be right in supposing the plural to be used for the angels. "Speak evil" is *blasphēmeō,* "to speak reproachfully of, rail at, revile, calumniate."

Translation. *In the same manner nevertheless, also these who are beguiled with sensual images and carried away to an impious course of conduct, defile indeed the flesh, and set at naught authority, and speak evil of preeminence.*

(9) In contrast to the treatment accorded the holy angels by these false teachers, Jude now presents the case of Michael the archangel, and his treatment of a fallen angel, Satan. Mayor says, "The story here narrated is taken from the apocryphal *Assumptio Mosis,* as we learn from Clement. . . . Charles, in

his edition of the *Assumption* thus summarizes the fragments dealing with the funeral of Moses: (1) Michael is commissioned to bury Moses, (2) Satan opposes his burial on two grounds: (a) he claims to be the lord of matter (hence the body should be handed over to him). To this claim Michael rejoins, 'The Lord rebuke thee, for it was God's spirit which created the world and all mankind.' (b) He brings the charge of murder against Moses (the answer is wanting). The story is based on Deuteronomy 34:6 (R.V.), "He buried him (*mg.* he was buried) in the valley . . . but no man knoweth of his sepulchre unto this day.' "

Alford says, "St. Jude took the incident from primitive tradition, which tradition, slightly modified, is also given by the prophet Zechariah (3:1-3). That the incident is related as a matter of fact, and not as an argument is evident by the very form of it. That, being thus related as a matter of fact, it *is* matter of fact, is a conclusion which will or will not be made, according as we are or are not persuaded of the authenticity of our Epistle as a part of canonical Scripture; and according as we esteem that canonical Scripture itself." All of which means that since we regard the Epistle of Jude part of the canonical scriptures, and therefore verbally inspired, and because the author treats the subject matter as fact, we are to regard it as such.

The word "archangel" is *archaggelos,* from *archē,* "first in rank," and *aggelos,* "angel," chief of the angels. Michael, the archangel, is spoken of in Daniel 10:13, 21; 12:1; I Thessalonians 4:16. His name means "who is like God?" He was regarded as the special protector of the Jewish nation. "Contending" is *diakrinō,* "to dispute." "Disputed" is *dialegomai,* "to argue." "Durst" is *tolmaō,* "to dare." "Railing accusation" is *krisis* (accusation) "judgment," and *blasphēmia* (railing), "detraction, reviling." Thayer translates, "a judgment pronounced in reproachful terms." Vincent offers, "a judgment of railing." He explains, "a sentence savoring of impugning his dignity." Michael remembered the high estate from which he (Lucifer) fell, and left his sentence to God." The word "rebuke" is in the optative mode in Greek, the mode that expresses a wish or a desire. The translation could read, "May the Lord rebuke thee." The particular word for "rebuke" here is *epitimaō*, "to rebuke another but without any effect upon the person rebuked, the latter not being convicted of any wrongdoing on his part nor brought to the place of conviction or confession, and for either one of two reasons; either the person is innocent, or he is incorrigible, that is, his heart is so hard that he refuses to be convicted of his sin or to confess it. Satan is incorrigible. Jude knew it, and therefore used that particular word. There is another word, *elegchō*, which speaks of a rebuke that brings out either conviction or confession of sin.

Translation. *Yet Michael, the archangel, when disputing with the devil, arguing concerning the body of Moses, dared not bring a sentence that would impugn his dignity, but said, May the Lord rebuke you.*

(10) Mayor comments: "The libertines do the contrary of what we are told of the respect shown by the angel even towards Satan; they speak evil of that spiritual world, those spiritual beings, of which they know nothing." "Speak evil" is *blasphēmeō*, "to speak reproachfully, revile, calumniate."

Jude uses two different words for "know" in this verse. The first is *oida*, speaking of mental comprehension and knowledge, and referring to the whole range of invisible things (Vincent). The second is *epistamai*, "to understand." Vincent says that it was originally used of skill in handicraft, and refers to palpable things, objects of sense, the circumstances of sensual enjoyment.

"Brute beasts" is *alogos* (brute) "without reason," and *zōon*, "a living being, an animal." The word *zōon*, "a living being," gives prominence to the vital element, whereas *thērion*, "a wild beast," gives prominence to the bestial element. Here Jude refers to the false teachers as in a class with unreasoning animals. "Naturally" is *phusikōs*, "by instinct." Mayor, commenting on the words, "in those things they corrupt themselves," says: "The natural antithesis here would have been, 'these things they admire and delight in.' For this Jude substitutes by a stern irony, 'these things are their ruin.'"

"Corrupt" is *phtheirō*, "to corrupt, to destroy." Thayer chooses the meaning in Jude 10, "to destroy." It is passive in voice, thus, "by these things they are being brought to ruin."

Translation. *But these on the one hand revile as many things concerning which they do not have absolute knowledge, and on the other hand as many things, by instinct, like the unreasoning animals, which they understand, by these they are being brought to ruin.*

(11) "Woe" is *ouai*, "an interjection of grief or of denunciation," here, the latter. "Way" is *hodos*, "a road, a way," metaphorically, "a course of conduct, a way, manner of thinking, feeling, deciding." The Scofield Bible speaks of Cain as the "type of a religious, natural man who believes in a God and in 'religion,' but after his own will, and who rejects redemption by blood. Compelled as a teacher of religion to explain the atonement, the apostate teacher explains it away."

"Gone" is *poreuomai*, "to take one's way, set out, to go on a journey," metaphorically, "to follow one, to become his adherent." The Scofield Bible defines the error of Balaam as follows: "The 'error' of Balaam must be distinguished from his 'way,' and his 'doctrine.' The 'error' of Balaam was that, reasoning from natural morality, and seeing the evil in Israel, he supposed a righteous God *must* curse them. He was blind to the higher morality of the Cross, through which God maintains and enforces the authority and awful sanctions of His law, so that He can be just and the justifier of a believing sinner. The 'reward' of v. 11 may not be money, but popularity, or applause." "Ran greedily" is *ekcheō*, "to pour out." The verb is in the passive voice here. Thayer says that in this voice the verb "is used of those who give themselves up to a thing, rush headlong into it." Vincent says, "A strong expression, indicating a reckless, abandoned devotion of energies." "Reward" is *misthos*, "dues paid for work, wages."

"Error" is *planē*, "a wandering, a straying about, whereby one, led astray from the right way, roams hither and thither," metaphorically, "error, a wrong opinion," relative to morals or religion (Thayer). Mayor commenting on the error of Balaam says: "Balaam went wrong because he allowed himself to hanker after gain and so lost communion with God. He not only went wrong himself, but he abused his great influence and his reputation as a prophet, to lead astray the Israelites by drawing them away from the holy worship of Jehovah to the impure worship of Baal Peor. So these false teachers use their prophetical gifts for the purpose of self-aggrandisement, and endeavor to make their services attractive by excluding from religion all that is strenuous and difficult, and opening the door to every kind of indulgence." As to the sin of Korah, the Scofield Bible defines it as "the denial of the authority of Moses as God's chosen spokesman, and intrusion into the priest's office." "Gainsaying" is *antilogia,* "to speak against," hence, "a contradiction."

Translation. *Woe to them, because in the way of Cain they took their way, and to the error of Balaam they abandoned themselves for a reward, and in the gainsaying of Kore they perished.*

(12) "Spots" is *spilas.* Vincent's note is illuminating: "Only here in the New Testament. So rendered in A.V., because understood as kindred to *spiloi* (II Pet. 2:13); but rightly, as Rev., *hidden rocks.* So Homer, (Odyssey, III, 298), 'the waves dashed the ship against the *rocks* (spiladesin) . . . These men were no longer mere *blots,* but elements of danger and wreck." The word was used of rocks covered by water and thus hidden. "Feasts of charity" is *agapē,* the word for God's love. It was used of the love feasts in the early Christian Church, a fellowship meal eaten by the Christians when they came together for worship. It was eaten at the local church, which in the first century always was in a person's home. There were no church edifices until much later.

"Feast" is *suneuōcheō,* "to feast sumptuously with" someone. Nestle, in his Greek text, punctuates the words, "without fear" with "feast with you." That is, these false teachers have no compunctions of conscience about participating in the fellowship of evangelical believers, posing as Christians. "Feeding" is *poimainō,* "to feed, tend a flock of sheep." It is used of shepherds pasturing their flocks. Vincent translates literally, "shepherding themselves," and quotes the Rev., "shepherds that feed themselves," and remarks, "further their own schemes and lusts instead of tending the flock of God."

Jude likens these false teachers to clouds without water, literally "clouds that are waterless." "Carried about" is *paraphero;* the simple verb is *phero* "to carry"; and the prefixed preposition, *para,* means "alongside," the compound verb meaning "to carry alongside." Vincent says: "As clouds which seem to be charged with refreshing showers, but are *borne past* and yield no rain." The expression, "whose fruit withereth" is *phthinoporina,* made up of *phthino,* "to waste away, pine," and *opora,* "autumn." The latter word characterizes these trees as late autumn trees. Thus, the reference is to autumn trees without fruit, at the time at which they are expected to have fruit. So these false teachers, men from whom one might expect the ministration of the Word, are as devoid of spiritual food for the saints as are these autumn trees without fruit. These trees are described as twice dead. Vincent remarks, "not only the *apparent* death of winter, but a *real* death, so that it only remains to pluck them up by the roots."

Translation. *These are the hidden rocks in your love feasts, sumptuously feasting with you without fear, as shepherds leading themselves to pasture, waterless clouds carried past by winds, autumn trees without fruit, having died twice, rooted up.*

(13) "Raging" is *agrios,* "wild, fierce, untamed." Vincent says, "Rev. *wild,* which is better, as implying *quality* rather than *act.* Waves, by nature *untamed.* The *act* or expression of the nature is given by the next word." "Foaming out" is *epaphrizo,* "to foam up, to cast out as foam." Thayer says that these false teachers are "impelled by their restless passions. They unblushingly exhibit in word and deed, their base and abandoned spirit." Concerning the expression, "wandering stars," Vincent says: "Possibly referring to comets, which shine a while and then pass into darkness. 'They belong not to the system: they stray at random and without law, and must at last be severed from the lights which rule while they are ruled' (Lumby)."

Translation. *Wild, untamed sea waves, foaming up their own shames, wandering stars, for whom the blackness of the darkness has been reserved forever.*

(14, 15) Enoch is the Old Testament person of that name (Gen. 5:18-24), the man who "walked with God." The quotation is from the apocryphal Book of Enoch. This book, known to the Church Fathers of the second century, lost for some centuries with the exception of a few fragments, was found in its entirety in a copy of the Ethiopic Bible in 1773 by Bruce. It consists of revelations purporting to have been given to Enoch and Noah. Its object is to vindicate the ways of divine providence, to set forth the retribution reserved for sinners, and to show that the world is under the immediate government of God. "Of these" is *toutois,* in dative case. Enoch prophesied with respect to these false teachers of these last days. The translation should read, "prophesied with respect to these." "Ten thousands of His saints" is literally, "His holy ten thousands." The word "myriad" is the English spelling of the Greek word here, which latter word means in the singular, "ten thousand," and in the plural as it is here, "an innumerable multitude, an unlimited number." The translation could also read, "His holy myriads." These would not be limited to saints, but would also include angels. The word "saints" is the A.V. translation of *hagios* which is an adjective meaning "holy," but can also be used as a noun to mean "saint." Here it is in the same case as "myriads" and therefore has an adjectival function. "Convince" is *elegchō,* "rebuke so as to bring the sinner to either a conviction or confession of his sin." "Ungodly" is *asebēs,* "destitute of reverential awe towards God, impious."

"Hard speeches" is *sklēros,* "hard, harsh, rough, stiff," of men, metaphorically, "harsh, stern, hard." When used with *laleō,* "to speak," it is used of one who speaks roughly.

Translation. *And there prophesied also with respect to these, the seventh from Adam, Enoch, saying, Behold, there comes the Lord with His holy myriads, to execute judgment against all and to convict all those who are destitute of a reverential awe towards* go on a journey," metaphorically, "to order one's life." The *God, concerning all their works of impiety which they impiously performed and concerning all the harsh things which impious sinners spoke against Him.*

(16) "Murmurers" is *goggustēs,* "one who discontentedly complains," here, against God. The word is used of the cooing of doves. It refers, not to a loud, outspoken dissatisfaction, but to an undertone muttering. "Complainers" is *memspimoiros,* from *memphomai,* "to find fault with," and *moira,* "a part or lot." The compound word means, "blamers of their lot, complaining of one's lot, discontented." "Walking" here is *poreuomai,* "to word speaks of a planned course of conduct. "Lusts" is *epithumia,* "a passionate craving," good or bad, according to the context, here, evil. The word "lust" today refers to an immoral desire, but in A.D. 1611 when the A.V. was translated, it meant what the Greek word means, strong desire or craving, good or evil, depending upon the context. "Swelling" is *huperogkos,* "overswollen," metaphorically, "immoderate, extravagant," expressive of arrogance.

"Having men's persons in admiration" is *thaumazō prosōpon,* "admiring countenances." The Revised translates, "showing respect of persons." Mayor comments: "As the fear of God drives out the fear of man, so defiance of God tends to put man in His place, as the chief source of good or evil to his fellows."

Translation. *These are complainers against their lot, ordering their course of conduct in accordance with their own passionate cravings, and their mouth speaks immoderate, extravagant things, catering to personalities for the sake of advantage.*

(17-19) The Greek has a pronoun which is not handled by the A.V. It is, "But as for you (in contradistinction to the apostates), divinely-loved ones." The word "beloved" does not refer to Jude's love for those to whom he is writing, but to the fact that the saints are beloved ones of God. The word is *agapaō,* the distinctive word for "love" used in John 3:16, for instance. "Separate themselves" is *apodiorizō,* "by drawing boundaries *to disjoin, part, separate* from one another." The Revised has "make separations." Vincent says: "Cause divisions in the Church. Of those who draw a *line through* the Church and set *off* one part from another." "Sensual" is *psuchikos*. Vincent says: "As *psuchē* denotes life in the distinctness of individual existence, 'the centre of the personal being, the I of each individual,' so this adjective derived from it denotes what pertains to man, the *natural* personality as distinguished from the *renewed* man . . . The rendering *sensual*, here, is inferential: *sensual* because *natural* and *unrenewed*."

Alford has an illuminating note: "The *psuchē* is the centre of the personal being, the 'I' of each individual. It is in each man bound to the spirit, man's higher part, and to the body, man's lower part; drawn upwards by the one, downward by the other. He who gives himself up to the lower appetites, is *sarkikos* (fleshly): he who by communion of his *pneuma* (spirit) with God's Spirit is employed in the higher aims of his being, is *pneumatikos* (spiritual). He who rests midway, thinking only of self and self's interests, whether animal or intellectual, is the *psuchikos* (sensual), the selfish man, the man in whom the spirit is sunk and degraded into subordination to the subordinate *psuchē* (soul). In the lack of any adequate word, I have retained the 'sensual' of E.V., though the impression which it gives is a wrong one: 'selfish' would be as bad, for the *psuchikos* may be an amiable and generous man: 'animal' would be worse, 'intellectual,' worse still. If the word were not so ill-looking in our language, 'psychic' would be a great gain." Moulton and Milligan in their *Vocabulary of the Greek Testament* quote from a papyrus fragment as follows, "my human natural powers," where the word "natural" is *psuchikos*. They quote Souter, "the principle of life and the basis of its emotional aspect, animating the present body of flesh, in contrast to the higher life." The word is used of worldly wisdom in James 3:15, and translated "sensual." James is speaking of the wisdom (*sophia*) which does not come down from above, but is earthly (*epigeios*) as opposed to the wisdom which came down from above; it was sensual (*psuchikē*) human, the domain wherein all that is essentially human holds sway in that it pandered to self-esteem; and it was devilish (*daimoniōdēs* demonical) in that it raised up the "very devil" in the hearts of both opposer and opposed (Mayor).

The question before us now is whether *pneuma* (spirit) refers here to the Holy Spirit or to the human spirit of these false teachers, the word "spirit" being defined as that part of man which gives him God-consciousness, and enables him when in possession of salvation to worship and serve God. Mayor and Robertson think that the word here refers to the Holy Spirit. Vincent and Alford say that it refers to man's human spirit. Mayor after taking the position that the Holy Spirit is in view here, quotes Plumptre as follows: "the false teachers were so absorbed in their lower sensuous nature that they no longer possessed, in any real sense of the word, that element in man's compound being, which is itself spiritual, and capable therefore of communion with the Divine Spirit." Alford says: "not directly the Holy Spirit of God . . . but the higher spiritual life of man's spirit in communion with the Holy Spirit. These men have not indeed ceased to have *pneuma* (spirit), as a part of their own tripartite nature: but they have ceased to possess it in any worthy sense: it is degraded beneath and under the power of the *psuchē*, the personal life, so as to have no vitality of its own." Vincent says: "the higher spiritual life. So the adjective *pneumatikos,* (spiritual), is everywhere in the N.T. opposed to *psuchikos,* natural. See I Corinthians 15:44, 46." The present writer decided with Vincent, Alford, and Plumtre, on the basis of the contrast implied which is not between the *psuchikos* of man and the Holy Spirit, but between man's *psuchikos* and man's *pneumatikos.* Of course, since these false teachers are devoid of the higher spiritual life and its accompaning sensibilities, it is clear that they do not have the Holy Spirit.

Translation. *But, as for you, divinely-loved ones, remember the words which were spoken previously by the apostles of our Lord Jesus Christ, that they were saying to you, In the last time there shall be mockers ordering their course of conduct in accordance with their own passionate cravings which are destitute of reverential awe towards God. These are those who cause divisions, egocentric, not holding the spirit.*

(20, 21)   Again, Jude contrasts the saints to whom he is writing with the false teachers, in the words, "But as for you, (in contradistinction to these false teachers), divinely-loved ones." "Building up" is *epoikodomeō*, "to build upon, build up," to finish the structure of which the foundation has already been laid, metaphorically, "to give constant increase in Christian knowledge and in a life conformed thereto" (Thayer). The papyri afford the following example, "build on it (a sound foundation) your firmness and unshaken resolve" (Moulton and Milligan). "Faith" does not refer to faith as exercised by the saint, for it is described as "most holy," but to the Christian faith, Christianity. The saints are exhorted to build up their Christian lives on the foundation of all that God has done for them in salvation, such as making them a partaker of the divine nature and giving them the indwelling Holy Spirit, together with the Word of God. Mayor says: "The faith here is called 'most holy' because it comes to us from God, and reveals God to us, and because it is by its means that man is made righteous, and enabled to overcome the world."

The words, "praying in the Holy Ghost" show how the saints are to build themselves up on their most holy faith. That is, prayer is the vital factor in the Christian life which activates all the other departments of the Christian experience. "Ghost" is the translation of *pneuma*, the word in other places rendered "Spirit." "Ghost" is obsolete English as used here for the word "spirit." "In the Holy Ghost" is locative of sphere. That is, all true prayer is exercised in the sphere of the Holy Spirit, motivated and empowered by Him. That means that if the saint expects to really pray, he must be Spirit-filled or Spirit-controlled. The fullness of the Holy Spirit is the prerequisite to effectual praying. The Spirit, when yielded to, leads us in our petitions and generates within us the faith necessary to acceptable and answered prayer. The expression "praying in the Holy Ghost" is also instrumental of means. We pray by means of the Holy Spirit, in dependence upon Him.

Jude exhorts the saints, "Keep yourselves in the love of God." They are to do this by means of the two things just mentioned, building themselves up in their Christian lives and by praying in the Holy Spirit. "Keep" is *tēreō*, "to attend to carefully, take care of, guard." The word is expressive of watchful care and is suggestive of present possession (Thayer). "In the love of God" is locative of sphere. The exhortation is to the saints, to keep themselves within the sphere of the love of God. That is, they are to see to it that they stay within the circle of His love. Alford says: "within that region of peculiar love wherewith God regards all who are built up on the faith and sustained by prayer." This is the love that God is, and the love with which He loves the saints. The saints are exhorted to so build themselves up on their Christian foundation and so pray in the power of the Holy Spirit, that they as a result keep themselves in the place where God is able to shower all of His love upon them. In other words, they are to so live that they will keep themselves in the place of blessing. There is no hint here that God will stop loving them, but that they by sin in their lives would make it impossible for God to give them blessings in the fullest sense.

"Looking" is *prosdechomai*, "to receive to one's self, to admit, give access to, to expect, wait for." The meaning of this word seems to point to that part of eternal life which will be given the saint at the Rapture, namely, the glorification of his physical body. The reader will not fail to observe the studied reference of Jude to the Three Persons of the God-head in these two verses.

Translation. *But, as for you, divinely-loved ones, building yourselves up constantly in the sphere of and by means of your most holy Faith, and as constantly praying in the sphere of and by means of the Holy Spirit, with watchful care keep yourselves within the sphere of God's love, expectantly looking for the mercy of our Lord Jesus Christ resulting in life eternal.*

(22, 23) There is some question among textual critics regarding the Greek text here. Both Nestle and Westcott and Hort agree on the Greek which requires the rendering, "And upon some, on the one hand, be having mercy, (those) who are in doubt; be saving (them), snatching (them) out of the fire. Upon others, on the other hand, be showing mercy in fear, hating even the undergarment completely defiled by the flesh."

However, Alford and Mayor read *elegchō*, "to bring to a confession and conviction of sin," rather than *eleeō*, "to have mercy on." Mayor then translates, "reprove them because of their doubts," or "convince them when they dispute with you." Alford translates, "And some indeed convict when contending with you."

The particle *men* appears in verse 22, and *de* in verse 23. When these are used together as they are here, they show contrast. This would decide for the reading given by Alford and Mayor, *elegchō*, "to convict," instead of *eleeō*, "to show mercy," since there is a contrast between these two actions, whereas there is no contrast between the act of showing mercy of verse 22 and the act of saving in verse 23. Thayer in his treatment of *men* and *de* in verse 22 says, "the one indeed — and but the other," showing contrast. These considerations decide the present writer for Alford and Mayor, even though in doing so he must set aside the findings of Nestle and Westcott and Hort in this instance.

In the words, "pulling them out of the fire," Jude has in mind Zechariah 3:2, "a brand plucked from the burning." Commenting upon the words "with fear," Vincent says: "lit., *in fear*, i.e., of the contagion of sin while we are rescuing them," and Mayor: "The faithful are urged to show all possible tenderness for the fallen, but at the same time to have a fear lest they themselves or others whom they influence should be led to think too lightly of the sin whose ravages they are endeavoring to repair."

Translation. *And some indeed on the one hand be convicting when contending with you; be saving, snatching out of the fire, others on the other hand, upon whom be showing mercy in fear, hating even the undergarment completely defiled by the flesh.*

(24, 25) Mayor comments on the final benediction and ascription as follows: "I have bidden you to keep yourselves in the love of God; I have warned you against all impiety and impurity. But do not think that you can attain to the one, or guard yourselves from the other, in your own strength. You must receive power from above, and that it may be so, I offer up my prayer to Him, who alone is able to keep you from stumbling, and to present you before the throne of His glory, pure and spotless in exceeding joy. To Him, the only God and Saviour belong glory, greatness, might, and authority throughout all ages."

"From falling" is *aptaiseos*, from *ptaiō*, "to stumble, to sin, to make a mistake," and alpha privative which negates the word. The word means in classical writers, "sure-footed as a horse that does not stumble" (Xenophon), and thus of a good man (Epictetus, Marcus Antoninus) (Robertson). "Present" is *histēmi*, "to cause or make to stand, to place."

Translation. *Now, to the One who is able to guard you from stumbling and to place you before the presence of His glory faultless in great rejoicing, to the only God our Saviour, through Jesus Christ our Lord be glory, majesty, might, and authority before all time, both now and forever. Amen.*

THE
EXPANDED TRANSLATION
OF
JUDE

Read this letter through at a single sitting.
Read it repeatedly, and see how the truths
in it become clearer and clearer every time
you read it.

THE EXPANDED TRANSLATION
OF
JUDE

Jude, a bondslave of Jesus Christ and brother of James, to those who by God the Father have been loved and are in a state of being the permanent objects of His love, and who for Jesus Christ have been guarded and are in a permanent state of being carefully watched, to those who are called ones. Mercy to you, peace, and love be multiplied.

Divinely-loved ones, when giving all diligence to be writing to you concerning the salvation possessed in common by all of us, I had constraint laid upon me to write to you, beseeching (you) to contend with intensity and determination for the Faith once for all entrusted into the safe-keeping of the saints. For certain men entered surreptitiously who were of old predicted with reference to this judgment, (men) destitute of reverential awe towards God, putting anarchy in the place of the grace of God, and denying the only absolute Master and our Lord Jesus Christ.

Moreover, after mature consideration, I desire to remind you, (who) know all things once for all, that the Lord, having saved the people out of Egypt, then destroyed those who did not believe. And angels who did not carefully guard their original position of preeminent dignity, but abandoned once for all their own private dwelling-place, with a view to the judgment of the great day, in everlasting bonds under darkness, He has put under careful guard. Just as Sodom and Gomorrha and the cities about them, in like manner to these, having given themselves out and out to fornication and having gone off to a different kind of flesh, are

*set forth as an exhibit, undergoing the punishment of everlast-
ing fire.*

*In the same manner nevertheless, also these who are beguiled
with sensual images and carried away to an impious course of
conduct, defile indeed the flesh, and set at naught authority, and
speak evil of preeminence. Yet Michael, the archangel, when
disputing with the devil, arguing concerning the body of Moses,
dared not bring a sentence that would impugn his dignity, but
said, May the Lord rebuke you. But these on the one hand revile
as many things concerning which they do not have absolute knowledge, and on the other hand as many things, by instinct, like the
unreasoning animals, which they understand, by these they are
being brought to ruin.*

*Woe to them, because in the way of Cain they took their way,
and to the error of Balaam they abandoned themselves for a
reward, and in the gainsaying of Kore they perished. These are
hidden rocks in your love feasts, sumptuously feasting with you
without fear, as shepherds leading themselves to pasture, waterless clouds carried past by winds, autumn trees without fruit, having died twice, rooted up. Wild, untamed sea waves, foaming up
their own shames, wandering stars, for whom the blackness of
the darkness has been reserved forever.*

*And there prophesied also with respect to these, the seventh
from Adam, Enoch, saying, Behold, there comes the Lord with
His holy myriads, to execute judgment against all and to convict
all those who are destitute of a reverential awe towards God,
concerning all their works of impiety which they impiously performed and concerning all the harsh things which impious sinners
spoke against Him. These are complainers against their lot,
ordering their course of conduct in accordance with their own
passionate cravings, and their mouth speaks immoderate, extravagant things, catering to personalities for the sake of advantage.*

*But, as for you, divinely-loved ones, remember the words which
were spoken previously by the apostles of our Lord Jesus Christ,
that they were saying to you, In the last time there shall be mockers ordering their course of conduct in accordance with their*

own passionate cravings which are destitute of reverential awe towards God. These are those who cause divisions, egocentric, not holding the spirit.

But, as for you, divinely-loved ones, building yourselves up constantly in the sphere of and by means of your most holy Faith, and as constantly praying in the sphere of and by means of the Holy Spirit, with watchful care keep yourselves within the sphere of God's love, expectantly looking for the mercy of our Lord Jesus Christ resulting in life eternal.

And some indeed on the one hand be convicting when contending with you; be saving, snatching out of the fire, others on the other hand, upon whom be showing mercy in fear, hating even the undergarment completely defiled by the flesh.

Now, to the One who is able to guard you from stumbling and to place you before the presence of His glory faultless in great rejoicing, to the only God our Saviour, through Jesus Christ our Lord be glory, majesty, might, and authority before all time, both now and forever. Amen.

SCRIPTURE INDEX

SCRIPTURE INDEX